Frederic William Farrar, Thomas De Quincey, James Hogg

The Wider Hope

Essays And Strictures On The Doctrine And Literature Of Future Punishment

Frederic William Farrar, Thomas De Quincey, James Hogg

The Wider Hope
Essays And Strictures On The Doctrine And Literature Of Future Punishment

ISBN/EAN: 9783337088118

Printed in Europe, USA, Canada, Australia, Japan

Cover: Foto ©Andreas Hilbeck / pixelio.de

More available books at **www.hansebooks.com**

THE WIDER HOPE

" LIFE'S MYSTERY—deep, restless, as the ocean—
    Hath surged and wailed for ages to and fro ;
Earth's generations watch i s ceaseless motion
    As in and out its hollow moanings flow.
Shivering and yearning by that unknown sea,
Let my soul calm itself, O Christ, in Thee !

Life's sorrows, with inexorable power,
    Sweep desolation o'er this mortal plain ;
And human loves and hopes fly as the chaff
    Borne by the whirlwind from the ripened grain.
Ah ! when before that blast my hopes all flee,
Let my soul calm itself, O Christ, in Thee !

Between the mysteries of death and life
    Thou standest, loving, guiding, not explaining ;
We ask, and Thou art silent ; yet we gaze,
    And our charmed hearts forget their drear complaining.
No crushing fate, no stony destiny,
O Lamb that hast been slain, we find in Thee !

The many waves of thought, the mighty tides,
    The ground-swell that rolls up from other lands,
From far-off worlds, from dim, eternal shores,
    Whose echo dashes on life's wave-worn strands,—
This vague, dark tumult of the inner sea
Grows calm, grows bright, O risen Lord, in Thee.

Thy piercèd hand guides the mysterious wheels ;
    Thy thorn-crowned brow now wears the crown of power ;
And, when the dread enigma presseth sore,
    Thy patient voice saith, 'Watch with Me one hour.'
As sinks the moaning river in the sea
In silver peace, so sinks my soul in Thee ! "

HARRIET BEECHER STOWE.

THE WIDER HOPE

Essays and Strictures

ON

THE DOCTRINE AND LITERATURE OF

FUTURE PUNISHMENT

BY

NUMEROUS WRITERS, LAY AND CLERICAL

INCLUDING

Archdeacon FARRAR; The Very Rev. E. H. PLUMPTRE, D.D.;
The late Principal TULLOCH; Rev. WILLIAM ARTHUR;
Rev. HENRY ALLON, D.D.; Rev. JAMES H. RIGG, D.D.;
The late Rev. J. BALDWIN BROWN,
ETC.

With a Paper

"ON THE SUPPOSED SCRIPTURAL EXPRESSION FOR

ETERNITY"

BY

THOMAS DE QUINCEY

AND A BIBLIOGRAPHICAL APPENDIX OF RECENT WORKS ON ESCHATOLOGY

AS CONTAINED IN THE BRITISH MUSEUM

NEW YORK

E. P. DUTTON & CO.

31 WEST TWENTY-THIRD STREET

1890

"THERE is one question which combines with the interest of speculation and curiosity an interest incomparably greater, nearer, more affecting, more solemn. It is the simple question—'WHAT SHALL WE BE?' How soon it is spoken! but who shall reply? Think how profoundly this question, this mystery, concerns us—and, in comparison with this, what are to us all questions of all sciences? What to us all researches into the constitution and laws of material nature? What—all investigations into the history of past ages? What to us—the future career of events in the progress of states and empires? What to us—what shall become of this globe itself, or all the mundane system? What WE shall be, *we ourselves*, is the matter of surpassing interest."

JOHN FOSTER.

CONTENTS.

	PAGE
PREFATORY NOTE	xi

ON THE SUPPOSED SCRIPTURAL EXPRESSION
FOR ETERNITY—

I. Thomas de Quincey	3

FUTURE PUNISHMENT—

II. The late Professor J. H. Jellett	33
(Provost of Trinity College, Dublin.)	
III. The late Principal Tulloch	43
IV. Rev. William Arthur	55
V. The late Rev. J. Baldwin Brown	67
VI. Rev. John Hunt, D.D.	77
VII. The late Rev. R. F. Littledale, D.C.L.	89
VIII. Rev. Edward White	105
IX. Rev. Professor Salmon, D.D.	115
(Provost of Trinity College, Dublin.)	
X. The Very Rev. E. H. Plumptre, D.D.	129
(Dean of Wells.)	
XI. Rev. Henry Allon, D.D.	149
XII. Rev. James H. Rigg, D.D.	175
XIII. The late Canon Birks	197
XIV. The Rev. Professor Gracey	213
XV. The late A. J. B. Beresford Hope	231
XVI. A Layman	245
(The late W. B. Rands, Author of "Lilliput Levee," etc.)	
XVII. The Rev. Professor Mayor	265

viii   CONTENTS.

                                                                         PAGE

ETERNAL HOPE—

    XVIII. (*Reply*) Archdeacon FARRAR . . . 295

ÆONIAN METEMPSYCHOSIS—

    XIX. (*Sequel*) FRANCIS PEEK . . . 315

MERCY AND JUDGMENT –

    XX. "PREFATORY AND PERSONAL" OPENING TO "MERCY AND JUDGMENT." Archdeacon FARRAR 377

    XXI. THE "CONCLUSION" OF "MERCY AND JUDGMENT." Archdeacon FARRAR . . 399

APPENDIX—

    RECENT WORKS ON ESCHATOLOGY CONTAINED IN THE LIBRARY OF THE BRITISH MUSEUM . 409

₊ *PREFATORY NOTE BY THE EDITOR.—*JAMES HOGG.

"THE wish, that of the living whole
  No life may fail beyond the grave,
  Derives it not from what we have
The likest God within the soul?

. . . . .

I stretch lame hands of faith, and grope,
  And gather dust and chaff, and call
  To what I feel is Lord of all,
And faintly trust the larger hope."

―――――

"OH yet we trust that somehow good
  Will be the final goal of ill,
  To pangs of nature, sins of will,
Defects of doubt, and taints of blood.

That nothing walks with aimless feet;
  That not one life shall be destroy'd,
  Or cast as rubbish to the void,
When God hath made the pile complete.

. . . . .

Behold, we know not anything;
  I can but trust that good shall fall
  At last—far off—at last, to all,
And every winter change to spring.

So runs my dream, but what am I?
  An infant crying in the night:
  An infant crying for the light:
And with no language but a cry."

TENNYSON.

" THERE'S a wideness in God's mercy,
  Like the wideness of the sea;
There's a kindness in His justice,
  Which is more than liberty.

There is no place where earth's sorrows
  Are more felt than up in heaven;
There is no place where earth's failings
  Have such kindly judgment given.

There is welcome for the sinner,
  And more graces for the good;
There is mercy with the Saviour;
  There is healing in His blood.

．　．　．　．　．　．

For the love of God is broader
  Than the measures of man's mind;
And the heart of the Eternal
  Is most wonderfully kind.

But we make His love too narrow
  By false limits of our own;
And we magnify His strictness
  With a zeal He will not own.

There is plentiful redemption
  In the blood that has been shed;
There is joy for all the members
  In the sorrows of the Head."

From *" Souls of men, why will ye scatter ?"*
BY F. W. FABER, D.D.

PREFATORY NOTE.

A SHORT explanation is necessary to enable the reader to understand how this book has grown.

Thirty-seven years ago, while engaged in the Editorship of the new series of *The Instructor* (my Father's Weekly Magazine), I had frequent conversations with THOMAS DE QUINCEY on matters relating to the Future State.

He reviewed, amidst other problems of the soul, our dim knowledge of that momentous question—the duration of future punishment, to which the yearning human spirit ever turns with awe. He dwelt on the great mysteries surrounding us, which the children of men must be content now to " see through a glass, darkly ; " and the lights and shadows of belief, which, age by age, perplex and agitate anxious, storm-tossed minds—in their honest endeavour to arrive at the true teaching of Scripture.

Again and again, during the discussion of these solemn and moving subjects, he recurred to the interpretation of the expression for *Eternity*, until at length, one day in the autumn of 1852, he said to me, "*If I write this, dare you print it?*" With a full sense of the far-reaching responsibility, I replied, "I dare." Accordingly, the essay which opens this volume was written, and soon afterwards published, viz. — in the number for the first week of 1853. It attracted much attention throughout the English-speaking world, and provoked criticism of a very mixed nature, privately, and in the Press. Thirty-seven years ago, it will be remembered, the rigour of theological opinion, particularly in the Modern Athens, operated with a severity differing greatly from what now prevails. I will only remark, that I have always felt satisfied at having done what lay in my power to promote a clear understanding of these Greek words, by enabling the distinguished author to offer to thoughtful men a contribution so deserving of their attentive consideration.

This remarkable essay—a legacy of DE QUINCEY's keen intellect and scholarly power—has been, perhaps, in some respects, even more fully appreciated in the recent literature of Eschatology than on its first appearance. I refer especially to its influence on the American mind,—it having been for a long time widely disseminated throughout the United States.

. . . . . .

In November and December 1877, Canon FARRAR preached in Westminster Abbey five striking sermons which appeared in February 1878, under the title, *Eternal Hope*,—a volume which excited universal attention in theological circles, and amongst thinkers of all branches of the Christian Church. The book has now passed through fourteen editions, of which eight appeared in the first year of publication.

Amidst the mass of comment which saw the light touching the Canon's work and its subject, the most noteworthy gathering was a group of Essays and Strictures, contributed by a number of eminent writers, clerical and lay, of various Schools, to the pages of *The Contemporary Review*.

By the kind assent of these Authors I am able to present, in a convenient form, this collection of papers—one which, I trust, will prove permanently valuable to students of Scripture truth and devout speculation. In the case of the seven Writers who have now passed "within the vail," I have received from their representatives the concurrence which allows me to include the comments in question.

To Archdeacon FARRAR I owe the additional kindness of permission to attach from his later volume—*Mercy and Judgment*—those sections which show the result of his careful historical researches and mature conclusions affecting the subject. It is right to state that he has in no way interfered either with the arrangement or revision of this matter or his original "Reply."

For the Bibliographical Appendix, I am chiefly indebted to Mr. G. W. FORTESCUE, the Superintendent of the British Museum Reading Room. In addition to what has issued from the British Press, the department of Eschatology has been well kept up at the Museum by the judicious purchase of American and Continental Works in recent years. Mr. FORTESCUE's Subject Catalogue (1880-1885), published by authority of the Trustees, is a valuable labour-saving apparatus, and by his courtesy I include the unpublished "Continuations" on this subject to the present date. The "Press Marks" attached will facilitate reference to the works at our National Library.

The section of the Appendix drawn from the last Edition and Supplement to Poole's *Index to Periodical Literature* (a work which affords evidence of the ability in this field of our American cousins), gives a ready key to many valuable articles strewn about in fugitive literature.

Proof sheets of the various papers (II. to XVII.) have been revised by the Authors or their representatives, and, in some cases, emendations made to elucidate the text or the writer's position. References in the present tense to writers now deceased have not been altered. Changes of personal title incident to Ecclesiastical preferment are noted once.

I have to thank the Editor and Proprietors of *The Contemporary Review* for their primary assent, which encouraged me to pursue the combination now happily effected by the junction of so many copyright interests.

The cordial expressions of sympathy with my purpose, and the co-operation afforded by the able and distinguished men who have promoted this object, are extremely gratifying. They have sustained me in this somewhat arduous attempt to consolidate and preserve these varying shades of opinion, entertained by serious students of Life and Scripture, on that solemn question in which every human being is so profoundly concerned.

JAMES HOGG.

Easter Day, 1890.

ON THE SUPPOSED SCRIPTURAL
EXPRESSION FOR ETERNITY

I.

ON THE SUPPOSED SCRIPTURAL EXPRESSION FOR ETERNITY.

BY THOMAS DE QUINCEY.

FORTY years ago[1] (or, in all probability, a good deal more, for we have already completed thirty-seven years from Waterloo, and my remembrances upon this subject go back to a period lying much behind that great era), I used to be annoyed and irritated by the false interpretation given to the Greek word *aiōn*, and given necessarily, therefore, to the adjective *aionios* as its immediate derivative. It was not so much the falsehood of this interpretation, as the narrowness of that falsehood, which disturbed me. There was a glimmer of truth in it; and precisely that glimmer it was which led the way to a general and obstinate misconception of the meaning. The word is remarkably situated. It is a Scriptural word, and it is also a Greek word; from which the inevitable inference is, that we must look for

---

[1] Written about the close of 1852.—*H.*

it only in the *New* Testament. Upon any question arising of deep, aboriginal, doctrinal truth, we have nothing to do with translations. Those are but secondary questions, archæological and critical, upon which we have a right to consult the Greek translation of the Hebrew Scriptures known by the name of the Septuagint.

Suffer me to pause at this point for the sake of premising an explanation needful to the unlearned reader. As the *reading* public and the *thinking* public is every year outgrowing more and more notoriously the mere *learned* public, it becomes every year more and more the right of the former public to give the law preferably to the latter public, upon all points which concern its own separate interests. In past generations, no pains were taken to make explanations that were not called for by the *learned* public. All other readers were ignored. They formed a mob, for whom no provision was made. And that many difficulties should be left entirely unexplained for *them*, was superciliously assumed to be no fault at all. And yet any sensible man, let him be as supercilious as he may, must on consideration allow that amongst the crowd of unlearned or half-learned readers, who have had neither time nor opportunities for what is called "erudition" or learned studies, there must always lurk a proportion of men that, by constitution of mind, and by the bounty of nature, are much better fitted for thinking, originally more philosophic, and are more capaciously endowed, than those who are, by accident of position, more learned. Such a natural superiority certainly takes precedency of a merely artificial superiority; and, therefore, it entitles those who possess it to a special consideration. Let there be an audience gathered about any book of 10,100 readers: it might be fair in these days to assume that 10,000 would be in a partial sense illiterate, and the remaining 100 what would be rigorously classed as " learned." Now, on such a distribution of the readers, it would be a matter of certainty that the most powerful intellects would lie amongst the illiterate 10,000, counting, probably, to 15 to 1 as against those in the learned minority. The inference, therefore, would be, that, in all equity, the interest of the unlearned section claimed a priority of attention, not merely as the more numerous section, but also as, by a high probability, the more philosophic. And in proportion as this unlearned section widens and expands, which every year it does, in that proportion the obligation and cogency of this equity strengthens. An attention to the unlearned part of an audience, which fifteen years ago might have rested upon pure courtesy, *now* rests upon a basis of absolute justice. I make this preliminary explanation, in order to take away the appearance of caprice from such occasional pauses as I may make for the purpose of clearing up obscurities or difficulties. Formerly, in a case of that nature, the learned reader would have told me that I was not entitled to delay *him* by elucidations that in *his* case must be supposed to be superfluous: and in such a remonstrance there would once have been some equity. The illiterate section of the readers might then be fairly assumed as present only by accident; as no abiding part of the audience; but, like the general public in the gallery of the House of Commons, as present only by sufferance; and officially in any records of the House whatever, utterly ignored as existences. At present, half-way on our pilgrimage through the nineteenth century, I reply to such a learned remonstrant —that it gives me pain to annoy him by superfluous explanations, but that, unhappily, this infliction of tedium upon *him* is inseparable from what has now become a duty to others.

This being said, I now go on to inform the illiterate reader, that the earliest translation of the Hebrew Scriptures ever made was into Greek. It was undertaken on the encouragement of a learned prince, Ptolemy Philadelphus, by an Association of Jewish emigrants in Alexandria. It was, as the event has shown in very many instances, an advantage of a rank rising to providential, that such a cosmopolitan version of the Hebrew sacred Writings should have been made at a moment when a rare concurrence of circumstances happened to make it possible; such as, for example, a king both learned in his tastes and liberal in his principles of religious toleration ; a language, viz., the Greek, which had already become, what for many centuries it continued to be, a common language of communication for the learned of the whole οἰκουμένη (*i.e.* in effect of the civilised world, viz. Greece, the shores of the Euxine, the whole of Asia Minor, Syria, Egypt, Carthage, and all the dependencies of Carthage, finally, and above all, Rome, then beginning to loom upon the Western horizon), together with all the dependencies of Rome, and, briefly, every state and city that adorned the imperial islands of the Mediterranean, or that glittered like gems in that vast belt of land, roundly speaking, 1000 miles in average breadth, and in circuit running up to 5000 miles. One thousand multiplied into five times 1000, or, otherwise expressed, a thousand thousand five times repeated, or, otherwise, a million five times repeated, briefly, a territory measuring 5,000,000 of square miles, or forty-five times the surface of our two British islands,—such was the boundless domain which this extraordinary act of Ptolemy suddenly threw open to the literature and spiritual revelation of a little obscure race, nestling in a little angle of Asia, scarcely visible as a fraction of Syria, buried in the broad shadows thrown out on one side by the great and ancient settlements on the Nile, and on the other by the vast empire that for thousands of years occupied the Tigris and the Euphrates. In the twinkling of an eye, at a sudden summons, as it were from the sounding of a trumpet, or the Oriental call by a clapping of hands, gates are thrown open, which have an effect corresponding in grandeur to the effect that would arise from the opening of a ship canal across the Isthmus of Darien, viz. the introduction to each other—face to face—of two separate infinities. Such a canal would suddenly lay open to each other the two great oceans of our planet, the Atlantic and the

Pacific ; whilst the act of translating *into* Greek and *from* Hebrew, that is, transferring out of a mysterious cipher as little accessible as Sanscrit, and which never *would* be more accessible through any worldly attractions of alliance with power and civic grandeur or commerce, *out of* this darkness *into* the golden light of a language the most beautiful, the most honoured amongst men, and the most widely diffused through a thousand years to come, had the immeasurable effect of throwing into the great crucible of human speculation, even then beginning to ferment, to boil, to overflow —that mightiest of all elements for exalting the chemistry of philosophy—grand and, for the first time, adequate conceptions of the Deity. For, although it is true that, until Elias should come—that is, until Christianity should have applied its final revelation to the completion of this great idea—we could not possess it in its total effulgence, it is, however, certain that an immense advance was made, a prodigious usurpation across the realms of chaos, by the grand illuminations of the Hebrew discoveries. Too terrifically austere we must presume the Hebrew idea to have been ; too undeniably it had not withdrawn the veil entirely which still rested upon the Divine countenance ; so much is involved in the subsequent revelations of Christianity. But still the advance made in reading aright the Divine lineaments had been enormous. God was now a Holy Spirit that could not tolerate impurity. He was the Fountain of justice, and no longer disfigured by any mode of sympathy with human caprice or infirmity. And, if a frown too awful still rested upon His face, making the approach to Him too fearful for harmonising with that perfect freedom and that childlike love which God seeks in His worshippers, it was yet made evident that no step for conciliating His favour did or could lie through any but *moral* graces.

Three centuries after this great epoch of the *publication* (for such it was), secured so providentially to the Hebrew theology, two learned Jews—viz. Josephus and Philo Judæus—had occasion to seek a cosmopolitan utterance for that burden of truth (or what they regarded as truth) which oppressed the spirit within them.

Once again they found a deliverance from the very same freezing imprisonment in an unknown language, through the very same magical key, viz. the all-pervading language of Greece, which carried their communications to the four winds of heaven, and carried them precisely amongst the class of men—viz., the enlightened and educated class—which pre-eminently, if not exclusively, their wish was to reach. About one generation *after* Christ it was, when the utter prostration and, politically speaking, the destruction of Jerusalem and the Jewish nation, threw these two learned Jews upon this recourse to the Greek language as their final resource, in a condition otherwise of absolute hopelessness. Pretty nearly *three* centuries *before* Christ it was (284 years, according to the common reckoning), when the first act of communication took place between the sealed-up literature of Palestine and the Greek catholic interpretation. Altogether, we may say that 320 years, or somewhere about ten generations of men, divided these two memorable acts of intercommunication. Such a space of time allows a large range of influence and of silent, unconscious operation to the vast and potent ideas that brooded over this awful Hebrew literature. Too little weight has been allowed to the probable contagiousness, and to the preternatural shock, of such a new and strange philosophy, acting upon the jaded and exhausted intellect of the Grecian race

We must remember, that precisely this particular range of time was that in which the Greek systems of philosophy, having thoroughly completed their evolution, had suffered something of a collapse; and, having exhausted their creative energies, began to gratify the cravings for novelty by remodellings of old forms. It is remarkable, indeed, that this very city of Alexandria founded and matured this new principle of remodelling applied to poetry not less than to philosophy and criticism. And, considering the activity of this great commercial city and port, which was meant to act, and *did* act, as a centre of communication between the East and the West, it is probable that a far greater effect was produced by the Greek translation of the Jewish Scriptures, in the way of preparing the mind of nations for the apprehension of Christianity, than has ever been distinctly recognised.

The silent destruction of books in those centuries has robbed us of all means for tracing innumerable revolutions, that nevertheless, by the evidence of results, must have existed. Taken, however, with or without this additional result, the translation of the Hebrew Scriptures in their most important portions must be ranked amongst what are called

"Providential" events. Such a king—a king whose father had been a personal friend of Alexander, the mighty civilising conqueror, and had shared in the liberalisation connected with his vast revolutionary projects for extending a higher civilisation over the globe,— such a king, conversing with such a language, having advantages so absolutely unrivalled; and again, this king and this language concurring with a treasure so supernatural of spiritual wisdom as the subject of their ministrations, and all three concurring with political events so auspicious—the founding of a new and mighty metropolis in Egypt, and the silent advance to supreme power amongst men of a new empire, martial beyond all precedent as regarded *means*, but not as regarded *ends* —working in all things towards the unity of civilisation and the unity of law, so that any new impulse, as, for instance, impulse of a new religion, was destined to find new facilities for its own propagation, resembling electric conductors. under the unity of government and of law,—concurrences like these, so many and so strange, justly impress upon this translation, the most memorable, because the most influential of all that have ever been accomplished, a character of grandeur that place it on the same level of interest as the building of the first or second temple at Jerusalem.

There is a Greek legend which openly ascribes to this translation all the characters of a miracle. But, as usually happens, this vulgarising form of the miraculous is far less impressive than the plain history itself, unfolding its stages with the most unpretending historical fidelity. Even the Greek language, on which, as the natural language of the new Greek dynasty in Egypt, the duty of the translation devolved, enjoyed a double advantage : *First*, as being the only language then spoken upon earth that could diffuse a book over *every* part of the civilised earth ; *secondly*, as being a language of unparalleled power and compass for expressing and reproducing effectually all ideas, however alien and novel. Even the city, again, in which this translation was accomplished, had a double dowry of advantages towards such a labour, not only as enjoying a large literary society, and, in particular, a large Jewish society, together with unusual provision in the shape of libraries, on a scale probably at that time unprecedented, but also as having the most extensive machinery then known to human experience for *publishing*, that is, for transmitting to foreign capitals all books in the readiest and the cheapest fashion, by means of its prodigious shipping.

Having thus indicated to the *unlearned* reader the particular nature of that interest which invests this earliest translation of the Hebrew Scriptures, viz. that, in fact, this translation was the earliest *publication* to the human race of a revelation which had previously been locked up in a language destined, as surely as the Welsh language or the Gaelic, to eternal obscurity amongst men, I go on to mention that the learned Jews selected for this weighty labour happened to be in number seventy-two; but, as the Jews systematically reject fractions in such cases (whence it is that always, in order to express the period of six weeks, they say *forty days*, and not, as strictly they should, *forty-two days*), popularly, the translators were called "The Seventy," for which the Latin word is *septuaginta*. And thus in after ages the translators were usually indicated as "The LXX," or, if the work and not the workmen should be noticed, it was cited as *The Septuagint*. In fact, this earliest of Scriptural versions, viz. into Greek, is by much the most famous; or, if any other approaches it in notoriety, it is the Latin translation by St. Jerome, which, in this one point, enjoys even a superior importance, that in the Church of Rome it is the authorised translation. Evidently, in every Church, it must be a matter of primary importance to assign the particular version to which that Church appeals, and by which, in any controversy arising, that Church consents to be governed. Now, the Jerome version fulfils this function for the Romish Church; and accordingly, in the sense of being published (*vulgata*), or publicly authorised by that Church, it is commonly called *The Vulgate*.

But, in a large polemic question, unless, like the Romish Church, we uphold a secondary inspiration as having secured a special privileged translation from the possibility of error, we cannot refuse an appeal to the Hebrew text for the Old Testament, or to the Greek text for the New. The word *aionios* (αιωνιος), as purely Grecian, could not connect itself with the Old Testament, unless it were through the Septuagint translation into Greek. Now, with that version, in any case of controversy, none of us, Protestants alike or Roman Catholics, have anything whatever to do. Controversially, we *can* be concerned only with the original language of the Scriptures, with its actual verbal expressions textually produced.

To be liable, therefore, to such a textual citation, any Greek word must belong to the *New* Testament. Because, though the word might happen to occur in the Septuagint, yet, since *that* is merely a translation, for any of us who occupy a controversial place, that is, who are bound by the responsibilities, or who claim the strict privileges of controversy, the Septuagint has no virtual existence. We should not be at liberty to allege the Septuagint as any authority, if it happened to countenance our own views; and, consequently, we could not be called on to recognise the Septuagint in any case where it should happen to be against us. I make this preliminary *caveat*, as not caring whether the word *aeonios* does or does not occur in the Septuagint. Either way, the reader understands that I disown the authority of that version as in any degree affecting myself. The word which, forty years ago, moved my disgust by its servile misinterpretation, was a word proper to the *New* Testament; and any sense which it may have received from an Alexandrian Jew in the third century before Christ, is no more relevant to any criticism that I am now going to suggest, than is the classical use of the word *aeon* (αιων) familiar to the learned in Sophocles or Euripides.

The reason which gives to this word *aeonian* what I do not scruple to call a *dreadful* importance, is the same reason, and no other, which prompted the dishonesty concerned in the ordinary interpretation of this word. The word happened to connect itself—but *that* was no practical concern of mine; me it had not biassed in the one direction, nor should it have biassed any just critic in the counter direction —happened, I say, to connect itself with the ancient dispute upon the *duration* of future punishments. What was meant by the *aeonian* punishments in the next world? Was the proper sense of the word *eternal*, or was it not? I, for my part, meddled not, nor upon any consideration could have been tempted to meddle, with a speculation repellent alike by the horror and by the hopeless mystery which invest it. Secrets of the prison-house, so afflicting to contemplate steadily, and so hopeless of solution, there could be no proper motive for investigating, unless the investigation promised a great deal more than it could ever accomplish; and my own feeling as to all such problems is, that they vulgarise what, left to itself would take its natural station amongst the freezing horrors that Shakspeare dismisses with so potent an expression of awe, in a well-known scene of *Measure for Measure*. I reiterate my protest against being in any way decoyed into the controversy. Perhaps I may have a strong opinion upon the subject. But, anticipating the coarse discussions into which the slightest entertainment of such a question would be every moment approaching, once for all, out of reverential regard for the dignity of human nature, I beg permission to decline the controversy altogether.

But does this declinature involve any countenance to a certain argument which I began by rejecting as abominable? Most certainly not. That argument runs thus — that the ordinary construction of the term *aeonian*, as equivalent to *everlasting*, could not possibly be given up when associated with penal misery because in that case, and by the very same act, the idea of eternity must be abandoned as applicable to the counter-bliss of Paradise. Torment and blessedness, it was argued, punishment and beatification, stood upon the same level; the same word it was, the word *aeonian*, which qualified the duration of either; and, if eternity in the most rigorous acceptation fell away from the one idea, it must equally fall away from the other. Well; be it so. But that would not settle the question. It might be very painful to renounce a long-cherished anticipation; but the necessity of doing so could not be received as a sufficient reason for adhering to the old unconditional use of the word *aeonian*. The argument is—that we must retain the old sense of *eternal*, because else we lose upon one scale what we had gained upon the other. But what then? would be the reasonable man's retort. We are not to accept or to reject a new construction (if otherwise the more colourable) of the word *aeonian*, simply because the consequences might seem such as upon the whole to displease us. We may gain nothing; for by the new interpretation our loss may balance our gain; and we may prefer the old arrangement. But how monstrous is all this! We are not summoned as to a choice of two different arrangements that may suit different tastes, but to a grave question as to what *is* the sense and operation of the word *aeonian*. Let the limitation of the word disturb our previous estimate of Paradise, grant that it so disturbs that estimate, not the less all such consequences leave the dispute exactly where it was; and if a balance of reason can be found for limiting the extent of the word *aeonian*, it will not be the less true because it may happen to disturb a crotchet of our own.

Meantime, all this speculation, first and last, is pure nonsense. *Aeonian* does not mean *eternal;* neither does it mean of limited duration ; nor would the unsettling of *aeonian* in its old use, as applied to punishment, to torment, to misery, etc., carry with it any necessary unsettling of the idea in its application to the beatitudes of Paradise. Pause, reader; and thou, my favoured and privileged reader, that boastest thyself to be unlearned, pause doubly whilst I communicate my views as to this remarkable word.

What is an *aeon?* In the use and acceptation of the Apocalypse, it is evidently this, viz., the duration or cycle of existence which belongs to any object, not individually for itself, but universally in right of its genus. Kant, for instance, in a little paper which I once translated, proposed and debated the question as to the age of our planet the Earth. What did he mean? Was he to be understood as asking whether the Earth were half a million, two millions, or three millions of years old? Not at all. The probabilities certainly lean, one and all, to the assignment of an antiquity greater by many thousands of times than that which we have most idly supposed ourselves to extract from Scripture, which assuredly never meant to approach a question so profoundly irrelevant to the great purposes of Scripture as any geological speculation whatsoever. But this was not within the field of Kant's inquiry. What he wished to know was simply the exact stage in the whole course of her development which the Earth at present occupies. Is she still in her infancy, for example, or in a stage corresponding to middle age, or in a stage approaching to superannuation? The idea of Kant presupposed a certain average duration as belonging to a planet of our particular system; and supposing this known, or discoverable, and that a certain assignable development belonged to a planet so circumstanced as ours, then in what particular stage of that development may we, the tenants of this respectable little planet *Tellus*, reasonably be conceived to stand?

Man, again, has a certain *aeonian* life; possibly ranging somewhere about the period of seventy years assigned in the Psalms. That is, in a state as highly improved as human infirmity and the errors of the earth herself, together with the diseases incident to our atmosphere, etc., could be supposed to allow, possibly the human race might average seventy years for each individual. This period would in that case represent the "*aeon*" of the *individual* Tellurian; but the "*aeon*" of the Tellurian RACE would probably amount to many millions of our earthly years; and it would remain an unfathomable mystery, deriving no light at all from the septuagenarian "aeon" of the individual; though between the two aeons I have no doubt that some secret link of connection does and must subsist, however undiscoverable by human sagacity.

The crow, the deer, the eagle, etc., are all supposed to be long-lived. Some people have fancied that in their normal state they tended to a period of two[1] centuries. I myself know

[1] I have heard the same normal duration ascribed to the tortoise, and one case became imperfectly known to myself personally. Somewhere I may have mentioned the case in print. These, at any rate, are the facts of the case: A lady (by birth a Cowper, of the Whig family, and cousin to the poet Cowper; and, equally with him, related to Dr. Madan, Bishop of Peterborough), in the early part of this century, mentioned to me that, in the palace at Peterborough, she had for years known as a pet of the household a venerable tortoise, who bore some inscription on his shell indicating that, from 1638 to 1643, he had belonged to Archbishop Laud, who (if I am not mistaken) held the bishopric of Peterborough before he was translated to London, and finally to Canterbury.

nothing certain for or against this belief; but, supposing the case to be as it is represented, then this would be the *aeonian* period of these animals, considered as individuals. Among trees, in like manner, the oak, the cedar, the yew, are notoriously of very slow growth, and their aeonian period is unusually long as regards the individual. What may be the *aeon* of the whole species is utterly unknown. Amongst birds, one species at least has become extinct in our own generation; its *aeon* was accomplished. So of all the fossil species in zoology, which Palæontology has revealed. Nothing, in short, throughout universal nature, can for a moment be conceived to have been resigned to accident for its normal *aeon*. All periods and dates of this order belong to the certainties of nature, but also, at the same time, to the mysteries of Providence. Throughout the Prophets, we are uniformly taught that nothing is more below the grandeur of Heaven than to assign earthly dates in fixing either the revolutions or the duration of great events such as prophecy would condescend to notice. A day has a prophetic meaning, but what sort of day? A mysterious expression for a time which has no resemblance to a natural day — sometimes comprehending long successions of centuries, and altering its meaning according to the object concerned. " A time," and " times," or " half a time "—" an aeon," or " aeons of aeons" —and other variations of this prophetic language (so full of dreadful meaning, but also of doubt and perplexity), are all significant. The peculiar grandeur of such expressions lies partly in the dimness of the approximation to any attempt at settling their limits, and still more in this, that the conventional character, and consequent meanness of ordinary human dates, are abandoned in the celestial chronologies. Hours and days, or lunations and months, have no true or philosophic relation to the origin, or duration, or periods of return belonging to great events, or revolutionary agencies, or vast national crimes ; but the normal period and duration of all acts whatever, the time of their emergence, of their agency, or their reagency, fall into harmony with the secret proportions of a heavenly scale, when they belong by mere necessity of their own internal constitution to the vital though hidden motions that are at work in their own life and manifestation. Under the old and ordinary view of the apocalyptic *aeon*, which supposed it always to mean the same period of time—mysterious, indeed, and uncertain, as regards *our* knowledge, but fixed and rigorously certain in the secret counsels of God—it was presumed that this period, if it lost its character of infinity when applied to evil, to criminality, or to punishment, must lose it by a corresponding necessity equally when applied to happiness and the golden aspects of hope. But, on the contrary, every object whatsoever, every mode of existence, has its own separate and independent *aeon*. The most thoughtless person must be satisfied, on reflection, even apart from the express commentary upon this idea furnished by the Apocalypse, that every life and mode of being must have hidden within itself the secret *why* of its duration. It is impossible to believe of *any* duration whatever that it is determined capriciously. Always it rests upon some ground, ancient as light and darkness, though undiscoverable by man. This only is discoverable, as a general tendency, that the *aeon*, or generic period of evil, is constantly towards a fugitive duration. The *aeon*, it is alleged, must always express the same idea, whatever *that* may be; if it is less than eternity for the evil cases, then it must be less for the good ones. Doubtless the idea of an *aeon* is in one sense always uniform, always the same, viz., as a tenth or a twelfth is always the same. Arithmetic could not exist if any caprice or variation affected these ideas — a tenth is always more than an eleventh, always less than a ninth. But this uniformity of ratio and proportion does not hinder but that a tenth may now represent a guinea, and next moment represent a thousand guineas. The exact amount of the duration expressed by an *aeon* depends altogether upon the particular subject which yields the *aeon*. It is, as I have said, a radix; and, like an algebraic square root or cube-root, though governed by the most rigorous laws of limitation, it must vary in obedience to the nature of the particular subject whose radix it forms.

Reader, I take my leave. I have been too loitering. I know it, and will make such efforts in future to cultivate the sternest brevity as nervous distress will allow. Meantime, as the upshot of my speculation, accept these three propositions :—

A. That man (which is in effect *every* man hitherto), who allows himself to infer the eternity of evil from the counter eternity of good, builds upon the mistake of assigning a stationary and mechanic value to the idea of an aeon; whereas the very purpose of

Scripture in using this word was to evade such a value. The word is always varying, for the very purpose of keeping it faithful to a spiritual identity. The period or duration of every object *would* be an essentially variable quantity, were it not mysteriously commensurate to the inner nature of that object as laid open to the eyes of God. And thus it happens, that everything in this world, possibly without a solitary exception, has its own separate *aeon:* how many entities, so many *aeons.*

B. But if it be an excess of blindness which can overlook the aeonian differences amongst even neutral entities, much deeper is that blindness which overlooks the separate tendencies of things evil and things good. Naturally, all evil is fugitive and allied to death.

C. I separately, speaking for myself only, profoundly believe that the Scriptures ascribe absolute and metaphysical eternity to one sole Being, viz., to God; and derivatively to all others according to the interest which they can plead in God's favour. Having anchorage in God, innumerable entities may possibly be admitted to a participation in divine aeon. But what interest in the favour of God can belong to falsehood, to malignity, to impurity?

To invest *them* with aeonian privileges, is in effect, and by its results, to distrust and to insult the Deity. Evil would *not* be evil, if it had that power of self-subsistence which is imputed to it in supposing its aeonian life to be co-eternal with that which crowns and glorifies the good.

FUTURE PUNISHMENT

II.

FUTURE PUNISHMENT.

BY THE LATE PROFESSOR J. H. JELLETT
(Provost of Trinity College, Dublin).

THE success of a book is often an important phenomenon of the age or generation in which it appears. Due in part to causes peculiar to no place or time, in part, perhaps, to causes which may be called accidental, the success of a book is often truly indicative of the generation which has welcomed it. It is successful, partly for its literary merit, partly too for its truth; but these causes combined are often insufficient to account for the phenomenon. It is successful because it discusses some question which is just then of surpassing interest, or because it gives vivid expression to a conception or a belief which is at that time present to the minds of men with a more than ordinary force. The successful books of a generation furnish, therefore, to the historian of thought, evidence of the highest value.

When he has assigned to the genius, the learning, and the truthfulness of the author, all that is justly due to them, and when he has found, as he will often find, that all together were insufficient to produce the effect, he will look for the conspiring causes, not to the author but to his readers, and may thus obtain precious materials for the intellectual or moral history of the time.

It is not too soon to speak of Canon Farrar's *Eternal Hope* as a successful book. Short as the time is which has elapsed since its publication, it has been long enough to leave no doubt of the feeling with which the public have received it. It is not too soon to call a book successful, which ran through its first edition in three weeks.

In seeking the causes of this success, we naturally look, in the first place, to the intrinsic merits of the book. Among these, that which is perhaps most conspicuous is the absolute truthfulness of the author. These sermons are stamped throughout with that kind of eloquence which is inspired by earnest conviction, and by that only. They are thoroughly Christian in spirit, and it would be unjust to call them violent; but they are certainly impassioned. The author believes a certain doctrine, against which a large part of his book is directed, to be a blot on popular Christianity; and this doctrine meets no tenderness at his hands. He repudiates controversy (p. 99); yet if this word be understood in its ordinary sense, it seems hard to give any other name to a book whose main object is to teach men to reject and even detest a very common article of belief. But his controversial writing, although impassioned, and sometimes even bitter, is honest and truthful.

Another cause which has contributed in no small degree to the popularity of these sermons, is the harmony of their central principle with a feeling, which is every day gaining a stronger hold over the minds of men. Every day which passes over religious controversy sees increased weight given to the verdict of the moral sense upon any doctrine which is proposed for man's acceptance. The right of this faculty to pronounce, if not decisively, yet with very great authority, upon the moral character of any asserted truth, and the influence which this sentence ought to have upon man's belief, are every day more fully acknowledged. Every day sees an increase in the number of those who will not consent to receive a doctrine on external evidence only, without examination of its moral character. Many would give to the moral faculty the absolute right to reject as untrue any doctrine appearing to it immoral, whatever amount of (apparent) Scriptural evidence may be adduced in its favour. Indeed, the well-known canon of Bishop Butler—that "if in revelation there be found any passages the seeming meaning of which is contrary to natural religion, we may most certainly conclude such seeming meaning not to be the real one"[1]—can hardly mean less. But, even from many who stop short of this conclusion, a controversialist would scarcely obtain a hearing who should deny to the human mind the right to judge of the intrinsic morality of any doctrine which it is asked to believe.

This principle is indeed no new one; we have seen that it is at least as old as Bishop Butler; but it was probably never so fully and generally admitted as it is now. Had it been always so, certain theories, which are the disgrace of theology, might never have seen the light. It is the earnest advocacy of this principle which places Canon Farrar's book in

---

[1] Analogy, Part 2, chap. i.

harmony with a great mass of religious thought in the present day. It may fairly be called the central principle of his Sermons. The popular doctrine of eternal punishment—the doctrine that "when we think of the future of the human race, we must conceive of a vast and burning prison, in which the lost souls of millions and millions writhe and shriek for ever, tormented in a flame that never will be quenched" (p. 55)—is condemned because it is repugnant to the moral sense. It is indeed true that his most bitter denunciations, clothed in language as strong as he can make it, are reserved, not for the doctrine itself, but for the additions which theologians—those especially of the Calvinistic school—have engrafted upon it. Yet if these additions to the popular belief be examined, it will be found that they are in reality no more than two,—namely, the dogma of reprobation, and the notion that the happiness of the blest is intensified by witnessing the suffering of the damned. All the rest which he denounces with such scathing eloquence—the frightful pictures drawn by Dante and Milton, by Tertullian and Jeremy Taylor—do but give definiteness to the common creed. Any one who believes that, for the great majority of mankind, the future life will be one of endless torture, must, if he would realise his belief to himself, draw a picture of a like horrible kind. Men's belief is not indeed usually so definite, but, if it mean anything, it must mean this or something like it.

It would be impossible to reproduce here the author's discussion of the supposed Scriptural proofs of the doctrine of endless punishment. It must suffice to mention one of these supposed proofs which turns upon the meaning of the word αἰώνιος in such passages as Matt. xxv. 46. It has been contended that, if this word, when applied to the punishment of the wicked, is to be understood of a limited time, the same word, when applied to the happiness of the righteous, must be understood with a similar limitation. In reply to this argument, Canon Farrar remarks, as Mr. Barlow had remarked before,[1] that if every passage in the New Testament in which the word occurs were struck out, there would remain ample Scriptural proof of the immortality of the righteous.

But the question may be considered in a more general way. Even if it be conceded that, according to the most probable interpre-

---

[1] Eternal Punishment and Eternal Death, pp. 89, 90.

tation of the texts which are supposed to contain the doctrine of endless punishment, they do contain this doctrine, it may still be asked—Does this decide the question? There is no infallibility attached to the process of interpretation. The reasoning by which the inspiration of Scripture itself is ascertained is not infallible. Probability is all that we can attain to. When, therefore, we find the testimony of Scripture, as interpreted by us, to be opposed to a moral intuition, the logical dilemma is this: 1. Scripture may be wrong. 2. Our interpretation of it may be wrong. 3. The moral intuition may be wrong. The canon of Bishop Butler would lead us to prefer the second alternative. Popular theology invariably prefers the third. The truth seems to be, that no absolutely general rule can be laid down, although much may be said in support of the canon of Bishop Butler. But the canon of popular theology is wholly indefensible. No faculty of the human mind is infallible, and the moral faculty may err like the rest. But no faculty is less *likely* to err. A canon which rejects, generally, its decision in favour of the decision of the exegetical faculty, cannot therefore be justified.

It remains to inquire what judgment Canon

Farrar has himself formed on this great question. Here, it may be observed that his classification of the "main views of eschatology" is open to a slight logical objection. As no question is made of the final destiny of "the good," the views of eschatology which he considers can differ only in the position which they assign to those who, at the close of their earthly life, are not among "the good." These views he classes as follows: 1. Universalism, or the belief that all men will ultimately be saved; Annihilationism (also called Conditional Immortality), or the belief that after a finite amount of retributive punishment the wicked will be destroyed; 3. Purgatory, or the belief in an intermediate state of purification; 4. The endless punishment of the wicked. This classification is founded on the answer given, not to a single question, but to two, one only of which is properly eschatological. These questions are: 1. What is man's ultimate destiny? 2. Is that destiny decided at the close of this life? The third of Canon Farrar's classes depends on the answer given to the second or non-eschatological question, and, as might be expected, this view is not absolutely inconsistent with any of the others. The supposition of an intermediate state may co-exist with a belief in either universal redemption, annihilation, or endless punishment. The true division would seem to be threefold, as the ultimate fate of all men must be either happiness, misery, or annihilation. Of these alternatives, Canon Farrar rejects the third altogether. He rejects the second, if it take the form of inflicted punishment, but not if it take the form of the suffering which vice brings with it. In this sense he thinks that the punishment of sin may be endless. But it is never hopeless. The path of repentance is never barred. There is no proof that man's probation ends with this life; and therefore, although the second alternative may be true, *in his sense*, yet the first is not impossible; nay, there are some indications of its truth.

It is thus plain that Canon Farrar is not dogmatic in his positive teaching; and for this no cautious thinker will blame him. His main purpose is the repudiation of the popular notion of hell. The part of his book which is inspired by this purpose, although not containing many new thoughts, is marked by a strain of indignant eloquence, and will well repay perusal.

III.

BY THE LATE PRINCIPAL TULLOCH.

THE question raised in Canon Farrar's volume, *Eternal Hope*, is an intensely interesting one. There will always be a peculiar fascination in questions pertaining to the future, especially in so far as they touch the issues of the great mystery of good and evil. The more profoundly this mystery is felt by thoughtful minds, the more in certain moods will they crave to penetrate "behind the veil," and to lay hold of something definite on which to rest their hopes or fears. The more at the same time will all sober minds feel how really impenetrable the veil is, and that no light of real *knowledge* can be carried beyond that sphere of time and space which now conditions all our powers of knowing.

If theology had admitted long ago the limitations of its knowledge, it would have been well for its progress. A true principle of Agnosticism, reverently admitted and applied, might have saved it, if not from the assaults of the modern principle which passes under this name, yet from some of its excesses. A more reticent theology might have been spared some of the humiliations of a time like ours, in which not only the higher but the common intelligence passes so reluctantly beyond the bounds of experience, and is quietly dropping, even from the skirts of its thought, many notions once universally received and acknowledged. The definiteness which mediæval, and, hardly less, Protestant theology sought to carry into questions which, by their professed nature, allowed of no adequate definition, has recoiled upon it disastrously, till its right to be a branch of knowledge at all has been disputed; and the spiritual sphere within which alone it finds its function has been denied any reality. So extreme a recoil as this will in the end bring its own redress; but there may be "a bad time" before the balance of thought swings round again; and theology is glad to be content, like other sciences, with its *own* sphere of facts, and its own order of generalizations. The new "experience theology" of Holland, with all its deficiencies, may mark the meeting-ground of the modern mind with such a sphere at least as real in human experience as any physical or mental series of facts, and claiming no less recognition and scientific explanation. This theology in the meantime is seeking rest in a mere moral idealism; but if the spiritual is admitted at all as *fact*, it will carry with it in the long run, as its necessary implicates, the old realities, however purified, of Divine revelation.

The good to be got out of all this tendency is the deeper appreciation of facts, the closer and wider study of all the phenomena of the spiritual life, as exhibited in the whole course of man's spiritual history. Religious thought must keep near to religious experience, and only with great caution stretch its wings beyond. Whatever transcends all contact with the farthest reaches of this experience must be beyond dogmatic affirmation, with whatever plausibility or authority it may be commended to us.

It is one of the great excellences of these Sermons, and of the interesting letter appended to them by Professor Plumptre, to whom they are dedicated, that they bring into view the principle of experience in dealing with the subject. Here, as in other cases, the profound though obscure genius of Butler anticipated the true order of procedure, viz., that of working onward from the operation of moral law in the present life towards any possible idea of the future. Seizing clearly the facts of good and evil here as verified in the moral consciousness, the conclusion seems inevitable that these facts will run out in the future as they have here begun. Every man will receive according to the things which he hath done, whether they be good or evil—"in *exact proportion.*" "Every one," in other words, "shall be *equitably* dealt with." This is an assured principle, Butler maintains, of the Divine administration which is by no means to be explained away "after it is acknowledged in words." And he adds, "All shadow of injustice, and indeed all harsh appearances, in the various economy of Providence, would be lost, if we would keep in mind *that every merciful allowance shall be made, and no more required of any one than what might have been equitably expected of him from the circumstances in which he was placed.*"[1]

The clear hold of this law of moral sequence, as embedded in life and building up its structure every day in ourselves or in others, must prevent all wise and cautious minds no

---

[1] Analogy, Part 2, chap. vi.

less than Butler's from affirming that the doom of sin may not be irreversible. As no one may dare to limit the mercy of God, so no one can tell to what awful depths the wickedness of man may reach, or what irremediableness of punishment may cleave to it "in the way of natural consequence." In its own character wickedness possesses no element of cure, nor even of exhaustion. It grows by what it feeds on, and shows sometimes a portentous power of self-development. It may make a hell upon earth; and that therefore it may make a hell in the future everlasting as itself, he must be a rash man who would deny. This the essential tendency of evil, when left to itself,—to intensify, to accumulate, and perpetuate its own misery,—is what makes the weak point in all schemes of Universalism or Restorationism. Like so many optimist theories, the idea that all men shall become good and be saved at last is opposed by the course of experience here. The hard facts of the present life are all against it, and how are we to judge of the future but by the present? Supposing even that new influences of good were brought to bear upon the human will, who can "estimate the hardening effect of obstinate persistence in evil, and the power of the human will to resist the law and repel the love of God?" Out of the very excess of love there sometimes comes a greater bitterness of hatred; out of the very light of good, a deeper darkness of evil. To assert, therefore, in the face of Scripture and experience, that "all men will be saved," is to make a very hardy assertion. About all such optimism there is a tinge of unreality. It may please the benevolent, but it can hardly satisfy the really thoughtful mind.

The theory of Conditional Immortality is vitiated by the same absence of supporting facts. It hangs in the air like so many of the older theories of theology—an imaginary hypothesis invented to explain difficulties, and not an induction resting on any basis of experience. It may or may not be true as a mere speculation. There can be no means of verifying, or even approximating to the verification of such an hypothesis, and the attempt to rest it on the letter of Scripture argues a misunderstanding of the idea of Revelation, more fatal because less excusable than the old literalism from which theology has suffered so much. "Rigid literalism," as Canon Farrar says, "is absolutely fatal to any true knowledge of Scripture." And one of the most eloquent passages of the third Sermon is devoted to a denunciation of the abuses which have sprung from a mere mechanical manipulation of Scriptural texts.

It is mainly by a higher and broader interpretation of the usual texts which have been employed on the subject that the author attempts to set aside what he calls the "common" or "popular" view of Future Punishment, not in favour of any new theory —this he distinctly repudiates—but in favour of an indefinite *trust* in the Divine mercy springing out of our ignorance of the future.

"Those," he says, "whose faith must have a broader basis than the halting reconciliation of ambiguous and opposing texts; they who grieve at the dark shadows flung by human theologians athwart God's light; they who believe that reason, and conscience, and experience, as well as Scripture, are books of God which must have a direct voice in those great decisions; they will not be so ready to snatch God's thunder into their own wretched and feeble hands; they will lay their mouths in the dust rather than make sad the hearts which God hath not made sad; they will take into account the grand principles which dominate through Scripture no less than its isolated expressions; and, undeterred by the base and feeble notion that virtue would be impossible without the horrors of an endless hell, they will declare their hope and trust—if it be not permitted us to go so far into this matter as belief and confidence— that even after death, through the infinite mercy of the loving Father, many of the dead shall be alive again, and the lost be found."

We quote this single passage for two reasons —because it gives the reader as clear a statement as we can find of Canon Farrar's own views on the subject of his volume, and because it indicates the tone of his treatment of the subject throughout. We do not venture to discuss either the one or the other. We have only said so much from a very general point of view, because it is the general line of thought raised by such discussions, rather than any special conclusion on one side or another, that interests us. Theories of one sort or another have done their work in theology—they have deepened thought; they have awakened conscience; they have led men to "search the Scriptures," if after a too narrow fashion. But they have also been fruitful in mischief, as the frequent product of false philosophy or a too ingenious logic. They have aimed at a wisdom above Revelation, a *gnosis* higher than that which maketh wise unto salvation. In so far as Canon Farrar's volume points to "a more excellent way," in reference to the great subject of future retribution, it is worthy of all praise. Its careful and enlightened discussion of the Scriptural terms associated with the subject, and which have played so sad and undue a part in its history, must convince all intelligent readers what need there is for caution and modesty of affirmation. No virtue is so constantly needed in theology as modesty—none, unhappily, is so constantly wanting. To a certain class of minds, theological modesty is supposed to indicate unfaithfulness, paltering with a double purpose. It is strange but true that, when the way is dark and the issues truly awful, most men will rather make a bold leap in the dark than a cautious and reticent advance. They must *know* something positive, even if they fill their mind with emptiness,— with notions which will often no more bear analysis than the terms of a contradictory proposition.

Canon Farrar's earnestness will do good if it make many only try to realise what they mean when they use glibly phrases of awful import. To make religious thought more real cannot be anything but a blessing to a time like ours, or to any time. He would have done even more good in this way, in our opinion, if he had not emphasised with so many dark strokes of rhetoric what he means by the " popular view." He should have remembered that the creed of no Church is responsible for the extravagances with which this view has been somehow set forth, from the frightful picture in the close of Tertullian's treatise *De Spectaculis* to the choice horrors which he quotes from Mr. Spurgeon. The spheres of theology and of popular rhetoric—the rhetoric even of an Augustine or a Jeremy Taylor—are quite apart. The caution which should always guide the induction of the one cannot be looked for in the other. The preacher has his own great function; he must rouse and penetrate,—at times he must startle and appal. But Christian theology must not be made responsible for the pictures of the pulpit, and still less of the devotional manual, whether it be Jesuitical or Evangelical.

This might form Canon Farrar's excuse for the too vehement sway of his own rhetoric, and the excess of his colour here and there. The volume is a volume of Sermons; but the vehement tone is not confined to the Sermons. It runs over into Preface and Excursus. A calmer and even a fairer tone towards what has hitherto been the "popular view," would have been more satisfactory. For, after all, the word "endless," of which it made so much, was not designed to cover more tl an the original Scriptural expression, whatever may be *its* true meaning. It was a mistranslation more than a "lie;" and the idea of Divine authority, rather than any love for "crude and glaring travesty," explains its place in past theology. Vehemence is a mighty weapon in the hands of the preacher; but it weakens the analysis of the critic, and blunts the genuine insight and tolerance of judgment which even the extravagances of Christian thought may claim from us.

IV.

BY THE REV. WILLIAM ARTHUR.

CANON FARRAR rightly condemns the practice of building doctrines on "isolated texts torn from the context," and not "on the whole scope and tenor of revelation." Few practices are more blameworthy, but of these, one is that of setting up doctrines without any texts to found them upon. The negative design of Canon Farrar's volume is to do away with the doctrine of eternal punishment; but its one positive design is to set up a Purgatory that is not Romish. And we believe that his only serious attempt to show that, according to Holy Scripture, any such Purgatory has an existence, rests upon the isolated text touching the spirits in prison, reinforced by the text from the Creed touching the descent into hell.

First invoking general principles, Canon Farrar strongly invokes also history and experience. What, then, according to him, are the general principles recognised in the Bible as those on which our Creator governs all things? He does not tell us. What, again, according to him, are the general principles on which it is shown by history and experience that our own world is governed? He does not tell us. He makes no assertion that history and experience teach that our world is governed on what we may call the painless principle,—that is, on the principle that the Creator, being perfectly benevolent, will never inflict pain on the creature; nor any assertion that Holy Scripture declares such to be the principle whereon He does govern. Neither does Canon Farrar assert that history and experience have shown that among men benevolent government requires that all penalties, for whatever offence, should be terminable; or that Holy Scripture declares that to be a guiding principle of the government of God over both men and angels. But much of Canon Farrar's book will have to be recast should the day ever come when he recognises, with full consciousness, the fact, and the consequences of the fact, that these principles are not recorded in experience, not enunciated in Holy Scripture, but are contrary to the whole scope and tenor of one and the other.

Canon Farrar over and over again unconsciously assumes that the Universe ought to have been governed on the principle that the Ruler would never inflict pain on the subject. To Canon Farrar there may be something in a distinction between inflicting and causing to be inflicted, or in modern jargon, between inflicting by "interference" and inflicting as "a natural consequence." To us these are dialectic distinctions, not moral; distinctions of mode, not of intent; of contrivance, not of polity. So, while to Canon Farrar the distinction between inflicting physical pain and other pain seems to have much to do with the cruelty involved, to us when pain has to be inflicted, whether from ill-will or good-will, if cruel at all, the cruelty of inflicting an equal amount of pain, by physical rather than by other means, is not greater as compared with less, but is simply grosser cruelty as compared with more refined.

Canon Farrar never, indeed, says that it is an established fact in historical science that causing pain implies a delight in suffering; but he declaims as if nobody could doubt it. He never says plainly that inflicting punishment implies cruelty, but he declaims as if that were an accepted certainty. Numerous expressions, even explicit ones, occur in direct contradiction to the assumptions here indicated. Nevertheless, the assumptions underlie the current of thought.

That province in the government of God on which Dr. Farrar fixes his attention, is the rule maintained over men beyond the grave. In judging of what that must be, he seldom seeks guidance in the rule maintained amongst us on this side of the grave. He has to assume that the latter does proceed on the principle of rewards and punishments; but, on the other hand, he would sometimes appear to assume that a perfectly benevolent government would not resort to either of these expedients, against both of which objections can be raised. He does not for guidance turn at all to the palmary instance of Holy Writ— the procedure in the case of angels; nor to the cardinal fact there revealed that a younger race and an elder, the first inhabiting only this world though destined for another, the second inhabiting another world though conversant with this, the one consisting of spirits housed in flesh, the other of spirits not so housed, act and react one upon the other, and are, as to government, dealt with on common principles by a common Ruler.

Canon Farrar does not deny the existence of punishment. He is not at all times unconscious of the fact that it may be merciful, though, perhaps, he means merciful only to the offender, not in the wider sense in which punishment, without mercy to the doer of a wrong, may be saving mercy to the sufferer of the wrong, and protecting mercy to the community. Canon Farrar thinks he relieves the character of the Ruler from charges of cruelty by intimating that He does not inflict the tortures—say those of *delirium tremens*— " attached "—by whom ?—to certain acts, but that we ourselves inflict them. Though Canon Farrar vehemently denies that all who die impenitent suffer eternal punishment, he does not deny, he only wishes he could absolutely deny, that any do. But this admission, and it seems to be a real admission, reduces to—we know not what — pages and pages of hot epithets. He does not believe that the doctrine of the final salvation of all the wicked is firmly established. He treats the doctrine of the annihilation of spirits as incapable of proof. In the language of his own Church, he calls the Romish doctrine of Purgatory " a fond thing vainly invented." But he holds that not the substantive " Purgatory," but the adjective "Romish," expresses all that was invented. He enthusiastically preaches, as a grand amelioration of the universe and adornment of the faith, a Purgatory that is not Romish—a place or state after death of discipline somewhat penal, perhaps, but essentially purifying, whence all who under the discipline repent, pass to Heaven. This Purgatory not Romish is, so far as we can make out, substantially Greek, much resembling that taught by Plato in the "Gorgias" and the "Phædo." As to sin being put away by pain, and not by the grace and spirit of God, the doctrine of Canon Farrar holds closer to the Greek one than to the Romish corruption of it. Plato held that only by suffering could sin be separated from the soul. Rome holds that it is partly by suffering, and partly by the suffrages of survivors. Canon Farrar deliberately teaches that men who "pray, love, agonize, and strive to creep ever nearer to the light," may nevertheless so die that they will "have to be purified in that Gehenna of æonian fire." Here he is more Romish than Greek. Plato would have counted these among the better souls, bound for the Isles of the Blessed; though not among the rare ones, answering to the "saints" of Canon Farrar, whom Plato carries to still brighter abodes. Canon Farrar, however, joins Rome in following the Greeks in dividing men at death into the good, the bad, and the mixed, rather than, as Moses and the Prophets, as Christ and the Apostles divide them, all being in one sense mixed, ultimately into the wicked and the just.

Canon Farrar almost invariably couples with the doctrine of eternal punishment that of reprobation. Some may take the impression that he fancies that the two doctrines were first united in the Reformed Churches. The opening sentence in Calmet's *Dissertation on Predestination* tells a very different tale. But multitudes of Protestants who believe that the Lord Jesus, the most loving, but by far the most alarming, of all the Teachers in the Bible, taught in many forms, negative and positive, that they who will not repent will suffer an endless penalty, do not believe in reprobation, in necessity, in a judgment of any man by a light he never had, or in the final ruin of the majority of our race. They dare not say that any soul that prays, loves, and turns towards the light, will have to pass through a Gehenna of æonian fire. They proclaim for all such mercy unstinted and without reserve. For purification they look not at all to torture, but only to the blood shed by the Lord Jesus, and to the Spirit of God. For them human pains after death exist not, except for the finally impenitent, and only as punishment.

One of Canon Farrar's general principles is "God's severity is all love." If so, the converse follows, that the love of God is sometimes severity. What, then, becomes of all the notions that punishment implies cruelty? Suppose a monster in power wishing to fill London with horrors; how could he more speedily effect his purpose than if, professing fatherly love for all, he issued an edict simply enacting, " Punishment is abolished; and no one shall in person, goods, or repute suffer for any deed done." Canon Farrar, however unintentionally, has so employed learning and eloquence as to confound in the popular apprehension the malignant part played by personal cruelty and private revenge with the beneficent office of public punishment. He overlooks the fact that correction and revenge, both personal affairs, may be fully enacted between two persons alone. A father governing one child may rule on principles impossible to a father governing two, still more to one governing ten, and still more to one governing a tribe. A father might resolve that as to Cain all that was wrong should come right, but how as to Abel already killed? how as to all others who had lives to lose? Canon Farrar overlooks the fact that punishment proper is not a personal matter, but one of public obligation and interest. "Not," said St. Paul, speaking of his solemn act of judgment, "for his cause that did the wrong, nor for his cause that suffered the wrong," but for the cause of the common weal.

When what is called punishment is merely correction, it carries with it demonstration that pain may be inflicted even from personal goodwill. But whenever it aims at rectifying dangerous dispositions in others besides the one "corrected," then the goodwill is not primarily personal, but public; and the degree of the pain inflicted is no measure of cruelty, but of care for the general good. So also when punishment is deterrent. But the great end of punishment is protection, and at this end Canon Farrar hardly glances. Among mortals punishment is not only the fence of all rights and happiness, but of existence itself. Abolish punishment, and you spill out life by a thousand gurgling sluices. So greatly is the protective end of punishment the paramount one, that in grave cases it becomes the only one. In the "Crito" the sense of this truth felt by Socrates is displayed with almost Biblical grandeur. His penalty was not just; it was not terminable; it was not capable of being repaired to him, his friends, or his children. But he would not flee; no, sooner perish Socrates than perish law, was, in effect, the word of the wise man.

Canon Farrar does not seem to be very cautious in invoking history and experience in support of government by terminable penalties exclusively. What government has ever given a guarantee beforehand to all offenders that after a time all consequences of their offence shall cease, and that they shall not on account of it have anything more to suffer? Does past experience point to the conclusion that the effect of such a guarantee would be beneficent? Would it not be malignant? Among mortals, however, the uncertainty of life, the fear of death, the awe of a higher judge, would in part restrain the evil effect of prospective impunity. But how if both immortality and prospective impunity were assured? Might not a system of terminable penalties lead to an interminable repetition of offences, necessitating ever new punishments for fresh transgressors? May not Plato, in firmly fixing on the "incurable" as monuments of terrible suffering for ever, no longer for their own correction, but as an example, a warning to others, have better interpreted the plans of a benevolence that covers all ages and all worlds than do they who insist that every offender must have eventual impunity? The latter supposition, pushed to its consequences, requires that wrong should never be allowed; for if only forgiven, the reparation is, we repeat, to Cain, not to Abel. Here we come in face of the problem of problems, the origin of evil, the permission of wrong, the toleration of the wicked, what Butler calls "*the mystery of God*, the great mystery of His suffering vice and confusion to prevail." In all his impetuous flights Canon Farrar barely grazes the surface of that mystery, like a bird skimming over a still but unfathomable deep.

V.

By the Late Rev. J. Baldwin Brown.

THOSE who have taken any fair measure of the wrong which the Kingdom of Heaven has suffered in all ages at the hands of its scribes and priests, will not wonder at the fervid, and indeed passionate, eloquence with which Canon Farrar pleads against the most terrible of all the dogmas by which they have distorted the righteousness of the Divine government, and clouded the glory of the Divine love. Such a book as Canon Farrar's *Eternal Hope* is deeply significant. Some of us have been for years witnessing against the doctrine of everlasting torment, as horrible in itself, even according to Calvin's confession, and staining with deep dishonour the justice as well as the love of God. But we have been as "voices crying in the wilderness," compared with the testimony which is uplifted by one who speaks with the weight of ecclesiastical dignity, and from the high places of the Anglican Church.

When a man of Canon Farrar's position and influence feels himself so pressed in spirit to preach the Eternal Hope that he can no longer forbear, and gives forth a work so charged with intense conviction as this, the controversy enters on a new phase, and is manifestly nearer to its end.

I do not attempt to criticise Canon Farrar's book in detail, for this simple reason. I have myself been led, under the pressure of the same influences, to very much the same conclusions, which I published three years ago, in an examination of *The Doctrine of Annihilation in the Light of the Gospel of Love*, and I could but repeat what I then expressed. I can only rejoice at finding that the conclusions to which I was then led, after much anxious thought, and under a very painful sense of responsibility, are sustained by the high authority and the ample learning of the eminent writer who has pleaded so eloquently for the Eternal Hope. Like Canon Farrar, I am unable to accept the dogma of the Universalists, after full consideration of the learned and impressive arguments which I have read upon the subject. I believe too deeply in the sacredness of human freedom to accept a doctrine which seems to me to set an imperative bound to its decisions; nor can I find it set forth, in any clear, developed form, in the vision of the future which is revealed in the Word of God. But I hold, and each year I seem to hold more firmly, that the love of God which is in Christ Jesus our Lord cannot be the one Divine power in the universe which, for man at any rate, is paralyzed by the hand of Death. Justice, holiness, fidelity to truth, wrath against sin,—these, we are told, and we joyfully believe, live on and rule through all eternity; but one thing, if this awful dogma be true, Death paralyzes—the hand of the Divine love. And this, when it is once fairly looked at in the light of Scripture and of reason, is blankly incredible. Whatever else may or may not work on through eternity, we are bound to believe that the love which moved the Father to redeem the world at such infinite cost, must work on, while there is one pang in the universe, born of sin, which can touch the Divine pity, or one wretched prodigal in rags and hunger far from the home and the heart of God. And while we know the wrath of God against evil, which is a dread reality, though always within the sphere of His love, and see that sin can only be purged through terrible pain, we have the right to clasp to our hearts all the hope that can grow out of the assurance, that so long as the God who *is* Love lives and reigns, the mercy which redeemed the world must be the regnant power through all the ages and in all the spheres. This surely must be the meaning of the vision of "the Lamb in the midst of the throne," bearing visibly the symbols of the Cross and Passion. All that the Cross symbolizes is there represented as exalted to the throne of universal dominion, the vital centre of the Divine order of the universe, "for ever and for ever."

Eternal Hope! It expresses, in brief, the words with which I closed the treatise to which I have referred: "I plead for the hope of the destruction of the work of the devil in the universe, by the salvation of all that bears the trace of the touch of the hand of God. Sin withered under the curse of the souls that were once its victims; the devil spoiled of his dark dominion, not by the fiat of omnipotent will, but by the hand of omnipotent love. Hell destroyed; Christ triumphant; gathering the spoils of His Cross and Passion here and in all the worlds." This is the Eternal Hope. The term is happily chosen, and the book will be as "glad tidings of great joy" to many a sad and burdened heart; justifying as it does the soul's deepest convictions and most passionate longings, by the best thoughts of the world's wisest teachers in all generations; by the valuable light which it sheds on the ideas and the beliefs of the generation to which the Gospel was first preached; and by the true meaning of the Word of God, which it ably expounds. The textual criticism is of great value; it forms, too, an important feature of a work of great interest, which should be read in connection with this—*Salvator Mundi*, by the Rev. Samuel Cox.

And now that we are emerging from the terrible shadow of this doctrine, we look back with a shudder, and ask ourselves, How was it possible that Christian men should believe it, and should connect such unutterable horrors with the administration of a Being who has given to us, in Calvary, the measure of His love? How could it ever be preached as a leading feature of the Gospel of the Kingdom to mankind? And there is another and darker question behind. The Christian world having believed and preached it all these ages, dare we wonder that Christendom is so little like a Kingdom of Heaven? In order to get light on these questions, it is needful to remember that the doctrine grew *pari passu* with sacerdotal ideas. It is emphatically the dogma of the priest, which he has wielded, and mainly with no base purpose, as a means of influence over men. It gave to him a ready and powerful means of terrorising a rough and brutal generation, and with what awful force he used it the students of mediæval literature will very well understand. But it would have defeated its own end, and become powerless through excess of horror, but for the priestly "power of the keys." There were always the sacraments, the priest's absolution, and the great purgatorial discipline between the human soul and the naked terror during the mediæval period; and so men were not afraid to paint out in the most loathsome and harrowing forms the physical torments of the damned, because they had a ready refuge to offer in the very mild condition of submission to the direction of the Church, which is the Christian attitude of soul in the judgment of Rome. And I venture to think that the same sacerdotal leaven in the Anglican Church has exercised the same influence, and has in some measure mitigated the sharp pressure of the doctrine on the hearts and consciences of its members; while we of the Evangelical Nonconformist Churches have felt it in its full force. We retain the Augustinian doctrine in its most explicit form, and we preach that the doom of the impenitent sinner is " everlasting burning." No priestly word or act is recognised in our Churches which can mitigate for a moment " the horrible decree ;" and the only " way of escape," as we are fond of phrasing it, is by what is constantly represented as a terribly narrow and difficult path. It is here, in the Churches which inherit the Puritan traditions, that the grisly form of the terror is to be seen. Canon Farrar has quoted some truly awful passages from President Edwards. I have quoted others in the work to which I have referred. But it is only fair to remember the anguish of mind which these doctrines inflicted on those who felt bound to preach them. They agonized in spirit until they felt sure that, if God's glory and the good of man demanded it, they were ready themselves to endure to the utmost what they believed that God was purposed to inflict on the great mass of mankind.

But the idea could only hold a hardly-disputed sway while the conception of the Divine order of the universe, which Augustine developes in the *De Civitate Dei*, was supreme— the two great households of light and of darkness in dire, constant, and hopeless antagonism. Calvinism is essentially a fighting creed; grand in its affirmations for all time, but in its negations and anathemas possible only in an age of stern strife between hopelessly irreconcilable antagonists, in which the sufferings of the beaten stir grim satisfaction, like the pains of traitors overthrown in war. Moreover, in ages when high-handed despotism was the normal form of government, men were more able, without a revulsion of horror, to connect stern, tyrannous methods with the rule of God.

But when the idea of the one great family of man, in which the saints were to be the ministers to the sinners, began to steal into human hearts largely through that great uprising of the human which is known as the Revolution, and which had deeper roots than is commonly suspected in the Word of God, men began to feel more sharply the incompatibility of this terrible dogma with the very first principles of the Gospel. New and benign ideas of the duty of a ruler, and his relation to the ruled, have been winning their way during these last generations, and are now accepted throughout the civilised world. Looking from earthly to heavenly things, men are forced to ask themselves, What rule is this which the Church through all these ages has been setting before Christendom as Divine? Great searchings of heart and stirrings of conscience are inevitable under such conditions. Let us thank God that they are breaking forth benignly in such works as these. How terribly Europe has been brutalised by the pictures of torture with which, from Bæda down to Orcagna, mediæval historians, preachers, painters, and poets made it familiar, one hardly dares to estimate. How many generations will pass before the hold on man's nobler nature, which has been lost by the Gospel of Terror, will be regained by the Gospel of Love!

VI.

BY THE REV. JOHN HUNT, D.D.

IF there be any doctrine ever taught in the name of Christianity which can claim to be really Catholic, it is the doctrine of never-ending punishment. This has been believed by the majority of Christians in all ages, in all Churches, and, with very insignificant exceptions, of all sects. Fathers, Schoolmen, and Reformers, zealous Roman Catholics and ardent Protestants, have agreed that this is an undeniable portion of the Catholic faith. We cannot deny that it is a Catholic doctrine, but is it Christian? Dr. Farrar says that the Scriptures, interpreted in the light of "modern criticism," are "absolutely silent" as to "endless torture." Like transubstantiation and many other *Catholic* doctrines, it is founded on taking literally words which were never intended to have a literal meaning.

It is a vast triumph for "modern criticism," if it has overthrown the interpretation which the great body of Christians in all ages have put on certain passages of Scripture. This, however, is but one symptom of the revolution which is overtaking the theology which has long sheltered itself under the name of Catholic or orthodox. It comes finally to the long-disputed question of authority or reason—whether we are to believe doctrines because of the Catholic consent of ages and generations, or if our belief is to be regulated by the results of investigation?

The party of progress in the Church of England, to which Dr. Farrar belongs, receives as a certain truth the axiom of Bishop Butler, that "reason is the only faculty whereby we have to judge of anything, even of revelation itself." If, then, any doctrine taught in the name of Christianity is not reasonable, there is so far a presumption that it is not really a doctrine of revelation. Moreover, as the doctrines of Christianity are, on Butler's principle, part of the evidence of its being a Divine revelation, the existence in Christianity of the doctrine of endless punishment would go a long way to invalidate its claim to be of Divine origin. The argument is, reason tells us that the doctrine of endless punishment is incompatible with the justice and mercy of

God, and therefore cannot be Divine. Attempts have been made to answer this argument by considerations drawn from the existence of evil, from present suffering, from the incapacity of human reason to judge of God's doings, and from our ignorance of the whole scheme of the Divine government. But the capacity of man to judge of God's justice is everywhere assumed in the Bible; the faith that He will do right in the end is a necessary part of our belief in God at all; and the case of present evil and suffering is altogether different from that of evil and suffering which shall never end. All present irregularities may be put right; God has before Him a whole eternity in which He can rectify the wrongs of this present life, but the very terms "endless evil and suffering" preclude the possibility of their ever being so rectified as to be compatible with the Divine attributes of justice and mercy. In this case the subject is within the competence of man to judge, for he is told that endless suffering is to depend on his actions in this present life, and reason declares that nothing which the worst of men could possibly do within the compass of his threescore and ten years could possibly deserve such a punishment as the endless torment of Catholic or orthodox theology.

We lay an emphasis on the word Catholic, for some of those who claim this appellation as the antithesis of Protestant have of late been trying to charge the awful hell on those who, at the Reformation, are said to have departed from the Catholic faith. Dr. Farrar seems partly to have admitted their plea; but the whole argument rests on the clumsy invention of purgatory, which is to purify by physical torments, not the lost, but the souls that are not sufficiently pure to enter into Paradise. There still exists the awful hell for the lost, which is as conspicuous in the Romish Church as it ever was in any Protestant community. To take the Roman Catholic books that first come to our hands, here is a passage from Bouhour's Meditations, translated in a book of devotion for English Roman Catholics :—

"What misery can be equal to that of being miserable so long as God shall be God ? . . . These unhappy children of wrath not only suffer during eternity, but they suffer eternity during each moment of their existence. Eternity is engraven on the flames which torment them ; it makes a part of all their sufferings ; it is ever present to their minds. O tormenting thought ! O miserable condition ! To burn for ever ! to weep for ever ! to rage for ever !"

Here is another passage from the Meditations

of St. Francis de Sales, which are printed in the *Garden of the Soul*:—

"Represent to yourself a dark city all burning and stinking with fire and brimstone. . . . The damned are in the depth of hell within this woeful city, where they suffer unspeakable torments in all their senses and members. . . Consider above all the eternity of their pains, which above all things makes hell intolerable."

To those who are really lost the Church of Rome, no more than orthodox Protestants, allows the possibility of amendment after this present life.

To reject endless punishment is to overturn the foundation of the whole system of theology which is known as Catholic, but it is also to remove what to many is an insuperable difficulty in the way of believing Christianity. The great question then is, Can it be done fairly, or can modern criticism really prove that the Scriptures are silent concerning never-ending punishment? The remark is made by old Thomas Hobbes, that though hell fire may be everlasting, those cast into it may not remain in it everlastingly. This is an ingenious solution of a pressing difficulty, but when ingenuity is necessary there is always ground for suspicion. Some have supposed that the wicked will be annihilated, or, in other words, that immortality will be granted only to them

F

that repent and amend. But this is a supposition which has no foundation in Scripture, and, like the other, is ingeniously invented to meet a difficulty. Restitution, or the ultimate salvation of all men, is the most reasonable hypothesis, and the one which could appeal to most passages of Scripture in the way of indirect intimation, but it cannot be said to be clearly taught in the New Testament.

To the English·reader of the Bible the plainest and most obvious doctrine concerning the future punishment of the wicked is that it shall be endless, in a place called hell, and with fire and brimstone; and the strongest words are those of Christ Himself, where He says of the wicked, that "their worm dieth not, and their fire is not quenched." Awful words to our ears when coming with the full meaning which they now convey to us. But had they this meaning when Christ spoke them? Did they convey this meaning to those who first heard them? This is surely a legitimate inquiry, and the meaning which Christ intended must be the proper meaning. Can a worm that never dies mean anything else but a worm that never dies? Can fire that is never to be quenched mean anything but fire that is never to be quenched? Certainly not, if we must take them literally, but does the discourse admit of this? A worm and a fire are material. It may be said that though they are only emblematic, yet they must mean that whatever the suffering is, it must be never-ending. And this would have been, so far as we can see, a fair inference; but it happens that Christ took the words from the last verse of Isaiah, where the reference is to material bodies and to a temporal punishment—in which case the worm cannot be literally never-dying, nor the fire unquenchable. Why should they be taken literally when spoken by Christ, if they are not to be taken literally, as obviously they cannot be, so far as duration is concerned, when used by Isaiah?

Dr. Farrar maintains that "hell" and "damnation" had not, when the Bible was translated, the terrible meaning which they have now. This may be partly true, but it cannot be doubted that the idea of a place of endless torment was familiar to the translators. Damnation has evidently changed its meaning for the worse. But the really important word is "eternal." The Greek αἰώνιος may or may not be translated "everlasting." It is used in many places in the Bible where it cannot mean endless, and its etymological meaning is the opposite of everlasting. The Master of Trinity College, Cambridge, in his notes to Archer Butler's *Lectures* (vol. ii. 182), points out a passage in Plato which no critic before had noticed, in which αἰώνιος is used as the antithesis of eternal. The word, however, was also used by the later philosophers, as Philo, Plotinus, and other Neo-Platonists, to mean eternal, not in the sense of having anything to do with duration, but as expressing the plenitude of being, in agreement with Spinoza's definition of eternity, "*per æternitatem intelligo ipsam existentiam.*" If we could suppose that Christ spoke the language of philosophy, and that the discourses in the fourth Gospel are reported literally, we might fairly conclude that by "eternal life" He meant absolute existence. The opposite of this—eternal death—would then be a mere negation, not suffering marked by any degree of duration, but the deprivation of absolute or real existence.

Etymology, metaphysics, and we may say, for the convenience of the argument, the fourth Gospel, may all be left out of the controversy; and the sole question to be settled is what Christ meant to say when He spoke of the future punishment of the wicked. The proper answer seems to be that He did not intend to convey any idea, either of the real nature or of the duration of the punishment. It was something so awful that the strongest metaphors with which the minds of His hearers were familiar were used to describe it; but still they were metaphors, and all taken from things temporal and material. The Bible, in fact, never introduces us to heaven or hell but under material figures, just as it rarely speaks of God except under the likeness of man, or with attributes which are in part common to God and man. And the reason of this probably is, that the multitude of men have no capacity for anything beyond this. Christ's language addressed to the multitude was metaphorical, and not literal. The judgment of God against sin is terrible, but the details of that judgment may not be definitely revealed, and we may not have capacities for understanding such a revelation if it were made.

We are thus, in the end, left to reason as to the duration of punishment, and reason has ever rebelled against the *Catholic* faith in never-ending suffering. In unbelievers, in rational apologists, and in Catholic saints and theologians, there has been in some form an objection to this belief, or a mitigation which went a long way to neutralize it. To all it is manifest that there is no such difference between the very best and the very worst of men, as that one should have a never-ending felicity, and the other be trampled under the feet of devils in never-ending torment. The distinction of baptized or unbaptized, Christian or heathen, Catholic or heretic, elect or reprobate, are all insufficient to make a difference so vast as that between heaven and hell, as commonly understood. And when we look at men as they actually are, the chief differences between them have depended on the circumstances of their birth, education, companions, and natural temperament; and when they die, the multitude, as Mr. Wilson, of Great Staughton, somewhere says, are "germinal souls." They are too bad for heaven, and too good for hell. Some may deserve many stripes, but others only a few. And that this is admitted by those who tenaciously cling to never-ending suffering is proved by the general reception of the doctrine of different degrees of rewards and punishments in a future life. Professor Plumptre, in a letter to Dr. Farrar, quotes remarkable passages on this subject from Butler and Paley; but he will also find the same doctrine as exactly stated in John Wesley's sermons. The idea that great revivalist preachers have owed their success to preaching the terrors of hell is exploded. They preached terror much less than is generally believed, and their success was not owing to this, but to their awakening the moral sense which found a hell wherever there was sin.

VII.

BY THE LATE REV. RICHARD F. LITTLEDALE, D.C.L.

CANON FARRAR'S volume of Sermons is one of four noticeable books which have recently appeared, in conjunction with many pamphlets, wherein the popular theology, as well of the Roman and Anglican Churches as of most Protestant communions, in respect of the condition of souls beyond the grave, is challenged or disputed. The three others are the Rev. Andrew Jukes's *Restitution of All Things*, the Rev. Samuel Cox's *Salvator Mundi*, and Mr. Edward White's *Life in Christ*.

I think that all dispassionate readers of these four works must come to agreement on one point, if no more—namely, that in the last three they are brought face to face with trained theologians, with men from whose conclusions they may indeed be constrained to differ widely, yet whose method and matter they must recognise as belonging to the sphere of scientific divinity. But in Canon Farrar's Sermons the amateur and neophyte is visible throughout; and the discourses themselves, while always cultured, often—perhaps too often—ornate, and sometimes impassioned, yet seldom rise to the dignity of sustained argument, or even of accurate thought, and never attain the level of matured theological knowledge. They are, to borrow a simile from forensic practice, declamatory appeals to a jury rather than reasoned pleadings before a judge; and although the preface and appendices are somewhat more chastened in style and more exact in method, yet they, too, exhibit a fragmentary and tentative character which is eminently unsatisfying, but which, it must in justice be said, the author apologetically confesses.

Nevertheless, these very defects have their value in the present state of the controversy with which the Sermons deal; for they supply ample proof that it has passed out of the domain of dead scholastic dialectics, and has entered into that of burning questions, to which the intellect and conscience of all thinking Christian men are imperatively demanding some prompt and unfaltering answer; and further, make it sufficiently plain that the answer which the popular theology has been tendering for centuries past will not be accepted much longer.

I disclaim any desire to uphold that theology (which I have never aided in propagating) when pointing out what seem to me certain flaws in Canon Farrar's method and statements; since, were I obliged to choose, I should prefer ranging myself at his side, rather than with Pinamonti, or even with Mr. E. H. Bickersteth, whose comparatively softened view appears in his remarkable poem, "Yesterday, To-day, and For Ever."

The most salient defect, then, in these Sermons is that they do little more than pull down. That is often a most necessary process, and all dwellers in crowded cities know full well how great is the gain in the mere sweeping away of noisome fever-dens, even if their sites be left bare and desolate, with no wholesome dwellings nor pleasant gardens to occupy them. And there is no question in my mind, at any rate, as to the imperative necessity of demolishing, and that speedily, the hyper-Augustinianism which still lingers amongst us. But we cannot wisely leave huge vacant spaces, like the wastes within the walls of Rome and of Constantinople, in men's minds, where once were some definite notions as to one of the most momentous topics which can exercise thought; and this is what Canon Farrar has practically, albeit undesignedly, done. There is much force in Mr. Cox's plea that the very limitations of our knowledge, and that ambiguity of the Scriptural indications which is admitted by all impartial scholars, must act in restraint of our constructing a complete and consistent theory which may be proffered as a full answer to inquiry, a convincing substitute for the discredited hypothesis; but Mr. Cox himself, not less than Mr. Jukes and Mr. White, does endeavour to set some positive teaching in the place of that which he seeks to displace. I can scarcely avoid the conclusion that the majority of those who heard Canon Farrar's sermons must have gone away with a much clearer notion as to what he denied than as to what he asserted and wished them to believe. And if so, he discharged no more than one-half of a teacher's function. It admits of no reasonable doubt that the popular theology is a very ineffective deterrent from sin, and that for exactly the same reason as caused the practical failure of the English penal code before Romilly softened it—namely, that as judges and juries

often then combined against the evidence to
acquit culprits, rather than inflict the disproportionate penalty of death for minor
offences, an element of great uncertainty was
introduced into the law, and almost perfect
impunity attended many serious crimes, so
that they were actually encouraged—a risk
obviated by the juster incidence of the present
code, which is more certain, though milder.
So, too, when men are taught that God has
only one penalty in His code—that of everlasting damnation—they cannot believe that
He will invariably inflict it, and each hopes to
get off altogether, not realising that every sin
must be chastised. Canon Farrar has scarcely
given this latter notion adequate prominence,
though subordinately mentioning it, and so
far has not supplied a clear deterrent for lower
natures—an error from which Mr. Jukes is
quite free. To my mind, further, even his
destructive argument is not put on the
soundest basis. There is not sufficient stress
laid anywhere on the cardinal fact that the
Scriptures of the New Testament contain two
parallel, and often seemingly contradictory,
sets of statements as to the Last Things; one
of which, even after being sifted jealously by
hostile criticism, does make for the popular

theology, and another which more than implies a full restoration, and the final victory of good over evil. It is as difficult to do justice to the inquiry if the evidence for the first half of these conflicting declarations be minimised, as it has proved to be when the second half is wholly disregarded; and on Canon Farrar's hypothesis, it seems almost impossible to account for the origin and spread of the popular theology at all. Unless it had a great deal more to go on than he is willing to allow, it could scarcely have arisen and maintained its position so long within the Christian Church.

The second point which is insufficiently illustrated, being indeed quite absent from the Sermons, and merely relegated to a casual note in one of the appendices, is the absence of any formulated decree of the Church Catholic in favour of everlasting punishment. That the question was raised and debated we know; that an attempt was made to procure a formal condemnation of Origen's doctrine on this head we know also; but the effort failed, and the question remains an open one to this day. There is a great significance in the fact that in the simplest of our symbols, the Apostles' Creed, and in the most universal of them, the

Nicæno-Constantinopolitan, we are called on to express our belief in the life, but not in the death, to come. And although the Athanasian Hymn may obviously be quoted adversely, it is to be noticed that it restricts itself in its closing verses to the citation of the exact words of Scripture, and does not undertake to gloss them for us, so that it can hardly be alleged as an interpretation. Dr. Farrar might very fitly have pointed out, in reply to the argument from the long prevalence of the popular theology in the Church, that an equal or greater prescription exists in favour of the tenet of Verbal Inspiration, which no Biblical scholar of repute now holds, since even those who declare that if we had the authentic text of every passage before us, each tittle of it would be infallibly and divinely true, do not assert that such a text exists for any one book of Scripture. But this tenet, like that of endless punishment, has never been formulated by the Church, and makes no part of any Conciliar decree or any Christian creed. This important fact ought to have been given prominence in connection with the proof tendered that St. Gregory Nyssen, and other eminent Fathers of an earlier date, followed the milder view, because it establishes that their opinion is still, to say the least of it, tenable, and has not been excluded, like some ante-Nicene phraseology on other points, by subsequent authoritative explanations or rulings. Dr. Farrar, while most usefully drawing attention to the unfamiliar fact that the Jewish Church has no tradition whatever in favour of endless punishment, has failed to group visibly with it that other fact, that Prayers for the Dead passed without break from Judaism into Christianity; so that, when once the true historical position of Christianity, as a continuous development of Judaism, is fully realised, the milder view seems antecedently more likely to be a part of the original deposit of the Gospel than the harsher one.

Another point where Dr. Farrar has understated his case, at the same time that he seems to lay almost undue stress on it, is his discussion, at pp. xxxiv, xxxv, 77, 78, and 80, 81, of the true meaning of the crucial word αἰώνιος, where he appears to exclude that meaning of infinity which it unquestionably often has, *e.g.* Exod. iii. 15; Job xxxiii. 12; Isa. xl. 28, lx. 19, etc. It is not enough to say that this term is confessedly ambiguous, without also saying that there are several Greek words perfectly free from any ambiguity, whose meaning of "endless" cannot be disputed, and which not only might, but almost certainly would, have been used had the Apostles and Evangelists designed to enforce that idea. Such are ἀτελεύταιος, ἀπέραντος, ἀθάνατος, ἄπαυστος, ἀέναος, ἄπειρος, perhaps διηνεκής, all of which are noticeably absent from the New Testament in this connection, as also are ἐς ἀεί and ἄνευ τέλους—a circumstance which does not seem to have been adequately pressed hitherto.

Beyond the negative statements of Dr. Farrar, there is, as already implied, a lack of positive ones. He does, indeed, in one place (p. xvi) just shrink from asserting Universalism, but he seems to accept it fully at p. 89; while his argument, if it may be so called, against Conditional Immortality, or Annihilationism, amounts to little more than that he does not like it. The real difficulties of Universalism—the metaphysical objection that it militates against the existence of free-will, and the consequent possibility of a volition of evil through eternity (especially in the case of evil spirits), and the moral objection that it fails to realise the true nature and effects of sin—he scarcely touches; and the chief objection to Annihilationism—its assertion of retrograde action on God's part, as reversing the process of creation—he does not touch at all. In fact, his mind, untrained in theology, and indeed in logic, as yet has reached only the stage of revolt; and even his pleas against the popular teaching, corroborative as they may be of sounder arguments, do not get beyond the *à priori* stage, and are open to the rejoinder that they avoid rather than solve difficulties. He has not, for example, more than distantly glanced at two cogent pleas severally urged by Mr. Jukes (who, by-the-bye, is an Anglican clergyman, not a Nonconformist, as Dr. Farrar reckons him), and by Mr. White — namely, that if the popular theology be true, then Christ has been completely defeated by Satan in the contest for the souls of men, since incomparably the larger spoils of battle rest with the latter; and the Incarnation has not affected the ultimate nature and destinies of mankind in general. So, again, while justly blaming the Reformers for tampering with the deposit of primitive Christianity, and for darkening the counsel of God by discontinuing prayers for the dead, he has quite failed to note the reason why Protestant teaching has for the most part, till the rise of Universalism, been so much harsher than Roman Catholic theology. The answer lies not in the mere denial of a purgatory, but in the abandonment by both Luther and Calvin of the ancient Christian doctrine of the Fall, and their substitution of a new theory for it. Catholics teach that the Fall deprived man of a certain supernatural grace which insured the due balance of his complex nature, and that he thereupon became wholly disorganized, and liable to find his higher will dominated by the lower, but was still the same creature, having good freely mixed with his evil. Luther and Calvin, on the other hand, fundamentally at one in their teaching, despite their marked surface differences, maintained that man by falling became a mere mass of absolute evil, without the smallest admixture of good, and even with no capacity for being developed into something better, so that he could be saved only by the legal fiction of the imputed righteousness of another, or else by the arbitrary favour of an autocratic decree, in each case quite irrespective of any personal equation, since even his virtues are only splendid sins. Once grant so much, and all mankind necessarily falls into the category of those whom all but the most extreme Universalists recognise as possible subjects of everlasting punishment—namely, such as have so wallowed in deliberate and wanton evil, that they have left nothing upon which, so to speak, even Omnipotence itself can work, so that there is no injustice in sentencing them to reap as they have sown.

But this monstrous teaching is false to the Bible, and also to all our moral sense and practical experience. We know that there is good as well as evil in man, and we may not call good evil to support a theory. And when once we recognise the germ of good in even the most wicked men, we are faced by this difficulty in the popular theology, that it assumes God to permit, if not to force, this good to be overpowered and assimilated by the evil in contact with it, and thereby contradicts the frequent analogy in the Old Testament borrowed from the smelting of ores. The metallurgist does not throw away nor destroy even "reprobate silver" (Jer. vi. 30), but purges it from its dross in his fiery furnace, drawing the purified metal thence to be wrought into costly fabrics (Isa. i. 25 ; Ezek. xxii. 18-23; Zech. xiii. 31; Mal. iii. 3); but God is, on this hypothesis, a less capable workman.

Another fruitful source of error which Canon Farrar has failed to point out is the popular teaching as to this life being a state of *probation*, a solitary chance, failure in which involves destruction, just as with us gun-barrels which cannot pass the test in the proof-house are invariably condemned, broken up, and cast into the fire—but only to be forged anew. There is no warrant in Scripture for this current opinion, which in truth necessitates a denial of God's foreknowledge, as not being able to trust His own work, nor to predict how it will turn out till He has tested it. He does indeed try and prove, but it is in the way of *education* and *purgation*, not of inquiry. " When He hath *tried* me, I shall come forth as gold" (Job xxiii. 10). " Behold, I will melt them, and *try* them" (Jer. ix. 7). Once grasp the notion that we have only one life given us to live, and that death is a mere episode in it, so that this world is but a lower class in God's school, and another stage of education in our unbroken personality and life beyond the grave awaits us in the intermediate state, whether that stage be downwards or upwards, according as we have used our opportunities here, and the whole scheme of redemption shows clearer.

Once more, Canon Farrar is not happy in his rejoinder to the argument urged even by

Mr. Keble, and repeated only a few days ago by Canon Ryle,[1] that to cast a doubt on the endlessness of punishment is to invalidate the argument for the endlessness of bliss, since both rest on exactly the same Biblical sanctions. There are three replies, cumulatively exhaustive, which he has failed to adduce. First, assuming the fact to be really so, there is all the difference caused by the rejoicing trust and confidence of the redeemed in the living protection of God in that City from which evil is for ever banished, and into which, consequently, temptation cannot make its way. Next, the fact is not, as alleged, that they do rest on the same Biblical sanctions, because though there is very much in Scripture which implies the termination of evil and the universal prevalence of good, there is very little to show for the everlasting duration of death, sin, and misery, and nothing whatever which can be made to hint at the possibility of another revolution, and the return of evil to power. Thirdly, the difference of the two eternities, hell and heaven, consists in the presence or absence of God. Let us put a

---

[1] Now Bishop of Liverpool. This was first published in 1878.

for each of these eternities or æons, and θ to denote Him. The assertion of the equality of the two, then, is that $a + \theta = a - \theta$, which can stand only if $\theta = 0$, the postulate of atheism.

Lastly, albeit Canon Farrar's forte is illustration, and argument his weak point, he has missed the opportunity of bringing a powerful sidelight to bear on that part of the popular theology which teaches that man's doom is irreversibly fixed at the moment of death, and that, if he be unrepentant at that particular instant of time, he is lost for ever. It is, that this view puts God on a moral level with the devisers of the most savagely malignant revenge known to history—the deed known in Italy as *la gran vendetta*. This differs from ordinary assassinations, in that the murderer does not strike his victim down at any time feasible, but dogs his steps till he finds him fresh from the committal of some sin accounted mortal in Roman Catholic theology, and then slays him before he has had a moment for repentance or confession, so as to insure his damnation as well as his death. When a hired bravo executes this vengeance, he exacts a much higher price than the ordinary tariff for his services. The horror with which we read of such a crime ought to make us all careful lest we should give our assent to the teaching which predicates it, only on an infinitely vaster scale, of the just and merciful God.

VIII.

BY THE REV. EDWARD WHITE

(Author of *Life in Christ*—A Study of the Scripture Doctrine on the Nature of Man, the Object of the Divine Incarnation, and the Conditions of Human Immortality).

CANON FARRAR'S Sermons, as the *Spectator* truly affirmed, are highly rhetorical; but I do not assent to the additional criticism that this quality diminishes their theological value. When, as in the present case, the rhetoric blazes up from a great depth of spiritual emotion, a zeal for God as the intelligibly just Judge of mankind—whether in its details of belief this zeal be less or more according to knowledge — the tremendous force of the language employed seems more helpful to wise and reverent thought on such a subject than would be the cold-blooded style of ordinary theological discussion. At all events, it is refreshing, just for once, to listen to a preacher who almost shook Westminster Abbey with the volcanic storm of his indignation in attacking what he holds to be the *mendacium mendaciorum* of Protestant divinity.

With Canon Farrar's earnest protest against confounding the good and evil principles in the universe I inwardly agree; believing, further, that the final, if indirect, result of this unconventional explosion of moral passion will be to awaken more serious thought on the present quality and future results of human conduct than has been known in our generation. Nevertheless, looking at the question here treated from the standpoint of the belief that redemption regards man's eternal being, as well as his blessedness, Canon Farrar's argument seems to me neither to rest on a quite solid basis, nor to reach a safe conclusion. All arguments respecting the future destinies of men which are restricted to the question of personal retribution, or to speculations on the Divine Character as involved in that retribution, must fail in solidity, and fail in reaching or overmastering the deep-seated scepticism of this generation, because failing in breadth of justice towards both biological and biblical science. Man's destiny in the future cannot be satisfactorily determined, on the ground either of reason or revelation, apart from previous study of man's *nature* as a whole; and the Divine communications on that destiny cannot be rightly apprehended apart from an understanding of their psychological and physical bases. Canon Farrar seems to start on his quest after truth in eschatology, as do both the more pronounced Universalists and the believers in endless suffering, from the assumption of the immortality of the soul; not simply from belief in its conceivable temporary survival, as the butterfly survives the chrysalis without being immortal, but in its absolute eternity in all cases, under the intention of God. Now, this natural eternity of souls appears to me to be confounded with a possible temporary survival, and, as a positive dogma, to be destitute of all evidence from nature or revelation. It is, in fact, the πρῶτον ψεῦδος which confuses all questions pertaining to the relations of God and man; it hinders men from rightly understanding the meaning and end of the Divine Incarnation, thereby concealing the glory of the Son of God as the "Life-giving Spirit;" and, finally, it tempts to the assertion of the doctrines either of universal salvation or of eternal suffering, both of which contradict, at least, the more obvious signification of ordinary Biblical language on the everlasting *destruction* of men who refuse to submit to the moral government of God.

I know that this denial of absolute immortality in mankind threatens an enormous revolution in popular thought, especially in England, where the belief in the immortal soul stands on a level of certitude with that of the existence of God. In France the alarm, from the prevalence of materialism, is not so great. Yet even in England the measure of the shock depends on the persons who cause it. This denial is listened to, indeed, with anger when it proceeds from Christian theologians. But when it comes, even in its most extreme form, from scientific biologists of the first rank, who, after careful study of the phenomena of brain-production and mind-evolution throughout living nature, and of the phenomena of waste and destruction in unfinished organisms, declare it to be the height of absurdity to maintain that the vital principle of every single human germ, born or unborn, which reaches some undefined point of development, *must live as long as the Creator Himself*,—why, even the theological public listens in placid or respectful silence. A similar opinion is received almost with reverent sympathy, when it is represented, by Mr. Rhys-Davids, in the *Contemporary*, as the faith of four hundred and eighty millions of Buddhists, all piously and sorrowfully toiling towards *Nirvana*, or extinction of individual being, on the other side of the continent of Asia. It is only when the mortality of the "soul" is maintained as a Christian dogma that it is dismissed, even by Canon Farrar, with indignation, as an opinion too debasing even to be considered with attention. Nevertheless, I must declare my steadfast consent to this conclusion, holding it not only for truth in ontology and biology, but also to be the basis on which Redemption proceeds from first to last. Tripartite man, we are taught, was created "in God's image;" he never was "a beast of the field;" he was formed in sublime relations with the Infinite. But his ascent from the lower plane of terrestrial mortality into assured immortal life depended on continued spiritual union with God, on voluntary subjection of the created to the Uncreated Will. That original purpose having been defeated by the action of infernal powers, and the prospect of life eternal vanishing through sin, restoration to " eternal hope" was possible only through a supernatural action of grace above law, involving a union of the Divine and Human natures in the person of Christ, and an inward and outward transformative change in the individual man, bestowing a "second birth" of both soul and body, in spiritual renewal and physical resurrection. So that unless men are born twice they will die twice. They must be "born again" or die the "second death." This, briefly stated, I take to be the drift of the Christian Revelation; and to describe this, as Canon Farrar does, as a "doctrine of Annihilationism," is as unreasonable as it would be so to describe some curative system introduced in order to save men's lives, *if they will receive it*, in a land where all were dying of fever or confluent small-pox.

It will be seen at once that all questions of human salvation, and of the future punishment of the "second death," assume wholly new aspects under such connected biological and theological views. What comes into prominence now, as the ground of hope for the endless future, is not the deathless nature of man, but the gift of God in the deathless nature of the Eternal Son, the Incarnate Life and Love; whose Person as Divine, and whose work in immortalising men, form the two subjects of that Fourth Gospel which is the chief glory of the Scriptures. What comes into prominence now is the action of that "Life-giving Spirit" (1 Cor. xv. 45), which operates on men under all various degrees of knowledge, in uniting them to Christ, "the Life of the world," and extends in some specified cases its gracious energy beyond the grave.

Under such views, wholly rejected by Dr. Farrar, yet strangely harmonising with the results of science in all departments, one is led to protest urgently against that old Origenist misapplication of the words "*the letter killeth*" (used by St. Paul to describe the destructive action of law) to which Canon Farrar lends his distinct approval,—a misapplication which makes a special virtue of non-natural interpretation, leading to the demand for some figurative sense to be imposed on the three most important series of terms in the records of Revelation: firstly, on all those which attribute man's eternal life to the Divine Incarnation, and restrict such endless life to the twice-born sons of God; secondly, on those which denounce *death, destruction of body and soul,* and *extermination,* to wicked men; and lastly, on those which declare that doom to be final and *eternal.* Thus it comes to pass, as has been shown at length elsewhere, that the very terms employed by Plato in the *Phædon,* and used for four hundred years before the Gospel, through the Greek-speaking world, to denote the extinction of life, are in the New Testament wrested from their obvious and historical meaning, in obedience to some imagined requirement of the sacred dialect, or some still more stringent requirement of a metaphysic resolved on maintaining the absolute eternity of one part of man's mortal nature.

Canon Farrar supports the popular allegation that, under this scheme of more literal interpretation, the wicked would be raised from the dead "only that they may be tormented and destroyed." But, indeed, this is to lose sight of the truth that the primary object of the Resurrection, in all cases, is represented in Scripture not simply as retribution, but, as Professor Stokes of Cambridge observes, as the visible vindication of the Divine Justice, in the historical "manifestation" of every individual human character, so that what God does with every man will satisfy the conscience of the universe. And the doctrine of the final destruction of the unrepenting remnant of God-rejecting men resolves itself into an awe-striking example of the survival of the fittest; the death of those who are "unworthy of eternal life," after the exhaustion of all redemptive processes on earth, and in some cases in Hades, being the result of the operation of the law of their nature, and not, as Mr. Erskine supposes, an act of arbitrary power on the part of the Almighty. And I am compelled unwillingly to express the persuasion that a line of religious instruction, which takes for its leading principle the notion that the principal aim of the Divine Revelation is to give to the generality of defiant men a cheerful and hopeful view of their ultimate destiny, differs *toto cœlo*, and even *toto inferno*, from the fearful doctrine of Christ and His Apostles, in its tone towards such persons, and will be attended practically, as experience shows, by widely different results.

IX.

BY THE REV. PROFESSOR SALMON, D.D.

THE question with which Canon Farrar's Sermons are mainly concerned is a difficulty of natural as much as of revealed religion. If we consider that we have sufficient reason, independently of Christianity, to believe in a future life, we have to form a theory as to what will be the future of those whose present life has been a moral failure. There certainly have been at least some whose earthly life has been quite the reverse of a season of discipline and moral improvement: they have spent it in learning new vices, and getting more hardened in old ones; they have died to all appearance irreformably wicked, and if they then enter on a life which can be described as anything like a natural continuation of the present one, they must do so under conditions infinitely less favourable than those under which they started here. Convinced that vice and misery must go together, we need not inquire about the happiness hereafter of such persons; it is enough to inquire about their goodness. Four theories may be started as to their future. First, it may be supposed that those whose reformation is hopeless, after death cease to exist. This hypothesis is difficult to reconcile with teaching the immortality of the soul as a doctrine of natural religion. Great moral depravity is known to be compatible with high physical vitality, so that we cannot well think of death as terminating the existence of very bad men, and of such only, without introducing a Divine miraculous intervention either for the destruction of those who perish, or for the bestowal of a new life on those who survive. In either case we travel out of the domain of natural religion. Secondly, it may be supposed that the existence of the wicked is temporarily continued beyond the grave, whether for the infliction of retributive punishment or for further probation, but that after unsuccessful trial their ultimate fate is annihilation. These two hypotheses agree in ascribing immortality to some men, not to others—thus really dividing the human race into two essentially different species; and the second is open to the further objection urged by Cicero against a similar theory of the Stoics, that it concedes the most difficult point—namely, that the soul can survive the dissolution of the body—and refuses to grant what is most natural to think —namely, that what has survived so great a shock must be immortal. The third supposition is, that all who leave this life pass into other scenes of discipline, so devised that all, without exception, are ultimately brought to virtue and happiness. There is nothing in natural religion, as Butler has remarked, which forbids us to think that human creatures, after leaving this world, may pass through different states of life and being. We may well believe that the constitution of all these states will be such as to "make for righteousness," and we cannot pronounce it incredible that, by the discipline of such states, virtue, here but inchoate, may hereafter be strengthened and perfected. But to say that such a process shall be absolutely without possibility of failure in any case, is to make an assertion opposed to the whole analogy of our present experience; and it is the more hazardous to attribute to future discipline this certainty of uniform success, inasmuch as many of the subjects of it enter upon it, as has been already remarked, in a condition far less favourable than that in which they started here. This third hypothesis, then, cannot be asserted on scientific grounds—that is to say, not because there is any present evidence that the constitution of nature is such as we think it ought to be; but solely on moral grounds, because our faith in the goodness of God induces us to believe that He will hereafter make it so, however little present signs of it there may be. Such an argument can at most inspire but a hope —it is far from yielding an assurance. We must have faith in the goodness of God, if we deserve to be called Theists at all; but we cannot, without extreme rashness, say that God will certainly justify His goodness in exactly the way we may pronounce most befitting Him. If we could have attained our present belief in His omnipotence and goodness without experience of the existing constitution of things, we should most certainly have declared it to be absolutely incredible that evil could find the place in it which it actually does. How the existence of evil can be reconciled with the Divine attributes is a problem which never has been solved. Such considerations as that by physical evil man's faculties are drawn out, that without the possibility of moral evil there would be no room for the highest kinds of virtue, etc., are not so much solutions as encouragements to hold fast our faith in God, and believe that He can hereafter justify His ways. Still, these considerations give us all the light we have, and we lose all explanation why God should have made us exposed to temptation here if we think it possible that He can hereafter, without annihilating virtue as well as vice, ordain a constitution of things in which the inducements to welldoing shall be so overpowering that wrongdoing shall be impossible.

It is credible that there are other worlds like ours, and equally credible that at any given period of time hereafter there may be one or more worlds in the same state of development as ours is now, and therefore not unlikely to present the same phenomena as those we have experience of. It is not defined in this third hypothesis how long a period of trial and discipline may be necessary for the reformation of a vicious person: the framers of the hypothesis feel no difficulty in conceding that it may be as long as you please, provided only it be not infinite. What, therefore, this third hypothesis requires us to assert is, that it is reconcilable with the Divine attributes that evil may exist in the universe to all eternity, and in any given individual for an indefinite time, but absolutely irreconcilable with them that its existence in the same individual should be eternal. To assert this requires more knowledge than I can pretend to possess concerning the Divine attributes—concerning infinity and eternity, and the relation of time to the absolute Being. If we have not evidence for any of the three suppositions enumerated, we must fall back on the only remaining fourth; and it appears to follow that the assertion of the immortality of the human soul involves, as a consequence, the admission of the possibility that there may be some from whom evil will never be eradicated.

It remains to examine how far these conclusions are modified by the acceptance of the Bible as a Divine revelation. It cannot be doubted that that book teaches the doctrine of the future life, and the only question is whether any of the hypotheses, which on the grounds of natural religion we have rejected as unproved, become credible as forming part of Christ's teaching. The first hypothesis may be set aside at once. It not only receives no countenance from, but is directly contradicted by a book which speaks as dis-

tinctly of future punishment for the wicked as
of future rewards for the good, and of a resurrection not only for the just but for the unjust.
The second hypothesis has no countenance
from Scripture, and, when combined with the
other doctrines of the Christian scheme, has
nothing attractive to recommend it, leaving us
as it does (to use Canon Farrar's words) with
"the ghastly conclusion that God will raise
the wicked from the dead only that they may
be tormented, and at last destroyed." Concerning the third hypothesis, the question is
not whether such hopes as natural religion
may have permitted us to form are confirmed
by Scripture, but whether they can be re-
tained without contradiction of the teaching
of Christ and His apostles. I have not
courage to discuss the meaning of Greek and
Hebrew words, because I ought to know
English better than either of these two lan-
guages, and I am very likely to go astray
about the meaning of the word αἰώνιος if I do
not rightly understand the meaning of the
word "eternal." I must own that I should
have been in danger of translating Canon
Farrar's title "Eternal Hope" as "a hope
destined never to be realised;" and I have not
a much clearer idea of the meaning of the

word "eternal," according to his use of it, than that it is an intensitive adjective which does not include the idea of endless duration. But there is no necessity for minute discussion, because the history of the religion proves summarily that if Christ revealed any doctrine of universal restitution, He did it so indistinctly that His followers failed to apprehend it. From the earliest times the popular and prevalent view among them was that which may be described as the popular view among Christians still. The doctrine of universal restitution, if ever taught at all among Christians, was but the private idea of speculative men, struggling for a bare toleration, and ultimately struggling in vain. Not to quote passages from the Book of Revelation, or any other canonical book, when Justin Martyr says that Christians held that the future punishment of the wicked would not be, as Plato imagined, for a thousand years only, but αἰώνιος, we certainly receive the impression that he attached the same meaning to that Greek word which uninstructed persons do to the English word "eternal." Canon Farrar speaks of the hope of heaven as the feeling which "inspired the martyrs as they bathed their hands in the torturing flame." But the most superficial acquaintance with early martyrdoms makes it plain that this is not a complete account of the feelings which kept the confessors stedfast. One has only to think of one of the martyrs of Lyons who cast away her fears when "reminded by the temporal punishment of the eternal fire in hell," or of Polycarp's answer to his judge, "You threaten me with fire that lasteth but for a season, and after a little is extinguished, and know not the fire of the future judgment and eternal punishment reserved for the ungodly." The martyrs could pray for their persecutors, whom they looked on as but the blinded instruments of Satan, but they did not include in their charity him whom they looked on as their real adversary, the crooked serpent whose condemnation they were making more sure. The most "merciful" of those against whom Augustine contends did not believe in any such complete triumph of good as would include the Devil and his angels. Even Origen, whose charity alone went so far, came short of teaching a complete expulsion of evil; for he cast doubts as well on the perpetuity of the goodness of the saved as of the evil of the lost. And it is needless to say how generally his views were repudiated by

Christians as transgressing the limits of permissible speculation. On the whole, if we investigate as a historical question what Christ's religion taught, unbiassed by our natural liking to think that it taught the things which we wish to believe to be true, we find no grounds to assert that Christianity has added anything to the strength of the hopes of universal restitution that natural religion may have led us to form.

When I ask myself how far the opinions here expressed agree with those of Canon Farrar, I am reminded of Brown's saying with regard to Reid's polemic against Hume: that both said the same things; only that what the one said in a loud voice, the other said in a whisper. Canon Farrar's Sermons were not intended for publication, and it would therefore not be fair to find fault with characteristics which no doubt made them more attractive to many of the hearers; and even one who does not find so florid a rhetoric to his taste, cannot without ingratitude complain that the perusal of the volume was made easy by its containing so many pages which might be skipped or skimmed. It is probably due to the hasty and essentially popular composition of these discourses that some things are whispered in them which I should have uttered more loudly, and some things shouted which I should have been content to say more quietly. And the doctrine which most of the hearers would carry away differs as much from that which is stated as the author's deliberate opinion in the preface, as the popular theology in the Romish Church often differs from what is defended in her schools. Nine hearers out of ten would have imagined that the preacher intended to teach Universalism; but we are told in the preface that he cannot venture to assert it, " partly because it is not clearly revealed to us, and partly because it is impossible for us to estimate the hardening effect of obstinate persistence in evil, and the power of the human will to resist the law and reject the love of God." Yet the vehemence with which he asserts that Christianity does not absolutely exclude hope for the future of the very worst of men, must have led many a careless hearer to think that he was asserting that there are good grounds for entertaining such a hope. On the other hand, I have no wish to defend against Canon Farrar the unwarranted additions which theologians of different schools have made to what Scripture has revealed on this subject. In his reaction, indeed, against the appalling descriptions of physical torment which some of these writers have given, Canon Farrar uses language which might easily have led his hearers to suppose that he thought any future physical suffering incredible. There have been some who have maintained that the dread of the agony of future remorse is no sufficient deterrent from sin; that this kind of mental pain is scarcely felt by those grosser natures which need most to be kept in check by fear of future retribution; and that even in those who are constituted so as to feel it most acutely, remorse for irremediable injury done to others by our misdoing can be banished from the mind by an effort of will in a way that the pain of a bad toothache cannot. Those who hold these views will be confirmed in them by observing the different ways in which mental and physical pain impress Canon Farrar's imagination. He can contemplate with moderate uneasiness the sinner suffering from the agonies of remorse and from the pain of loss; but that he should endure any pain of sense is a thought too dreadful for him to entertain. Again, I heartily join in Canon Farrar's protest against the prominence which certain have given to hell-fire in their preaching. I do so without disbelieving in the doctrine, which I prefer to keep in the background, because I but follow the method of the sacred writers. They do not teach that the wicked shall cease to exist, nor do they teach that they who reject the means which God has here provided for their restoration to virtue and happiness may rely on some means provided hereafter which they *cannot* resist. Yet they appeal most sparingly to the motives of hope and fear; and their statements as to the sanctions of God's law in rewards and punishments hereafter are addressed exclusively to the reason of their disciples, never to their imagination. As we do not commonly find that to paralyse a man's mind with terror at a danger is the best way of enabling him to avoid it, we have no reason to think that drawing fearful pictures of hell is the best way of keeping men from falling into it. We have no New Testament warrant for throwing any one's mind off its balance in such a way as to unfit him for discharging those ordinary duties of life by which he has been called to glorify God, and for yielding that obedience of love which is so much more noble than any that can be extorted by terror.

X.[1]

BY THE VERY REV. E. H. PLUMPTRE, D.D.

(DEAN OF WELLS.)

I DO not feel called on to review a book with which my own name has, through the kind feeling of the author, been very closely connected, nor to restate the views which I have expressed in the volume itself as to the great question of which he treats. I purpose accordingly confining myself in the present paper to some of the collateral issues which are involved in it, and shall be content if, by such sidelights as I am able to throw on them, I can help those who are, each of them, seekers after truth and eager to " vindicate the ways of God to man," if not to a *formula concordiæ*,—I do not profess to believe in the possibility of a " short and easy " *Theodikæa*,—yet at least to a tolerant understanding.

---

[1] Reprinted, by permission, from *The Spirits in Prison, and other Studies on the Life after Death*, by E. H. Plumptre, D.D., Dean of Wells. London: Isbister.

I. It will be felt, I imagine, that the most telling argument on the side of the popular belief that there is no room for an extension after death of the long-suffering of God, which we acknowledge as leading men, during this life, to repentance through the discipline of suffering,—that then all punishment, however equitable, must be simply retributive and not reformatory,—is found in the thought that in so doing you weaken the assurance of the penitent and the righteous that their trials are over when they sleep the sleep of death. As Keble has put it, in words which embody a widely spread conviction—

"But with the sinner's fear their hope departs,
   Fast linked as Thy great Name to Thee, O Lord."
            (*Christian Year: Second Sunday in Lent.*)

As bearing on this question, I purpose laying before the readers of this paper some private letters which passed between myself and a Roman Catholic priest, to whom I was led to send the sermon on the "Spirits in Prison," which I preached at St. Paul's, and published in 1871. It will be admitted, I think, that the objection is stated by him with a force and subtlety to which my own style of thought and writing can make but distant approaches, and that, if my answers carry conviction with them to any thoughtful mind, as I venture to hope they may do, it is rather through their intrinsic force than through any skill in the advocate.

Omitting portions of the letter which are strictly personal, my friend begins thus :—

I.

"MY DEAR SIR,—You will wish me, I think, to say how your sermon has struck me, and therefore, at the risk of being officious, I will venture to do so. It seems to me that you do not deny eternal punishment; but you aim at withdrawing from so awful a doom vast multitudes who have popularly been considered to fall under it, and to substitute for it in their case a purgatorial punishment, extending (as in the case of the antediluvians) through long ages ; at the same time, avoiding the word ' purgatory ' on account of its associations.

"There is nothing, I think, in this view incompatible with the faith of Catholics.

"What we cannot accept (any more than the mass of Protestants and of Divines of the Ancient Church) is one of your incidental statements, that man's probation for his eternal destiny, as well as his purification, continues after this life.

"Nor does this doctrine seem necessary for your main point ; for Catholics are able to hold purgatory without accepting it, merely by holding that there are innumerable degrees of grace and sanctity among the saved, and that those who go to purgatory, however many, die one and all with the presence of God's grace and the earnest of eternal life, however invisible to man, already in their hearts,—an assumption not greater than yours, for it is quite as great an assumption to believe, as you do, in the *future happiness* of those who die and make no sign, as to believe, as I may do, in the present *faith and repentance* of those who die and make no sign.

" And further still, I almost think that you yourself hold

as well as we this connection of grace with glory; for you say the 'Spirits in Prison' 'had not hardened themselves in the one irremediable antagonism to good which has never forgiveness' (p. 20); 'had not hardened themselves against His righteousness and love, and therefore were not shut out utterly from hope' (p. 7).

"Excuse the freedom of these remarks, and believe me to be,

"Yours very truly,

"*July* 26, 1871. ————."

I have not kept a copy of the whole of my answer to this letter, but I dwelt in it, as I have done in my letter to Dr. Farrar, on the fact that for a large number of human souls, whom the great mass of Christians recognise as heirs of immortality, there has been absolutely no possibility of any action that could test or develop character :—

"As yet I am compelled to believe that where there has been no adequate probation, or none at all, there must be some extension of the possibility of development or change beyond the limits of this present life. Take the case of unbaptized children. Shall we close the gates of Paradise against them, and satisfy ourselves with the *levissima damnatio* which gained for Augustine the repute of the *durus pater infantum*? And if we are forced in such a case to admit the law of progress, is it not legitimate to infer that it extends beyond them to those whose state is more or less analogous?"

II.

"*Aug.* 1, 1871.

"My Dear Sir,—Thank you for your very kind answer to my letter. My apology for writing to you again lies in the importance of the question which is opened in your sermon.

"Let me ask, then, will it be *possible* to extend the period of probation of any man beyond this life without extending it to all? and is not this a cruel prospect for all of those who are trying to live a good life with the hope of having done with sin and spiritual peril once for all, as the gain of dying? Also, is it not a suggestion cruel to all of us, who lose dear and virtuous friends, if we cannot rest in the security that they are beyond harm and reverse?

"And next, the barrier being once broken down between our present state and our future, are we not at once forced on to the further conclusion, to which the present day so much inclines already, that our future state is only a continuation (that is, so long as the soul endures) of the same sort of world as that in which we are now, to the disavowal of that series of catastrophes (Resurrection, general Judgment, Heaven, and Hell) which in physical matters is so contrary to the ideas of some of the most eminent physical philosophers of the day, who refer everything to the action of gradually operating laws? But if supernatural agency has no place in the future world, who will believe that it exists, or has existed, in this? And so Christianity ceases to be a direct Divine revelation.

"I know you will pardon my pertinacity for the motive which causes it.

"Very truly yours,

"———."

III.

"*Aug.* 5, 1871.

"My Dear ———,—You urge as against the hypothesis that there may be, on the other side of the grave, a trial time of some kind for those who have had no adequate probation, or none at all, here, that if there is a probation for any, it must extend to all, and that this is 'cruel' to those who have rejoiced for others, and who find hope for themselves, in the thought that death frees them from all the conflict and the danger which they have had to encounter during life. The logical force of this objection is, I apprehend, this, that it is improbable, whatever seeming evidence or counter probabilities there may be on the other side, that a theory involving such 'cruelty' as its consequence can be a true one.

"I will be bold to ask (1) whether, on the assumption that this consequence were involved in the view which I have maintained, the balance of 'cruelty' would be altogether on its side. If it were given to one of the blessed to elect between having the possession of eternal life in fee, on the one hand, or accepting it on the other, as the saints of God accept His favour now, with the feeling that nothing but their own sin can separate them from it, but that they need to watch and pray lest sin should separate them, with the condition attached to the latter alternative, that those who have failed to attain holiness here should not be shut out from hope, and to the former, that the door should be closed on them for ever, which choice would be most in the spirit of St. Paul (Rom. ix. 3), most after the mind of Christ (Gal. iii. 13)? Would not the decision, 'Let *me* be safe, safe for ever, and let them perish,' seem to us as a concentrated egoism raised to its highest power? Would not the word 'cruel' rise to our lips as applicable to the temper that could make such a choice? And if this be so,—if the natural instincts which fill us with a glow of admiration as we hear of some heroic self-sacrifice wrought by one who loves his neighbour better than himself, echo that judgment,—then may we not ask whether the charge of 'cruelty' can legitimately lie against a theory because it involves as a *possible* consequence that what we admire, rather than what we loathe, is the law of God's dealings with the spirits of the righteous?

"2. But I question whether the inference is a necessary one. It assumes that there can be no probation but under conditions identical with those under which we now live, the presence of temptations from without and from within to which all men are equally exposed. But that assumption is surely arbitrary. In the range of God's kingdom there may well be conditions, other than those which we now experience (such, for example, as the manner in which punishment is accepted), which may yet test whether the will is loyal, loving, obedient, or self-centred and rebellious. And if we were to reason from the analogy of our own experience, and the law of tendencies which is already partially developed, would it not seem natural to infer that, as we see here, in the ἕξις as distinct from the ἐνέργεια, an ever-increasing fixity of character, so that with many a falling-away from grace is a moral impossibility, so, when death brings them nearer to the presence of God, that fixity may become absolutely irreversible, with no more fear of change than is felt by the spirits around the throne ? And if, after the law of our nature, the habit reproduces itself in the energy, may we not, must we not, think of that character, which has been formed on earth by labours of love as well as by prayer and praise, as neither sleeping nor otiose while it waits for the Resurrection, but finding there also, in that other world, some scope for a like action ?

"3. But the argument from continuity, you urge further, tends to subvert the Christian's faith in events which are not continuous, but catastrophic, in their character, such as the Resurrection and the Last Judgment. The answer, however, is not far to seek, and it is (1) that our faith in those events, as such, rests on grounds altogether distinct from any argument drawn from analogy or experience, and that, if the grounds warrant our belief in them, the faith remains unshaken, whatever conclusions we may draw from analogy as to the intermediate state of souls ; and (2) that the theory which I am now defending gives a significance to the Final Judgment, of which the popular belief, in great measure, deprives it. Protestants and Catholics alike, for the most part, think of that judgment as passed, irrevocably passed, at the moment of death. The soul knows its eternal doom then, passes to heaven or hell or purgatory, has no real scrutiny to expect when the Judge shall sit upon the Throne ; while, on this view, the righteous award will then be bestowed on each according to the tenor of his life during the *whole* period of his existence, and not only during the short years or months or days of his earthly being. This gives, I venture to think, not a less, but a more, worthy conception of that to which we look forward as the great completion of God's dealings with our race.

"Yours very faithfully,
"E. H. PLUMPTRE."

IV.

"*Aug.* 9, 1871.

"MY DEAR SIR,—I feel the force of your answer to my objections, viewing both the objections and the answer in a strictly logical view, though in one respect I have misled you by omitting to state, as I had fully intended, what I meant by their logical issue.

"I meant to have stated it before concluding, and then forgot to do so, my letter having run to a greater length than I wished; and now, if I state it, or otherwise attempt to clear my meaning, I am sure you will not think I do so in a controversial spirit.

"Let me observe, then, that your argument in behalf of what I ventured to call the 'cruelty' of teaching that the probation (to stand or fall) of good men does not end with this life, may avail, in my opinion, with men of subtle intellects or of heroic natures (such as St. Paul, whom you instance), but will not serve for the run of men, or support them in their struggle here with evil. What's the good of my striving so hard to keep from sin and temptation, if I am not safe when I die, and my neighbour who gives himself to the world, the flesh, and the devil, and so dies, may, for aught I know, after this life get to heaven and I fail of it? Is it not best to go my own way here and chance the life to come? Men in general take broad practical views, and are moved by imagination rather than by speculation. Arguments after Butler's manner of what is unrevealed but possible, used by way of explanation of the great balk which the doctrine in question would be to them, will not meet their needs. It is hard enough to bear the view, as at present, of virtue suffering, evil triumphant. Would it not be a second trial, quite as great, nay, greater because unexpected, to have to believe that, this weary life passed, the end does not come after all? Such a teaching I have called cruel, unsettling as it is both to faith and to hope. Of course I cannot prove all this, but I submit it to your judgment.

"I grant, indeed, that if your view be revealed truth, then my argument about cruelty and unsettlement goes for nothing; and this is the very point to which I omitted to proceed in my letter to you. I meant the logical drift of what I urged to be this, Is this novel doctrine new, or is it apostolic? There are many truths which may be startling and even dangerous in places where they have been long forgotten; but if apostolic, we must return to them, and preach them at whatever cost. *Is this one of them? Must it be preached?* Certainly it has a heavy *onus probandi* on it, both as 'cruel' and as novel, and requires good evidence in order to be allowed. I had intended to have said with what interest I looked out for the testimonies of approved early writers in its behalf, which I understood you to promise in your advertisement, an interest founded on doubts whether you can fulfil your intention. Of course I was aware that several of the Fathers are in favour of a restoration of all things; but such a restoration does not imply probation to stand or fall continuing beyond this life, and this is the point which I doubt of your finding in the Fathers. I trust I have said nothing out of character with the sincere respect and goodwill with which I subscribe myself,

"Sincerely yours,

"———."

I left my courteous antagonist in possession of the last word, and contented myself with thanking him for his letter. Nor do I wish now to enlarge on that special point of the "cruelty" which it is alleged is involved in the idea of the extension, in some instances, of the probation or discipline, which in this life has been inadequate, beyond the limits of the grave. It is, however, I think, worthy of note (1) how wide a hope, extending to those who "die and make no sign," as well as to the unbaptized and the heathen, the Catholic Priest holds to be compatible with Catholic theology; and (2) that he admits, what some divines of his Church have denied, that the doctrine of a restoration of all things was held not by Origen only, but by "several of the Fathers." It is, I submit, obvious that although this theory of a restitution of all things is not identical with that which I have maintained, it is, at least, as compatible with the idea of probation after death as it is with the acknowledged fact that the present life is a time of trial and probation. Not the most fervent advocate of Universalism dreams of an absolute equality of blessedness. He is content to hope for a victory over sin, for the acceptance by each created spirit of the will of the Father as absolutely righteous, for the cessation, or at least the mitigation, of the sufferings of body and of mind which sin has caused. But if so, then the thought of an universal restoration is compatible with the belief in infinite grades of capacity for knowing God, yet more so with infinite variations in the effect produced on each separate consciousness by the memory of its own past; and thus, as this life is a probation for the next stage of our being, that, in its turn, may be a trial-time also, and the "lowest place" will differ from the highest, as the result of the total aggregate of the past; and so, strange as the paradox may seem, the belief in an universal restoration is compatible with a belief also in the eternity of punishment.

II. I would fain, had the limits of my space allowed me, have discussed the theory which has been called by some the gospel of Annihilation, but which its author prefers to proclaim as the doctrine of Conditional Immortality. I endorse, with hardly any reserve, what Dr. Littledale has said as to the merits of Mr. White's treatise on *Life in Christ*, in which that theory is developed. It is the work of a trained thinker. It is elaborate, exhaustive, systematic,—I would venture to add, almost too complete in its logical coherence. But it, too, has its vulnerable points. It is admitted by Mr. White and those who think with him, that it has never formed part of the accepted

Creed of Christendom, that in this respect it falls short of the authority which may be claimed, not only for popular eschatology, but for the extension of the hope of a discipline of purification after death, or for the ultimate restoration of every member of the great human family. He holds, of course, that he is reviving a lost article of a creed earlier than the Apostles' or the Nicene, of that which was held and taught by Christ and His Apostles, and he rests this belief on a lexical analysis, not, as others have done, of the adjective "eternal" or "everlasting" as attached to the retribution that falls on the ultimately impenitent, but of the verbs and substantives which are used in the New Testament to express that retribution itself. "To destroy," "to perish," "destruction," "perdition," "the lost," these bring to his mind the connotation, not of continued existence, in actual suffering, of body or of spirit; or of the privation of a blessedness which might otherwise have been attained, but of annihilation,—or, if he objects to that word as invidious and unphilosophical, of the cessation of conscious being. But is this true, we may ask, either of the verb ἀπόλλυμι, or of the noun ἀπωλεία? When the shepherd brought back the sheep which was lost (τὸ ἀπολωλός), when the father of the prodigal said that he had been lost (ἀπολωλὼς ἦν) and was found, when the woman that searched the house found the piece of money which she had lost (ἣν ἀπώλεσα), when the Son of Man declared that He came to seek and to save that which was lost (τὸ ἀπολωλός), is it possible to connect the word with the idea of the cessation of existence which Mr. White attaches to it as its usual or dominant signification? Is not the root-idea here, and indeed, for the most part, elsewhere, that of existence which does not reach its goal, which falls short of the end which God or man had designed for it? And this thought, as our translators have felt, attaches also to the noun for "destruction." Judas complained of the "waste" (ἀπωλεία) of the ointment which had been poured on his Master's feet. Peter, in his indignant repudiation of the sorcerer's proffered bribe, prayed that "his money might go with him to destruction," might fail to bring him any of the advantages which he counted on obtaining through it. The fact is that all systems built wholly or chiefly on the philological analysis of single words are, through the inevitable elasticity of human language, more or less precarious. As this is true of "destruction" and "perdition," so is it true also, in a yet greater measure, of the word "eternal" (αἰώνιος)[1] in which some have seen the pivot of the whole controversy. It cannot possibly exclude, as Mr. Maurice was led to think (*Theological Essays*, p. 436), the idea of duration, and connote only a state of being transcending that which is measured by the motion of the heavens, for the idea of duration is of the very essence of the noun, and men do not commonly use adjectives to deny that which is implied in the substantive from which they are derived.[2] It cannot necessarily involve the thought of endless duration, for it is used of things that were essentially temporary in their nature,—of the possession of Canaan by the seed of Abraham (Gen. xvii. 8), of the covenant which gave the throne of Israel to the house of David (2 Chron. xiii. 5). It cannot necessarily import

---

[1] It may be worth while noting that the Latin *æternus* is not only a translation of αἰώνιος, but absolutely a cognate form from the same root. *Æternus* is contracted from *æviternus*, and that is formed from *ævum*, and *ævum* is identical with αἰών.

[2] The language of patristic theology in speaking of the "Eternal Generation" of the Son may, I admit, be urged in favour of Mr. Maurice's view. That phrase, however, is not a Scriptural one, and therefore can throw little or no light on the New Testament use of the word "eternal."

a merely finite duration, for it is used also of the unchanging attributes of God (1 Tim. vi. 16) If we cannot hope that the word "*æonian*" will be naturalised in our English speech as its only true representative, we must yet remember as we use it, that it carries with it, as a word, the sense of undefined, and not of infinite, duration, and that there is nothing self-contradictory in language like that of Gregory of Nyssa, when he expresses the hope that "after an eternal interval" ($\mu\epsilon\tau\grave{\alpha}$ $\alpha\grave{\iota}\acute{\omega}\nu\iota\acute{o}\nu$ $\tau\iota$ $\delta\iota\acute{\alpha}\sigma\tau\eta\mu\alpha$) the discords of the earth may be harmonised in a Divine concord.[1]

In yet another point, Mr. White's argument seems to me to break down. He admits[2] that the belief in the perpetuity of man's existence was part of the creed of the Pharisees, and that creed, so far as it was not formally set aside, passed into the belief of Christendom and formed the substratum of the thought of the Apostles. When St. Paul cried out, in one great crisis of his life, "I am a Pharisee, the son of a Pharisee!" he deliberately identified himself with them in this belief of theirs, and so it entered into the first elements of Christian

---

[1] *De Anima*, Opp. ii. p. 689.   [2] *Life in Christ*, p. 201.

theology, as prayers for the dead entered, from the first, into the rudiments of Christian worship.

I recognise, with thankfulness, what many of those who oppose Mr. White's teaching as the Gospel of Annihilation seem to ignore, that he too admits agencies leading to repentance and reformation, extending beyond the limits of the present life, a gospel preached to the spirits in prison, a work of conversion, and therefore of probation, as carried on in Hades.[1] But I do not see—though, in this respect, I may be in error, through an incomplete study of his book—that he attaches sufficient weight to the words which appear in Matt. xxv. 46, as the "everlasting *punishment*" reserved for the doers of evil. There were two words which the Evangelist might have used, κόλασις and τιμωρία. Of these the first carries with it, by the definition of the greatest of Greek ethical writers, the idea of a reformatory process. It is inflicted "for the sake of him who suffers it."[2] The second, on the other hand, describes a penalty purely vindictive or retributive. St. Matthew chose—if we believe that our Lord

---

[1] *Life in Christ*, p. 344.
[2] Aristotle, *Rhet.*, i. 10.

spoke Greek, He Himself chose—the former word and not the latter.

We need, I will venture to add in conclusion, in discussing this momentous question, compared with which all other controversies within the Church that are now raging round us sink into the category of the "infinitely little," the temper of calmness and moderation. We see but a little way into the great mystery of permitted evil and of the ultimate victory of good, and our words should be wary and few. We need to remember that each of our little systems has commended itself to men of truest faith in God, and deepest love, and holiest lives; that each has drawn souls from darkness to light, and from the power of Satan unto God. If we are tempted to speak of those who preach the popular eschatology as placing a Moloch in the place of God, the names of Dante and St. Francis de Sales and Archbishop Leighton should rebuke the rash and ill-advised utterance. If we condemn those who proclaim the wider hope as subverting the sanctions of personal and social morality, and leading men to an antinomian indifference, the names of Origen and Gregory of Nyssa, of Maurice and of Erskine, should bid us hold our peace,

K

we condemn the righteous whom God has not condemned. The want of formulated system on which second-rate critics have dwelt as the characteristic defect of Dr. Farrar's Sermons is to me their chief charm, the witness to a calmness and sobriety of thought underlying all his passionate and glowing eloquence. He has given utterance to a protest against human exaggerations or distortions of a Divine truth, and such a protest on behalf of our instinctive convictions in the righteousness and love of God, can, for the most part, only express itself in the language of indignant horror. So it is, indeed, with other truths and other human inferences from them. We follow the sacramental teaching of Augustine and the mediæval Church until we find ourselves lodged in the conclusion that unbaptized infants are excluded from salvation. We accept the truth that eternal life depends on our knowing God as He is, until we stand face to face with the dogma that "all who do not keep the Catholic faith," as man has formulated it, shall "perish everlastingly." We receive the thoughts of grace, election, predestination, until they land us in the *horribile decretum*. We believe that man is justified by faith in Christ, until men press the conclusion, on the one hand, that we may continue in sin that grace may abound, and on the other that the millions of the heathen world are shut out from hope. We welcome the thought of a purifying discipline after death till it finds its practical outcome in the indulgences of Tetzel. Against these conclusions we feel that argument is at once needless and useless. The reason and conscience of mankind, in proportion as they are enlightened, protest against them. The teacher of a theology that shuns the falsehoods of extremes may well be content, in the question before us, to take refuge in that protest, and to echo St. Paul's cry—if you will, St. Paul's *scream*—of horror. "God forbid!" Μὴ γένοιτο! may well be with us, as with him, the end of controversy! Commending what we have been led to think ourselves to the calm thought of others, we may rest, as the patriarch rested of old, in the question, "Shall not the Judge of all the earth do right?"

XI.

By Rev. HENRY ALLON, D.D.

It is not easy exactly to define the place of oratorical rhetoric in the discussion of philosophical or theological questions. One shrinks somewhat from applications of it to questions such as that now under discussion. Pulpit declamation concerning Eternal Punishment, and vehement denunciations of opinions, on either side of the controversy, make one shudder; inasmuch as the very subject is one to be approached with only subdued feeling and measured words. Moreover, in popular address, neither can evidence be fully adduced nor judicial faculty maintained.

In all departments of thought indeed,— philosophical, scientific, and political, as well as theological,—there are topics, the determination of which depends upon exact exegesis or testimony, and fine discrimination of argument or of principles; and one instinctively feels that such should be withheld from oratorical treatment. I must therefore say that I have recoiled with something like pain from the discussion of this question in popular sermons. And this is the preliminary difficulty that I feel in dealing with Canon Farrar's book—as with other like publications. The preacher and the critic necessarily proceed by different methods. It is not easy to apply formulæ of exact thought to strong explosive declamation. Those who differ from me may deserve my oratorical denunciation, but the denunciation does not prove that they do. Nor in this particular matter can the impulses of moral sentiment be accepted as of themselves sufficient criteria of truth. So long as a question demands the processes of the witness-box and the function of the judge, it is difficult to conceive the good which rhetoric can effect. On all hands it will be admitted that this question has not yet advanced into such clear unencumbered view, as that there is room only for oratorical denunciation of the obstinately blind.

The use of rhetoric in controversy is to explode assumptions, and to give expression to moral instincts. So far, sermons in relation to theology, like popular lectures in relation to physical science, and speeches in relation to politics, have their use, and under certain conditions a great use. Both in social and in religious history oratory has done much to further the settlement of thought. It has assailed traditional assumptions, it has created a favourable atmosphere, and favourable sympathies, in which evidential and argumentative treatment has become living and practical. It has sometimes been like the destruction of old fortifications, by explosive power, clearing the ground for new foundations. If the treatment in the pulpit of the question of the eternal issues of sin could be restricted to this, it would be unobjectionable. But the question is hardly in a state for this process; the first essential requisite for its settlement seems to me to be a patient and comprehensive examination of evidence. Who are competent witnesses, and what is their testimony? In one sense evidence is always being taken concerning every great question; but there come crises—and this seems to be one—when the case is specially brought into court for a rehearing.

Whatever may be the authority of the verifying faculty of our moral nature, clearly the question under consideration,—viz., the nature and duration of the punitive consequences of sin in the life to come, cannot be determined by the subjective consciousness alone; although this may and must pass a verdict upon the external evidence adduced. It is primarily a question of fact, and not of mere moral feeling.

Some theories of the nature and condition of the future punishment of sin may be so incongruous and gross,—they may so contradict moral processes, and revolt the moral nature, —that we may be justified in saying *à priori* they cannot be true. Such theories may, therefore, justify vigorous denunciation like Canon Farrar's. Accretions of imagination and circumstance may gather round a root-idea,—not in ignorant and vulgar conception only, but in the constructions of religious faith by highly intelligent men,—which to the unsophisticated moral sense may make it repulsive and impossible. Such, for instance, are some of the accretions which in the Church of Rome, and in other sacerdotal Churches, have gathered round the root-idea of sacrifice; and have been accepted by the religious faith of men so transcendently able as those whose names are almost representative of their systems.

But it does not follow, because the accretions

are illicit, that the root-idea is false. It is at any rate conceivable that the entire structure of sacerdotalism may be overthrown, and the fundamental doctrine of sacrifice remain not only unimpaired by the process, but more firmly established. It is possible that the repulsive sequences of logical Calvinism may be traversed, and the supreme idea of God's immanence in human life and salvation be held fast, as indeed they are in many Churches. In both instances the accretions may fitly be denounced in popular oratory.

In like manner, the accretions which ignorant literalism, poets, and painters, and, above all, perhaps, priestcraft, have clustered round the root-idea of the retribution of sin in the future life, may be pulverised by a more spiritual conception; and yet it may remain true that the retributive sequences of sin are irreversible, and even unending. The argument which is to decide the question must deal not so much with the ignorant and popular perversion, nor with the imaginative forms of the painter, the poet, and the rhetor, nor with the metaphorical forms of Scripture representation even, but with the root-idea of retribution; and with the exact evidence that revelation, the moral sense, philosophy, and experience may furnish.

Thus reduced, it will hardly be maintained that the subjective consciousness of a man, however elevated and refined by pure religious feeling, is competent to demonstrate—(1) Whether the sequences of sin will in the future life be reversible? (2) Whether, if they are not, they are terminable? For all our information concerning the facts and the characteristics of the life hereafter, whether affecting the saved or the lost, we are necessarily dependent upon the testimony of revelation, whatever the verifying functions of our own reason and moral faculty. Naturally, therefore, our first inquiry is concerning the testimony of Christ, who hath "brought life and immortality to light."

Distinctively, and transcendently, He reveals to us our highest, and indeed all our certain knowledge concerning the life hereafter. It is His special mission to reveal these things. Necessarily, therefore, He has much to say concerning them; although it may be admitted that much of His teaching was not fully understood until the light of His own death and resurrection was thrown upon it.

It is in harmony with an obvious moral law, that the most terrible of all judgments concerning sin come from the lips of Him who, in infinite compassion, came to save us from our sin ; and the most unqualified and appalling words concerning the retribution of sin come from Him who "opened the Kingdom of Heaven to all believers." The measure of love is the power of hate, the measure of holiness is antagonism to sin.

It is not possible to attempt here any examination of our Lord's testimony concerning the future condition of unrepentant sinners. And nothing could be more misleading or unsatisfactory than to adduce any portion of His affirmations without an exhaustive examination of the whole. Our Lord's testimony is very ample, and it is very strong. It demands minute exegesis, not of words only, but of aims and circumstances. What in each instance was the relation of His assertion to its immediate occasion and purpose ? What was the relation of the phrases which He employed, and of the ideas which He propounded to those of the Old Testament Scriptures, and to contemporary Jewish thought ? How far did He conform in His expressions to the ignorances or prejudices of His time ? These are questions which demand a full critical examination ; which should be conducted, in the first instance, without any assumption of

His supernatural knowledge or infallible authority. They are questions purely of interpretation, and are solely of literary and historical determination.

I cannot think that our Lord's teachings on such a subject can be ruled by the possible exegesis of a single word, however crucial, or of a single phrase. Questions of popular meaning can scarcely be determined by the ingenuities of philology. Both the philological meaning of words and their *usus loquendi* must, of course, have due consideration; but we are surely justified in concluding that the substantial meanings which our Lord's words actually conveyed were the meanings which He intended; making, of course, due allowance for shades of meaning in the words chosen, and for imperfect understanding in His auditors. It would do violence to common sense, to intellectual respect, and to moral feeling, to suppose that His words conveyed a meaning diametrically opposite to that which He intended—that when He meant to say that retribution was terminable, He was understood to mean that it was unending. He would surely have corrected a misapprehension so false on such a subject. Undeveloped meanings there necessarily were, but these are vastly different from contradictory meanings. For example, He strove to instruct His disciples concerning the true character of His kingdom and of His death. The antagonistic conceptions which He failed to remove were due, not to purposed reserve on His part, nor to the use of ambiguous words and phrases, but wholly to their own strong prepossessions. No such conditions are found in connection with His teachings concerning the sequences of sin.

Perhaps it is unjustifiable to affirm a general conclusion without adducing in detail the evidence; which, of course, is here impracticable. Such affirmation must therefore be taken for what it is worth. Looking at our Lord's sayings broadly and popularly, and with such a degree of deference to possible meanings of words as popular teaching may admit, I cannot resist the conclusion that in the most absolute manner He affirmed and intended to affirm the finality of religious conditions after death. I purposely put it thus, because there seems to be ground for the further question whether the metaphors, phrases, and words which He employed do, or were intended to, convey the meaning of absolute unendingness. If, as collocated in phrases, words have any meaning; if, as related to ideas, metaphors have any relevancy, it seems to be indubitable that our Lord intended to teach that the moral issues of this life are not to be reversed in the life to come.

At any rate, this is the apparent meaning of most of His assertions; and if any can be found of a contrary purport, it is not enough to adduce the seeming exception; it is imperative that a satisfactory harmony of it with the general teaching shall be established. If this be our Lord's teaching, then, either (1) Our Lord consciously conformed His representations to certain popular ideas of His own day, knowing them to be erroneous—a supposition in relation to such a subject that I think would go far to overthrow His moral authority: or (2) His own knowledge was limited, and, like Plato, He only formulated the highest thought of His times, raising it by His own genius to greater heights; but not teaching indubitable fact, only moral probability—a supposition that in relation to such a subject would go far to invalidate His claim to be in any supernatural sense a teacher sent from God: or (3) He knew what was true concerning the sequence of sin in the future life, and meant His affirmations to be accepted as authoritative truth.

The first and second of these suppositions so

fatally undermine the authority of Christ as a teacher, they represent Him as so seriously compromising what must be regarded as most important truth, or so hopelessly failing to attain to it, that all claim of authoritative teaching in any supernatural sense, or in any other than a moral sense, must be denied to Him. And this, it must be borne in mind, is primarily a question of fact, not of moral idea. Theories of Universalism and of the reversibility of condition after death are no novelties in Christian speculation—they have been propounded in every Christian age, and were not unknown to pre-Christian Judaism. But if it has been left for this nineteenth century to establish them as the true theory of the future life, we are, I think, compelled to the conclusion that Christ did not attain to the highest truth concerning it; for such ideas are in no sense a development of His germinal meanings; they seem to me to be a contradiction to His direct assertions, and to involve a radical change in our conceptions of Him as an authoritative teacher. The theory that His teaching was not absolute may be the true one; but it is well clearly to understand how distinctly it is raised in these inquiries. A primary question here unquestionably is, What is the authority of Christ as a teacher concerning eschatology? If He be really the authoritative and infallible teacher that He has been supposed to be, what are His words, and what are their meanings?

Coming to the Apostolic writings, and placing them on the very lowest grounds of authority, they undoubtedly testify concerning early Christian opinion. Everywhere they avow implicit deference to the authority of Christ, and render Him Divine homage. They must, therefore, on the assumption of their genuineness, be accepted as faithfully and reverently setting forth—so far as the writers understood them—the doctrines which the early Christians had received from Christ. Most Christian men, however, regard the New Testament writers as guided and aided by a supernatural inspiration, which although not necessarily excluding individualities of perception and impression, and imperfections of knowledge, yet did secure, substantially, a faithful deposit of the great facts and doctrines of Christianity. According to this view, the unequivocal affirmations of Christian apostles concerning a matter so important as that now under discussion are also authoritative.

Here, again, detailed and exact exegesis is imperative, although it is impracticable in this paper. It is an obvious canon that meanings are to be determined not by passages exceptional and obscure, but by passages normal and explicit. Both must, of course, be adduced and examined, and their harmony must be established. But in no case is it legitimate that the explicit meanings of lucid passages shall be overruled by possible interpretations of passages that are obscure. For example, to rule the unequivocal meaning of such a passage as Rom. ii. by an ingenious and barely possible interpretation of such an obscure passage as 1 Pet. iii. 18-20, is to violate first principles of interpretation, and to adopt the methods of the polemic rather than those of the inflexible exegete. If either is to rule, the unknown should be ruled by the known, not the reverse.

In the Apostolic writings obscure passages occur relating to many subjects. There are in them "things hard to be understood," such as Peter found in Paul's Epistles. We are not forbidden to scrutinise these to the utmost; but with some, the issue will be such, that wise men will be contented to leave them without dogmatic affirmation, lest they should incur the issue which Peter deprecates.

There are also rhetorical passages concerning the work and kingdom of Christ, inspired by the great hope which was filling Christian hearts with the rapture of a new revelation, which are conceived in the lofty poetic form and largeness of Isaiah's prophecies. In such passages as Rom. viii. and Ephes. i. the writer does not demonstrate so much as he triumphs. It is prophetic song; and according to familiar rhetorical usage he puts universals for generals; not logically so as to admit of no exceptions, but rhetorically so as to affirm general characteristics. To take rhetorical passages of this order, and subject them to severe scientific tests, is just as illogical as to test Milton's Paradise by geographical and botanical science, or his representations of Satan by historic evidence. No one thinks of interpreting the later chapters of Isaiah by the canons of an exact theological treatise. Equally illegitimate is it so to construe the rhetoric of Paul's Epistles, or the sublime dramatic symbolism of the Apocalypse. Every composition claims to be construed according to the laws of its own structure.

Is it too much to affirm that, due allowance being made for rhetoric and poetry in certain passages, no authority can be drawn from

Apostolic writings for any theory of Universalism or of a second probation? To construe the great prophetic expressions of glorious hope which the predictions of the issues of Christ's mediatorial work elicit as exact and literal affirmations, and to explain these and passages of another character in their relations to each other as an unequivocal and insoluble antinomy, is to destroy the moral authority of the writers, and to represent them as making contradictory affirmations concerning a vital element of Christian teaching. Whatever difficulties certain statements may present, even though we can find no solution of them, it is surely scarcely allowable to make them neutralise each other. If a true and satisfying harmony cannot be found, the obvious course is to accept the statements that are unequivocal, and to be contented without affirmations concerning such as are obscure. Whether the Apostolic writings be inspired or not, their intellectual power and elevation demands that we do them this literary, not to say moral, justice. Their statements certainly produce the impression of finality, and seem intended to produce it. There is a kind of immorality even in the supposition that a great religious teacher, professing to speak authoritatively on such a theme, should use words so cunningly or dubiously, that, by an ingenious philology, he can be shown not necessarily to affirm what he apparently means. For those who regard the Christian apostles as having no supernatural authority, this line of argument may be legitimate enough, but it can scarcely be adopted by those who believe in any form of their Divine inspiration. If it really be that the moral sense refuses their apparent doctrine, the solution is not to be found in a philological manipulation of the latter; the true issue to be joined is their authority as teachers in relation to the moral sense. Any dogma of the New Testament—a book of popular religious teaching and not of scientific theology—which depends upon philological possibilities of texts, is of very precarious authority. Generally speaking, broad and apparent meanings must be accepted as the purposed meanings. Undeveloped meanings there are, and advancing theological science and spiritual life will more and more develop them—as, for instance, in the doctrine of the Atonement; but, again, it must be said, development is one thing, categorical contradiction another.

It appears to me that the explicit teaching

of the Apostolic writers is of finality in the awards and conditions of the life after death. If not, to say the least, their statements are unaccountably ambiguous, if not culpably misleading.

The Apocalypse—a book dramatic in its structure, and of the boldest symbolical character—admits of endless interpretations and controversies in the details of its meanings and references; but it may fairly be adduced in respect of its general representations of moral issues. Avowedly a prediction of the future of Christ's kingdom, it is vindicated by its profound spiritual ideas, and by its marvellous harmonies in the cycle of redemptive thought. Its place, as a general presentation of the issues of redemption and the final fortunes of Christ's kingdom, is imperative, if the cycle of revelation is to be completed. Nothing can be more unequivocal than its representations of the finality of all the moral and religious conflicts that it surveys. Whatever the false idea or power with which Christ comes into conflict, He is represented as finally and utterly destroying both it and its votaries. Make every reasonable allowance for the laws of dramatic art, and for the absoluteness of prophetic symbolism, yet if, as an indication of the future, the book has any prophetic or religious value at all, it cannot be construed as representing the direct opposite of eventual fact. Its one dominant note, concerning good and evil, is finality.

So far therefore as the testimony of the New Testament goes—which is the only external authority to which we can appeal at all—I see no way of evading its assertions of finality, save by exegetical processes, the ingenuity of which excites suspicion when applied as a solvent to the meanings of a popular religious book.

The question next arises, What is the relation of Scripture to the moral sense, and what verdict upon this great issue does the latter pronounce? I may be permitted to quote words printed some years ago, and with an entirely different reference :—

"To a man's own moral consciousness all teachings of religion must appeal. I do not hesitate to say that no word of God in the Bible, no element of the religious system of Jesus Christ, can achieve any practical religious hold upon us, unless it carries the assent of our own moral conscience. We might submit to it as to a supreme authority, we might accept it as a metaphysical theology, but unless it entered our conscience and possessed our religious convictions, it could not possibly excite our religious feeling, or rule our religious conduct. Do not let us be afraid of saying that our conscience, our moral sense, must in this sense be to us the ultimate test of all God's teachings. If the teachings do not justify themselves to our conscience when it is earnestly excited and we are sincerely solicitous to know the truth, they are, to say the least, utterly unsuited to us, and the probability is that we have misconceived them, and that they are not God's truths at all."—*The Life Eternal*, p. 66.

To the moral sense, therefore, the eschatology of the New Testament must appeal. Any doctrine concerning the issues of sin, that is morally contradictory to the conception of God as a holy and loving Father, as Jesus Christ has revealed Him to us, can scarcely be a true one. Our conception of God may itself be imperfect, and due allowance for its imperfection must be made. But when we are exercising our holiest thoughts about God, we may safely say that whatever broadly contradicts them, and compels us to qualify our ideas of God's holiness and love, must be untrue.

That the conception of God as an Almighty being, inflicting eternal torment upon His creatures by acts of material punishment, such as the mediæval Church represented, contradicts such elementary feelings, is fully conceded. Good men have had forcibly to subdue this feeling, to reason it down by logic, or to determine to believe in spite of it, because they deemed it authoritatively taught

—just as men avow other incredible ecclesiastical or theological dogmas—"they believe because it is impossible;" but this is both a wrong to the moral nature, and a spurious homage to revelation.

Almost by common consent, therefore, men are renouncing traditional beliefs in the material interpretations put upon the Scripture symbolism of retribution, and are inquiring concerning the moral ideas and processes which these represent.

Is there, then, in our moral nature, when purest and most devout, anything to which the idea of finality, as we have suggested it, is in moral contradiction.

So far as equity goes, accepting the law of retribution as graduated by the Apostle in Rom. ii.,—viz., that men's responsibility, and therefore their culpability, is limited by their light and their personal ability, their opportunity and their circumstances,—the moral sense cannot object. It is a rule of equity universally applicable.

But further, does our conception of the Divine love demand that all men shall ultimately be saved? This is very strongly affirmed; and so far as it is a mere feeling, there can be no reply to it. But in the light of reason and analogy it seems a very daring affirmation. May not the Divine love be as seriously called in question in connection with the very existence of moral evil? The real problem lies here; duration is only a secondary idea. It does not touch the principle of the Divine government and character, whether moral evil exists in this life or in the next. It may affect sentiment, and our ideal of the apotheosis of things, but it does not affect the principle.

The problem of moral evil cannot, of course, be argued here, nor perhaps anywhere else, but the *crux* of the entire moral difficulty about this great question of retribution lies here. Probably we shall never get beyond Tertullian's position, that moral freedom and endowment are a prerogative so great, that for it, the possibility, and even certainty, of sin may be well incurred. The demand for the Divine love, therefore, that, if it be really love, it must restore and save at the last all sinful moral beings, "the puir deil" included, resolves itself into a mere optimist sentiment, for which there seems to be no authority either in the statements of Scripture or in the necessities of our own moral consciousness.

The feeling that insists upon this seems to come perilously near to that which prompted

John Stuart Mill to denounce creation as it is as a blunder, and the present moral condition of men as something like a crime.[1] If, that is, God's love do not hereafter what, according to John Stuart Mill, it ought to have done here, it will, as now, be amenable to the reproach of defectiveness, unless extenuated by inability. These are perilous lengths to go on the ground of mere sentiment. Are we not continually discovering how little we know concerning the ways and possibilities of God's love? And do not the discoveries, when made, command the fullest assent of our moral consciousness? Could we have sat in judgment when moral evil first arose in God's creation, and have ventured to apply it as the test and measure of God's love, we should surely have been impelled to almost blasphemous conclusions; unless indeed our piety had made us dumb in utterest perplexity. *A priori* reasonings about the ways of Divine love, uncontrolled by essential moral principle, are both illicit and perilous.

Can we get any light from psychology? Is there any principle more portentous than that of the permanency of moral character, the

---

[1] Mill's Three Essays on Religion, pp. 36-38, 192.

accumulating power of evil, and the irreversibility of moral sequences? Is there any rational presumption in human nature, as we know it, that a renewed moral probation after death, necessarily commencing with considerable induration of feeling, will result in holier issues? Is there any moral probability, in the light of human history, that in the exercise of moral freedom *every human being* will repent of sin and accept the salvation of God? It would be unwarrantable to affirm this to be impossible. But he is a bold man who affirms it to be the probable issue; and he is bolder still who builds upon it a dogma, and preaches that as a gospel. The moral processes that go on in men—many of them most favourably circumstanced in relation to the influences of Christ's Gospel, children of pious homes, for instance—give no encouragement to such a theory. The suffering of penal consequences does not often produce a genuine moral repentance and reformation. Punishment as a reformatory influence appeals to a very low class of motives, and is very weak. The presumptions seem to be terribly adverse to the speculation. The conception of a literally universal repentance and holiness, considered in the light of actual exercises of human freedom, seems well-nigh incredible. It contradicts both experience and philosophy, and seems to resolve the strong love of God into something like a weak sentiment. It is a possibility, but scarcely a probability. It is not a basis upon which a doctrine can be constructed. It cannot be predicated in the light of any evidence that we possess. Every argument adduced to prove that Divine love must cause evil to cease is valid to prove that it should not have permitted it to begin.

There is to our consciousness nothing that is more certain and imperative than the inviolability of moral sequence. Nothing is more terrible than the self-propagating power of evil, and nothing is more certain than that God will not interfere with it, save by moral appeal. His love provides possibilities of salvation, but we have no reason for further imposing upon it the moral certainty of salvation. To say the least, the odds against the moral renovation hereafter of a man who here has sinned away his moral sensitiveness, almost his moral capability, are overwhelming and terrible.

Notwithstanding, therefore, the strongest predisposition to optimist views concerning this great and fearful problem, I feel compelled to the conclusion that the testimony both of Scripture and of the moral judgment is in favour of the finality of moral condition after death. From neither does the theory of a second probation in another life under other and more favourable conditions derive any support. Against the theory that the ultimate issue in the conflict between good and evil will be the necessary salvation of every individual moral being, the presumptions seem immense. It is contrary to all experience, and to all analogy; it puts unauthorised limits upon human freedom, and it restricts unwarrantably the ways and issues of God's holy love.

It does not follow, however, that finality of moral condition implies unending being, or unending consciousness of retribution. There is no moral necessity, either in the law of righteousness or in the correlative life of the saved, to suppose this; while both the philology and the symbolism are such as would probably find their adequate interpretation in the simple idea of finality,—the ending of sin and of sinful being: whether by the natural cessation of the latter,—which seems the most plausible,—or by other processes, we are not told; and in the entire absence of intelligent presumption we cannot speculate.

I am contented to leave this appalling question here; that is, with such contentment as alone is possible in the presence of the great and insoluble problems of moral evil. In my ignorance of what certainly will be, I can rest in the assurance that there is no creature of God that is not the object of His loving and holy solicitude; that He whose love is infinitely more tender and yearning than ours, and who gave His only begotten Son to save men, will do nothing from which any humane feeling of ours would shrink; and that He will leave unemployed no possible means of bringing His sinful creatures to Himself. Whatever can be done to redeem men from evil and to counteract its issues, the loving Father in heaven will do. It is not for me to prescribe or restrict His methods. I can trust His wise and holy love, even when most ignorant concerning its ways. I am sure that He will fully vindicate it, and that at last, without any qualification, all holy men will join in the ascription, "Just and true are Thy ways, Thou King of saints." And justice and truth are the highest ways of love.

XII.

By Rev. JAMES H. RIGG, D.D.

CANON FARRAR disclaims Universalism in his preface; but his hearers felt that he was preaching something not to be practically distinguished from Universalism; and how fine is the shade of colour which discriminates between his view and Universalism, may be understood from the last sentence but one in his volume (in the Appendix on Texts). " It may be asked," he says, " why, then, am I unable to adopt the Universalist opinion? The answer is simple. It is because one or two passages [of Scripture]—though far more than their due significance seems to have been attributed to them—seem to make it unwise to speak dogmatically on a matter which God has not clearly revealed." What is this but to say that he holds the opinion to be probable, but that he cannot venture dogmatically to affirm it, because it is " not clearly revealed"?

Now Universalism is a view to which all men, I should think, would naturally incline. I am conscious of having the strongest natural prepossessions in its favour. My human compassion, my own consciousness of sin, and some of the keenest promptings of my Christian sympathy, would combine to make me a Universalist, if, this world being what it is, and men being what they are, other feelings, more solemnly authoritative, and the deepest and most sacred reasons on the other side, did not forbid me to rest in such a conclusion, however pleasing and attractive. I wish accordingly, first of all, to touch upon the question of Universalism. In so doing, we shall in fact go down to the deepest ground of controversy with Canon Farrar.

The question of eternal punishment is essentially the question of individual responsibility, the question of self-determination as against fatalism, the question of moral character and agency. Does man, in any true moral sense, shape his own character and determine his own destiny? Is he, or is he not, merely the creature of circumstances? If man does not, in any true sense, shape his own character and determine his own course and destiny, it is evident that it cannot be just to hold him accountable, that it must be unjust to punish him, for being whatever he may be, however apparently evil, or for having done whatever he may have done, however malignant, or vile, or injurious it may have been, according to any moral standard. But then this conclusion must be just as true for this world as for any other, for time as for eternity.

It is further evident that, if we are all merely creatures of circumstance, not only must it be unjust to attribute guilt to us under any circumstances, or to inflict any punishment, but it might even be conceivable that if any man, however depraved and terrible a being he may seem to be, were to be placed, for a succession of years or of æons, in circumstances adapted to induce reformation and transformation of character, such reformation and transformation might be the result. This is, in fact, the principle which underlies Universalism. Universalists hold that by a course of salutary discipline and beneficent influence hereafter, continued sufficiently long, the worst of human beings may be and will be reclaimed and saved.

Universalism accordingly implies the doctrines of fatalism; it involves, though this has not always been seen, the denial of man' proper morality. It assumes that man is altogether moulded and made what he is by circumstances. It is incompatible, accordingly, with any admission of guilt; it makes sin to be nothing else but inconvenience or misfortune; it gives the lie to conscience, and declares the unrighteousness of all punishment whether by divine or human law. It is a doctrine entirely congenial with pantheism, if pantheism could be reconciled with the doctrine of a future life, of conscious and personal immortality. As, however, pantheism proper—which can be nothing more than atheism disguised under figurative forms of quasi-theistic speech—is not compatible with the hope of life after death, this Universalism, being thus placed between pantheism and theism, being pantheistic in its fatalism and in its antagonism to morality, whilst it is theistic in its faith in God and human immortality, is apt to ally itself with some sort of pantheizing theism. It is thus allied commonly in America, where Universalism was formerly very prevalent, especially in New England, but where, during the last forty years, it has quite lost its hold of the leading Churches, whether called evangelical or orthodox, has greatly declined in extent and influence, and has, for the most part, become identified with wild speculations hovering between theism and pantheism, and with undisguised laxity of morals. The same Universalists who speak great words about the universal fatherhood of God not seldom also hold the doctrines of free love. It has been my lot to meet with some of these Universalists in my visits to the States who, in extraordinary rhapsodies, mixed up all these things, and whose practice corresponded to their principles. These theistic pantheizers exhibit in their extreme results the tendencies of which I have been speaking, and which, in other instances of Universalism, are, for the most part, latent.

But there are also forms of theological doctrine, such as are and have been in different ages held by eminent, and indeed by excellent men, which approach somewhat towards the character of a pantheizing theism, and which tend distinctly towards Universalism. Most forms of Platonizing theological mysticism have been of this character. Many expressions and not a few passages are found in Mr. Maurice's writings which so identify God the universal Father with the personality of all men as to imply the necessary salvation of all men. Nor can it be doubted that Mr.

Maurice was a Universalist. Nevertheless, whether consistently or not, Mr. Maurice most strongly insists on the personal responsibility, the individual moral agency, of all men, on the necessity of retributory righteousness in the government of the world, and on the doctrine, accordingly, of punishment for sin, both in this world and in the world to come. What he refused to believe, what he rejected as incompatible with his own faith as to the necessary Divine sonship of every human being, was the thought of eternal separation from Christ for any human being. Christ, according to his view, is the Divine Son, with whom all men are so personally identified and united, that this identification and union constitutes them men, makes them responsible persons, defines their humanity. Being men, they must in Christ the Son themselves be sons, children of God, and "if children, then heirs, heirs of God, and joint-heirs with Christ." Christ, the Word, the Logos, is the Universal Reason, which "lighteth every man coming into the world." All sinners, accordingly, are, at the worst, no other than prodigals who must some day be brought home, although, in the meantime, they may have wandered very far away, have indulged in much riotous living, served very bad and hard masters, eaten many bitter husks, endured much suffering, and brought deep disgrace on themselves and shameful reproach on the name of their God and Father. To this school of thought it is evident that Canon Farrar strongly inclines.

To this theological school my late honoured friend, Canon Kingsley, confessedly belonged. Kingsley, however, found that this phase of his theology was not exactly adapted to the condition of his Eversley parishioners. It does not appear that he preached this side of his creed much to them. Indeed, an ordinary reader would conclude from his *Village Sermons* that he taught no other doctrine to sinners than that of eternal, of everlasting, punishment and retribution, and that he preached this doctrine with no ordinary plainness and energy.[1] Moreover, whilst always consistently and vehemently repudiating the Gehenna doctrine of all material cruelties and horrors which is painted in some extracts given by Canon Farrar, it is well known that in his later years[2] he became a

---

[1] See *Village Sermons*, pp. 31, 172, 206, 207, 212, 244.

[2] Canon Farrar would seem to dispute the statements which I make in the text. But Canon Kingsley himself is a higher authority as to his own views than even Canon Farrar.

stout upholder of the Athanasian Creed, which in his early manhood he repudiated with intense dislike. The considerations that led him so far to modify his earlier opinion, that counteracted so powerfully that tendency to Universalism which he shared with his master, Mr. Maurice, and which comes out so strongly in all his novels and in not a few of his sermons, were such as I have already indicated as arising out of the moral individuality and responsibility of man. No writer, no preacher, has ever insisted more strongly than Canon Kingsley, perhaps no one has dilated so eloquently, on the fearful and wonderful prerogatives and responsibilities involved in man's personality. No one could have a larger, deeper, keener sense of the awful royalty belonging to the personal consciousness of the fully awakened and responsible human being, standing up "in the image of God," choosing the right and refusing the wrong, invested with the amazing attribute of moral autonomy, making or marring his own fortunes, determining his own future, moulding his own destiny, both in this world and the world to come. Hence he wrote to the *Guardian* newspaper, in a letter explaining his later views as to the Athanasian Creed, the following pregnant sentence :—

"It is as well here to say that I do not deny endless punishment. On the contrary, I believe it possible for me and other Christian men, by loss of God's grace, to commit acts of ἀπασθαλια, sins against light and knowledge, which would plunge us into endless abysses of probably increasing sin, and therefore of probably increasing and endless punishment."[1]

Canon Farrar himself, indeed, though he looks with a prevalent hope, however vague, toward final issues hardly to be distinguished from Universalism, does in effect condemn Universalism in his preface, on the same ground as Canon Kingsley, when he admits that "it is impossible for us to estimate the hardening effect of obstinate persistence in evil, and the power of the human will to resist the law and reject the love of God." After all, therefore, Canon Farrar dare not deny, and, when it comes to a sharp point, does not deny, the doctrine of endless punishment. He makes much capital—makes, as I venture to think, an unfair use—of coarse materialistic descriptions of hell-torments, and he brings into view the possible disciplinary character of the intermediate state; but, though he would fain deny, and wishes to put out of view, if it

---

[1] Letters and Memories, vol. ii. p. 396.

were possible, the judicial threatening and the final issue of fixed and eternal separation from Christ's heaven and His Father's house, and of abiding punishment and doom, for self-hardened and impenitent sinners, he does not really venture to go this length. He has not, after all, completely purged himself of the taint of the "popular" doctrine. An enemy might turn some of his own artillery against himself. Consistency might require him either to go further, or to unsay some of the things which he has written.

In his sermon, for example, on the "Consequences of Sin," he gives a powerful description of the consequences, not only moral, but physical, of indulgence in evil passions, in the course of which he speaks of "an executioner of justice told off to wait upon drunkenness," and paints in terrible language the results, from generation to generation, of sins of uncleanness. He makes a vain attempt, it is true, to evade the natural inference as to the retributive justice of God— not only moral, but also, it may be, physical; and not only in this world, but in that to come. He seeks to salve the obvious inconsistency with some of his own appeals and assumptions foregoing, by affirming that God

does not inflict the horrors he describes on the
drunkard, but the drunkard on himself—the
God who loves us having attached this law of
retribution to drunkenness, "to save us from
handling fire." But here, in fact, he is only
using the very argument of orthodoxy in
defence of penal retribution—of future and
eternal punishment for sin. Nor does he at
all help his own argument, or embarrass the
position of those who uphold the ancient and
Catholic doctrine, by laying it down that "the
punishment of men is not an arbitrary interference, but a necessary law." So say those
whose views he misrepresents and opposes.
He himself, indeed, is compelled to add—thus
making the tribute and testimony to the truth,
wrung from his inner truthfulness, the more
decisive—"I do not mean that God never
directly interferes. He does. We see it daily
in the history of crime."

Canon Farrar would seem to have only
known the doctrine of Divine retribution and
eternal punishment as taught in its most
violent and lurid forms. He speaks of himself
as having been brought up to believe the
doctrine in a form of extreme horror (p. 47).
He evidently has been altogether unaware of
the manner in which great Nonconformist

divines have held and taught it. He may perhaps be surprised to learn that in the form (No. 4) in which he describes the doctrine in his preface, it has never been held by the highest class of theologians outside of the Church of England. Such a work as that by the late Dr. R. W. Hamilton, on *Future Rewards and Punishments*—one of the series of Congregational Lectures — he probably never heard of. If he had read it, he could not have written on the subject as he has done. Such want of reading and information can hardly, however, be admitted as a defence of the manner in which he has written. Much less can he be excused for taking such monstrous travesties of the doctrine as those branded by Dr. Guthrie as in any sort quotable representations of the orthodox doctrine held by such men as Dr. Guthrie himself.

As to the question of the intermediate state, there is much in Professor Plumptre's letter to Canon Farrar, printed in the Appendix, as there is much also in Professor Birks' writings on the same subject, which cannot but enter deeply into the minds of earnest Christian thinkers. Much which has been for many years floating in the thoughts of those who

have patiently pondered over the painful
depths of this awful and mysterious subject,
and studied the various hints and intimations
in relation thereto contained in the Scripture,
has found expression in what these eminent
clergymen have thus written. But though
such considerations as are therein suggested
must enter into the thoughts of those
whose burden it is to study the speculative
theology relating to the doctrine of the
future state, they hardly bear upon the
practical teaching and preaching necessary in
dealing with men and women who come under
the public ministry of the Word. The case of
infants has always been held a case exempt.
Where infancy ends, again—where, when, and
how full moral responsibility begins—are
questions which cannot be definitely answered.
The case of heathens, furthermore, is a case to
be judged apart. It must come under the
same general principles of moral responsibility
as that of Christians; yet must the heathen,
as St. Paul teaches, be differently judged.
That they, no less than the men of Christian
nations, are to be judged by the Son of Man,
and sent away to eternal punishment or eternal life, is clearly taught by our Lord Himself
in the parable of the sheep and the goats

(Matt. xxv.), where, indeed, the main scope of the parable seems to relate to the Gentile world—the great world of all nations, including those who might never have heard of Christianity. But in the case of heathens the thought of possibilities connected with the intermediate state cannot but come in. Doubtless, also, there would seem to be some in this country, and in other Christian countries, whose case and condition resembles rather that of infants, on the one hand, or men heathen-born and bred, on the other, than of those who have had Christian privileges and opportunities, or who underlie Christian responsibilities. What can we do but leave all such cases in the hands of the "Judge of all the earth," who must "do right"? It is of such classes that Professor Plumptre speaks, when he sums up together "infants, idiots, and the vast multitudes who have lived and died in the times of ignorance," as having had here "no real probation." Surely it is our wisdom to trust these matters of mystery to our Father in heaven.[1] There

---

[1] Our Lord's prayer for the men who crucified Him, "Father, forgive them, they know not what they do," cannot be lost sight of, when thinking of such cases as these. Deep lessons also are to be learned from His words of comfort and mercy to the penitent brigand, whose case, however, demands profounder study than has often been given to it.

could not but be vast unillumined spaces, vast questions left in impenetrable mystery, when our dim and feeble intelligences look out upon the infinite depth and height and compass of God's moral government of the universe. The practical question for us is as to our own responsibilities.

And here the clear teaching of Scripture seems to be that, for those to whom Christ is preached, this life is the one appointed period of probation. The text in the Epistle to the Hebrews represents the apostolic doctrine, "It is appointed unto men once for all (ἅπαξ) to die, and after death the judgment." The very point of that text would seem to be that there is to be no second probation; after death—not probation, but judgment; no second death, no second life in another body, no probation beyond the grave. But, leaving that, I refer to our Lord's own words to the wicked self-hardened Jews, "Ye shall die in your sins; whither I go, ye cannot come" (John viii. 21). This was to be their doom. Take away the probationary character of this life on earth, and that sentence of the Lord is emptied of its meaning. The whole teaching of our Lord is consistent with this central thought. What is the meaning of the urgent exhortations to men now—at this present time—"to pluck out the right eye," to "cut off the right hand," that so they might "enter into life,"—of the solemn warnings to them of their peril, the peril of "hell-fire"? That this last phrase is a strong figure, like those other and cognate figures of "outer darkness," and "weeping and gnashing of teeth," I do not at all dispute. But of what are all these phrases the figures, —what is the reality which they represent, unless it involve judicial punishment for those who in this life have proved themselves impenitent and disobedient,—unless for such it involves such banishment and doom, such abiding exclusion, and such bitter penalty, as cannot but cause irremediable sorrow and remorse? This doom, or submission and repentance—such is the alternative, the sharp and urgent alternative. Failing repentance, there was to be no entrance into life. Bearing in mind, also, all that exegesis teaches us as to the original and figurative nature of the expressions, it can be neither a light nor a reversible penalty for the rejection of Christ's truth and grace, as offered by Himself on earth, the nature of which is indicated by the figures of the undying worm and the unquenchable fire.

Apart, accordingly, altogether from the controversy as to the meaning of the word *æonian*, I can imagine no other conclusion possible as to our Lord's teaching but that it sets forth, by the most impressive figures, the doctrine of everlasting punishment for those who wilfully choose to pursue their own will and pleasure in this world rather than "seek first the kingdom of God and His righteousness." In this world is the period of probation, and the doom of sin and self-seeking is eternal. "Whoso seeketh his life shall lose it; but whoso loseth his life for My sake, shall find it unto life eternal." Judged by the whole tenor of our Lord's doctrine, this sentence pronounces for the rejecters of Christ an irreversible judgment.

Indeed, it does, I confess, appear to me to be an unreasonable and presumptuous thing to imagine that more powerful and affecting motives to repentance, and faith, and righteousness may be exhibited and applied in another world than are offered to the hearers of Christ's gospel, by the revelation of God's holiness and love, God's righteousness and mercy, in the incarnation and revelation of His Son. Yet such is the assumption which seems to underlie Canon Farrar's arguments and appeals. "If under the present state of things," says Canon Kingsley in his *Village Sermons*, "we cannot be holy, we shall never be holy." To the same effect I may quote Canon Farrar himself: "Do not think that repentance is an easy thing; and be quite sure of this, that the longer it is delayed, the less easy does it become, and the more terrible are the consequences, both here and hereafter, which the delay involves" (p. 152). But if this indeed be so, how little reason does there appear to be in assuming that those who have rejected in this life the Gospel of Christ, with all its motives to repentance, will certainly be brought to repentance, sooner or later, in the intermediate state! If Canon Farrar's words now quoted be well considered, they will be found to contain an admission fatal to any doctrine of Universalism or Restorationism, in whatever form.

The law of retribution is one to which universal conscience bears witness, which is inwoven through all the web of life, and forms the basis of all law and government, whether human or Divine. Let them be disguised ever so subtly, let them be employed ever so wisely, it will still be found that the motives of reward and punishment are, and cannot but be, employed in influencing and training human beings from the cradle to the grave. In the governments of this world, it need not be said, rewards and punishments are the weights and impulses systematically brought to bear on the community. But in society also, in civil and political life, the same class of motives, though often they may not be distinctly recognised, are always operating, and without them all things would either languish and stagnate into dreary immobility, or fall asunder into chaos. So, then, if God is indeed to influence and govern us for Himself and for the future, how else is even He to deal with us except on the same principles? He must deal with us as we are. It matters not whether the future for which we are to act and live lie in this world or another—we are still the same.

Canon Farrar's pleadings and appeals assume throughout that Divine punishment is meant to be merely corrective, and never strictly and personally penal. But if so, what is to be done with the finally impenitent sinner? What this principle amounts to—unless, going the whole length of Universalism, Canon Farrar should hold that there can be no such thing as final impenitence—is that the more wicked and hardened a man becomes, the more hopeless and irreclaimable, the less right and reason will there be in punishing him; that a perfectly hardened and impenetrable sinner will have purchased his impunity by his impiety, and may roam the universe at large, enfranchised from law, from fear, from obedience to God.

My last word will be in reference to the hypothesis of Mr. White and his fellows respecting Conditional Immortality. I have a high respect for Mr. White and for some of his brethren whom I know. I esteem them highly as Christian men, and I know them to be able men. But yet I can only refer to them here as witnesses to the great doctrine of retribution and final judgment. If any doctrine of Universalism or of intermediate discipline could have been regarded by them as satisfactory, they would not have yielded themselves up to the influence of an hypothesis so violent and so difficult—they would not, as an alternative, have betaken themselves to a position so untenable—as that which they actually hold. Their compromise is "contrived a double debt to pay"—to uphold the Scripture doctrines of eternal judgment and inevitable retribution, and yet to escape from the doctrine of endless conscious punishment and suffering as hitherto taught by Catholic orthodoxy. As a matter of fact, their doctrine is open to equivalent objections to those which are urged against the "popular" theology, and to other objections of an exceedingly serious character, alike from the ground of philosophy and of theology. But it is at least a testimony against such a theology as tends to do away altogether with the doctrine of a final and universal judgment, and with any foreboding of "the wrath to come." It is true that both the teaching of Canon Farrar and that of Mr. White concur in antagonism to the hitherto received orthodoxy. But it is no less true that, in opposing that orthodoxy, they neutralise and negative each other.

XIII.

By the late Canon Birks.

ETERNAL judgment, the real subject of Canon Farrar's work, is the most solemn and mysterious in the whole compass of the Word of God. My own thoughts were deeply exercised with it, in more than a year of Scriptural study, more than forty years ago. I longed to gain, and thought I did gain, so much increase of light as might lighten the pressure of a load felt almost insupportable, without incurring the guilt of impairing in the least the force of God's revealed warnings of wrath to come upon persevering and impenitent sin. Every attempt to throw fresh light on this solemn mystery demands not only reverence and humility, but caution and patience of thought, and an exclusion of loose and hasty speech, even more than the most exact researches in natural science.

Such were my convictions when I published thoughts bearing indirectly on this subject twenty-three years ago, and more directly still later. Experience and observation of all that has since been passing in the Church and the world has only deepened and confirmed them. Utter unbelief of God's warnings of judgment to come is one of the darkest features of the times in which we live. Some of the forms in which it has lately shown itself are portentous and alarming. Human additions, encrusting those warnings, and designed to increase their deterrent power over guilty consciences, have had just the opposite effect. They have concurred with other causes, fatalistic theories, the worship of majorities, and boasts of human progress, to produce widespread and ostentatious unbelief of the great and solemn truth: "God will bring every work into judgment, and every secret thing, whether it be good or evil." The warnings of Scripture are cast aside with contempt, as too terrible to be true.

No cure for this evil can be found, though sometimes sought, as I have had painful experience, by bringing loud charges of unsoundness in the faith against any who maintain the great truth itself, but refuse to accept current and popular opinions about hell, damnation, and the misery of the lost, as the sufficient test and standard of Christian orthodoxy. But as little can be gained, on the other hand, by vehement invectives and gushes of indignant declamation against those simple believers in the Bible who dare not give up any part of the creed of their childhood and of most Christians in past ages about " wrath to come," till they see surer grounds for rejecting it than the unwillingness of sinful hearts to believe anything so alarming, and an offered choice in its stead of three or four contradictory alternatives which exclude each other. It is not dealing reverently with God's warnings to say practically to a mixed audience, " Put on them almost any meaning you please, only do not accept the common view of them, since it is too terrible to be true."

Eternal Hope, the title Canon Farrar has chosen for his work, like eternal torture, is a phrase unknown to Scripture, though there is a close approach to both in 1 Cor. xiii. 13, Rev. xiv. 11, xx. 10. The sermons themselves, from their declamatory and illogical style, seem to me likely to aggravate the evil against which they are aimed, and to hinder, not help, the firm maintenance of the great truth itself of "eternal judgment," and its extrication from spurious human disguises or additions.

The Preface and the Appendix are in a calmer tone, and one better suited to the real requirements of the solemn subject they seek to unfold.

The sermons are followed by a list of authorities, whom Canon Farrar quotes in his favour, of those who have this one point of agreement with him, that they do not fully accept what he calls "the common view." Besides a rather vague allusion to twelve Fathers and one Schoolman, fifty divines or laymen of modern times are named, beginning with "the great and saintly Bengel," including nine bishops of our own Church, and ending with Père Revignan, "the most eloquent French preacher of recent days." Such a loose massing of authorities who differ widely from each other is unfair to the writers themselves. It has the worse fault of tending to confuse the whole question. It replaces the Divine counsel, "Prove all things, and hold fast that which is good," by repeating one of the worst faults of the loose, popular orthodoxy assailed in a negative form. It offers us the alternative, to "receive the fatal grist unsifted, husks and all," or else to be huddled up in a medley of opinions which have nothing in common, except that they all differ from some point or other of what is vaguely called "the common view." Most of the writers quoted hold either "Conditional Immortality" or "Universalism"—two views inconsistent with each other, and both of which the Canon disclaims and rejects. Such a heaping up of names may be a convenient missile in an assault on implicit faith and traditional orthodoxy, but its only natural tendency is to substitute a greater evil—a theological chaos of utter uncertainty and confusion of thought, and an utter shipwreck of all practical faith in the warnings of God.

The Preface begins with a startling remark: "Of the truths here propounded I have never since my early youth had the slightest doubt; but had I intended a controversial defence of them, it would have been far fuller and more impregnable than I can now make it." The claim *may* perhaps refer only to this one proposition, that there is some element or other in that complex total called "the common view," which is not according to the mind of the Holy Spirit and the true teaching of Scripture, and must be pruned away before we can attain to the full and perfect truth. But the words, in their natural sense, assert much more. These short and easy cuts to undoubting confidence in the perfect truth of one's own opinions are always suspicious, especially when claimed for a complex whole, professedly at variance with the usual judgment of Christian men. If the Canon, since his early youth, has never had the slightest doubt of the truth of any of the critical decisions on the sacred text and its proper version, and the theological dogmas which form the main substance of the work when it has been pruned of its redundant metaphors and poetical quotations, such a confidence on such a subject, so early and cheaply gained, seems to me the very mark of a guide whom it is wholly unsafe to follow.

The Canon notices four main opinions, and then defines his own :—

1. Universalism—the opinion that all men will ultimately be saved. Every man, he says, must long, with all his heart, that this were true. Yet he does not lay down any such dogma, partly because it is not clearly revealed, and partly because it is impossible for us to estimate the power of the human will to resist the law and reject the love of God.

There is here no sign of clear insight and a full and assured conviction, but rather of a still unsolved problem, in the Canon's mind, which leaves his heart and judgment at utter variance. He could wish the present world to be very different from what, in our experience, we find it to be. Still more, he could wish that the world to come should be very different from what Scripture seems to him to say that it will be. He is too honest to shut his eyes to present facts, such as he amplifies in the fifth sermon. He is honest enough to own that Scripture does not seem to say that all alike will be saved in the life to come. He is not honest enough to admit that it seems to affirm, in the strongest and clearest words, the exact reverse. His wishes, then, determine nine-tenths, or ninety-nine hundredths, of his creed. His honesty is satisfied by his holding that Scripture speaks truly of a broad way that leads to death, and that perhaps one in a hundred of very hardened criminals do walk therein. But such a compromise between the heart and the conscience, in my opinion, satisfies the claims neither of truth nor love.

2. Conditional Immortality, or Annihilationism, is the second main theory on the life to come. Canon Farrar " cannot at all accept it. It seems to rest too entirely on the supposed invariable meaning of a few words, and to

press that meaning too far. It rejects the instinctive belief in immortality which has been found in almost every age and race of man. And while it relieves the soul from the crushing horror involved in the conception of endless torment, it leaves us with the ghastly conclusion, that God will raise the wicked from the dead, only that they may be tormented and at last destroyed." The Canon, then, rejects along with "the common view" the two alternatives espoused by far the greater part of the authorities he quotes in his favour; and his own creed, by his own admission, is a compromise which fully satisfies neither his judgment nor his heart.

3. The third view is that of Purgatory. This he adopts as his own, but not in its Romish form, which our article calls "a fond thing, vainly invented, and grounded on no warranty of Scripture, but rather repugnant to the Word of God." Canon Farrar thinks the Reformers "rejected it in the rough, because it had been made too compact, specific, matured, and systematic to be capable of exact Scripture proof, and connected with too many deplorable abuses." He takes it as the master-key to the solemn message of God concerning the wrath to come. I do not see how the

abuses and secondary accidents of the doctrine can explain the entire contrast between the statement in the article and his own view. The Reformers left too much out of view, though they never denied, the wide distinction in Scripture between the state of souls after death and after the resurrection and final judgment. Canon Farrar, with less excuse, repeats the same faults. He speaks of his own view, that "souls who die in a state unfit for heaven may have perfected in them till the day of Christ the good work in this world begun." But this plainly does not touch the deeper question, Are there, or are there not, two classes in the great day itself, to whom the Judge then announces a different and opposite doom?

4. The Canon comes at last to the fourth alternative, which he calls "the common and popular view in our own Church." He has never dreamt, he says, of denying the great, awful, but neither unjust nor unmerciful doctrine of future retribution. "That there is a terrible retribution on impenitent sin, here and hereafter, that 'without holiness no man shall see the Lord,' that sin cannot be forgiven till forsaken and repented of, and that the doom on sin is both merciful and just, we are all

agreed." These are large and important admissions.

What, then, are the supposed accretions of the true doctrine which he repudiates and condemns? They are mainly four—(1) The physical torments and material agonies; (2) its endless duration; (3) that it is incurred by the vast mass of mankind; (4) that it is a doom passed irreversibly at the moment of death on all who die in a state of sin. "How frightful are the facts which they must face who hold these opinions is obvious to all, and I have given some proof in their own words! How a man with a heart of pity . . . can enjoy in this world one moment of happiness, however deeply he may be assured of his own individual salvation, is more than I can ever understand."

I own the force of this earnest appeal; but if relief came to my own mind at last, it was certainly not in the way in which Canon Farrar seems to look for it. I cannot, in the few pages here open to me, enter on so wide a subject. My views may be seen in the *Ways of God*[1] and *Difficulties of Belief*,[2] and I hope soon to add some further remarks on it in a

---

[1] Seeleys. 1863.
[2] Second Edition. Macmillan & Co. 1876.

second edition of my *Commentary on Isaiah*, now in the press. On the Canon's four points I would make one or two brief remarks.

First, the vehement dislike of any element of sensible pain in future punishment, when the doctrine itself is received, and also that of the resurrection both of the just and unjust, has no warrant either of Scripture or reason. To believe that in the life to come some will suffer intense mental anguish and agony through former sin, and that they will so suffer in the body after they have been raised from the dead, and still to conceive that a painless and unsuffering body will be the clothing or vessel of a spirit enduring intensest anguish and mental torment, is an opinion as plainly unreasonable as it is opposed to the natural meaning of the sacred text.

The Canon says with truth, "It is only when these topics fall into vulgar handling that we see them in all their intolerable ghastliness. Many true and loving Christians have held these views, and mourned with aching heart over what seemed to them the fatal necessity for believing them. Good men may and do hold this doctrine with pity and fear and trembling and awful submission; but let those suspect their own hearts to whom so terrible a dogma is so clear and precious and comforting, that they are quite distressed at the thought of losing it." The rebuke is deeply true. Nothing can be more hateful than such a temper, or more opposed to the lesson taught by the tears of the Lord over Jerusalem.

With regard to frightful pictures of future misery, like those of Tertullian in the Preface, of Henry Smith, and Jeremy Taylor, I would remind the Canon of his own picture in these sermons of the horrors of *delirium tremens* to the unhappy drunkard (p.142). If one drunkard more can be reclaimed by such dark colouring, there may be a full warrant for the preacher. But the principle in both cases is the same. I fear that in both the indulgence in drawing pictures of intense horrors is more likely to revolt some and deaden the feelings of others than effectually to reclaim. The Scriptures, at least, give us no pattern of such "ghastly" modes of impressing their warnings deeper on the consciences of men. Their warnings, those of Christ Himself, are the more impressive because the words are few and simple, severe in their calm grandeur of earnest caution— outer darkness, weeping, mourning, and gnashing of teeth.

Next, that in the present age the Church of the saved has been, from the time of Abel downward, a minority of the race, seems one of the clearest and plainest elements of the solemn truth revealed. We read nowhere of a broad way which leads to life, and a narrow which leads to death. No true relief from the pressure of a solemn truth can be found by reversing one of its most prominent and essential features. That relief is to be found, first, in a further truth, that besides the Church of the First-born, saved out of the trials of this world, and heirs of a special dignity, there will be countless and growing myriads of redeemed men in the generations of the world to come. And if further relief be still desired, it may be partly found in the thought, half accepted by the Canon himself, and by which he recedes further from Universalism than by the exception of a handful of hardened and stubborn criminals from the general gaol delivery of the universe, that, "as the very word damnation once implied, the *pœna damni*, the loss—*it may be for ever*—of the beatific vision, is, far more than physical torture, the essence of the sufferings of the lost."

The worst corruption of the Divine message of judgment to come is not that which includes in it the conception of penal fire and corporal suffering, which is an integral though secondary part of the revealed truth. It is that which shuts out from it, without any warrant in the letter or spirit of Scripture, any concurrent manifestation of the Divine mercy, not only towards others, but towards the very objects of the judgment itself. The most essential feature of it, implied in the words of Christ, is the conception of an irreparable, irreversible loss of a privilege now attainable, and, when the door has been shut, never after to be attained.

Canon Farrar, in this work, seems to himself to be uttering a bold and earnest protest against popular and current notions of the judgment to come, which dishonour God, are a hindrance and stumbling-block in the way of Christianity, and lay a sore burden on the hearts of Christian men. But the real risk and evil of his work is that its real character is to reinforce and strengthen a view already popular and widely current, not perhaps in creeds and Church formularies, but in the actual life and thoughts of men, and which almost wholly abrogates the Divine warnings.

The practical creed of millions, who have any faith at all in this Protestant land, is

Universalism, thinly disguised, with a few rare exceptions of atrocious and hardened criminals. It is the doctrine repeated in churchyards and at death-beds, drunk in by sorrowing friends, under the name of the consolations of religion, that each one, a few prodigious wretches excepted, when he dies, goes at once to heaven, and, without passing before any judgment-seat, enters into perfect bliss and perfect glory. This unlimited and prompt self-canonisation is the practical creed of millions in whom some remains of Christian faith are left. The creed which Canon Farrar enforces in these sermons is not quite so wide of the Scriptural truth. But in its classification of men into three classes—the saintly good, the neutral, and the hopelessly bad—and the proclamation to the middle class, tenfold and a hundredfold more numerous than both the others, of an endlessly renewed probation after death and the judgment, it adopts and gives fresh currency to some of the worst elements of a widespread popular delusion, which robs the Word of God of its warning power, and sets the consciences of men free from any real expectation of a judgment to come.

XIV.[1]

BY THE REV PROFESSOR GRACEY.

THESE Five Discourses already belong to the rapidly accumulating literature of the Future Life, and will probably hold rank hereafter among the curiosities of that literature. They present an instructive specimen of rationalistic theology, addressed, not to the rational, but to the sentimental. At almost every sentence the feelings are goaded into excitement, at times into painful agitation. Every sensibility is skilfully touched by one who has at command, through his elegance of style, his force of passion, his vividness of imagery, the whole gamut of sensationalism; and there is no pause given for a clear conception or a calm judgment of the multifarious matters hurriedly brought forward for acceptance.

The object of the volume has previously

---

[1] The Article is simply a reprint, as I have neither deemed it advisable to recast it, nor needful to make any reply to Dr. Farrar's brief notice.—*D. G.*

been discussed. The matters which chiefly interest us are Canon Farrar's processes of investigation and his conclusions. Many surprising antitheses are brought about in the course of the development of the theme, but none more surprising than that Canon Farrar has provided a common meeting-place for High Churchmen and Broad Churchmen, and that that meeting-place is Purgatory—the High Churchman's only complaint of the Canon being that he does not go deep enough and far enough. Towards the goal of his reasonings, however, Canon Farrar manfully clears his way, plying his axe against every obstruction with all the vigour of a backwoodsman. He is impetuously frank. He thinks aloud in his premises; but it must be owned that he sometimes seems to whisper his conclusions. Yet it is in these same whispered conclusions the value of the production must be sought.

None can doubt Dr. Farrar's transparent sincerity and straightforwardness of purpose. This is the most charming quality in the volume; it is also the most elementary in Christian service, and it may become widely pernicious unless associated with other essential qualifications of a "master in Israel." The Church and the world expect more from

Canon Farrar than the eruptive zeal of a youthful evangelist. His previous services, the solemn import of his present undertaking, demand at his hands severest accuracy of reasoning, of critical exposition, teachings consistent with themselves and with Scripture.

On scanning Canon Farrar's paragraphs, the higher the reader's expectations may have been in these respects, the keener will be his disappointment. There is discernible a vast underplay of subsidiary critical appliances, subordinate theological tenets, kept diligently moving, and floating forward the main thesis. Of these a complete analysis is here impossible—at any time it would be tedious —but a cursory notice is imperative. These *subsidia critica* form by no means a pellucid stream, but rather a turbid inundation of disintegrated theologies. The word "theology" may be taken as a sample: at the very sound of its syllables Canon Farrar seems to grow irate, and continually fastens it with a degree of contempt upon the opinions of those who differ from him, forgetful all the time that when he is doing anything to the purpose, he is setting up a theology of his own. Smiting theology with theology, Dr. Farrar rehearses the part of Diogenes treading on the pride of Plato, as Plato retorted, with equal pride.

Dr. Farrar discredits the poetry, the metaphors, and the parables of Scripture as having a potent voice in this debate, and thus thins away the deep shadows divinely thrown across the subject; and yet who so abundant in edging his statements with the surmises of modern poets, as if they were authentic, and should be listened to, singing of hope where Scripture sighs of despair? Canon Farrar arraigns the impenetrable prejudices of his opponents, and yet brings forward his own early boyish predilections as subordinate proofs of his theories. He inveighs against the ignorance of Scripture which stands in the way of his views, and is obliged himself to appeal to tradition. He denounces abiding by the hard literalness of isolated texts, but who more eagerly calls to his aid the verbal tinklings of Scriptural words wrenched from their contextual meaning, if they but chime with the sound of his declamation? He denounces Pharisecism, and yet he stands forth as the champion possessed of a "noble and trembling pity, so fearfully unlike the language of divines and schoolmen."

Even when Canon Farrar avowedly ceases

to speak with "natural passion," and observes "most accurate theological precision," his "most accurate theological precision" takes the shape first of vapid generalities, and then opens out into a mass of conflicting theological incongruities. What can be the meaning of Canon Farrar in setting Christian experience against the Word of God, as if bitter and sweet could issue from the same primal fount? Where is the consistency of Canon Farrar in bringing down the "old, sensible, admitted rule, 'Theologia symbolica *non est* demonstrativa,'—in other words, that phrases which belong to metaphor, to imagery, to poetry, to emotion, are not to be formulated into necessary dogma, or crystallized into rigid creed," and, after the brief pause of a single sentence, laying himself open to the censure of this "old sensible canon," by using such crude emotional ejaculations as the following: "In the name of Christian light and Christian liberty; once more in the name of Christ's promised Spirit; once more in the name of the broadened dawn and the day-star which has arisen in our hearts,"—intending them as arguments against what he calls the "ignorant tyranny of isolated texts"? When we inquire after the possible meaning, if meaning there be, in this remarkable triplet of invocations, the Canon vouchsafes it in the very last sentence of the volume. "The broadened dawn and daystar," of which he seems here to have a monopoly, there shrink into the attenuated form of the "candle of the Lord," which he will not deny to be the common heritage of the meanest of those who hold the "popular views."

The consistency of Canon Farrar is still more seriously compromised in his use of this "old, sensible, and admitted rule." He seems fond of the axiom, and it is in his hands a two-edged sword. In his article on *Hell*, in Dr. W. Smith's Dictionary of the Bible,—a critical composition addressed to critics,—Dr. Farrar introduces this wise saw to check the modern speculations of Dr. Trench and others, who said they saw something like purgatory in the parable of Lazarus. But now, when Dr. Farrar in these discourses is no longer writing *Conciones ad clerum*, but striking "sparks from the anvil of a busy life," which nevertheless are struck off "after years of thought," he can make this theological adage face the opposite way, and help the opinions he formerly smote : adding to the involutions of this consistency, he yet appeals to the article on *Hell* as of unimpaired authority.

I do not propose to follow Canon Farrar through the minutiæ of his criticism of the words "damnation," "hell," and "everlasting." I intend merely to point out what seems to me a fatal error of his style of treatment, which thwarts all efforts to get nearer a truthful solution of the subject by a single hairsbreadth. Both in the Sermons and in the critical elucidations by which they are flanked, Dr. Farrar first steeps the words in prejudice and then begins to examine them. When, with the accessories of much hysterical invocation of Unseen Powers, Dr. Farrar puts the question, "Where would be these popular teachings about hell . . . if we calmly and deliberately, by substituting the true translations, erased from our English Bibles, as being inadequate or erroneous or disputed renderings, the three words 'damnation,' 'hell,' and 'everlasting'?"—it is very easy to reply, The popular teachings would remain where they were before. We complain that the most literal rendering is not in all cases extant in the English version. This defect has not helped, but damaged our cause. It has furnished the excuse of a necessity of appeal to "the original," which has been sedulously worked as a most potent lever to move all those who, being themselves destitute of scholarship, are yet open to the delicate flattery of holding scholarly opinions. Perhaps no single feature of the recent advocacy of the various theories of Annihilation, etc., has caused them to loom with such portentous bulk before the public eye, as the appeal to "the original." We fear not the labours of the Revisers; we have therefore no need to utter admonitions; we expect their impartiality will strip many current speculations of much of their adventitious importance.

One can hardly conceive why the word "damnation" should have been investigated with such painful minuteness, its precarious position in our version being well known, and having for a long time deprived it of all decisive weight in this controversy. Why slaughter the slain by producing the Bishop of Chester's recent Charge, when in the very earliest "pleas for revision"—and the earliest emanated, I believe, from the Evangelicals—this word has been again and again stigmatised? Why bring it up as if a fresh discovery had been made, throwing all the odium of its harsh grating dissonance upon men who have for years repudiated it!

In a similar way Canon Farrar's treatment

of the word "hell" is misleading and defective. Is it indeed so universal a fact in our language as Dr. Farrar assumes that the English word "hell,"—cognate with the German "Hölle," and akin in meaning to the Hebrew "Sheôl" and the Greek "Hades,"—has been so much warped from its native signification as to be an utterly false name for the state and place of lost souls? Dr. Farrar's own usage proves the contrary. He retains the word. He tells us "hell is a temper"—so far adopting the "popular teaching"—without the remotest fear of being suspected of saying, "Hell is an *eternal temper*." To press the matter no further, this one instance is sufficiently cogent to show that it is at least fairly open to debate whether the notion of duration—of eternal duration—is embedded in the popular conception of the word "hell." Need it be urged in these days that as a translation is not made for scholars, but for readers of the "vulgar tongue," it is a fairer method in so momentous a matter to use a word which will convey the most approximate meaning of the original, rather than to transfer terms that are not English and can convey no definite meaning whatever, or a meaning only appreciable by those skilled in Rabbinical and classical lore? The deficiencies of the word in a critical point of view, as an exact equivalent of Hades in some passages, have been long ago detected and pointed out. The language of Dr. Farrar on this head conveys the impression that those of his way of thinking were the only persons or the first Protestants to find fault with the vagueness of the rendering of Hades, Gehenna, and Tartarus by one word only. So far from this being the case, as far back as two centuries ago—to probe the matter no further—we find John Howe, certainly one of the Masters of English Theology, appending a remarkable note to his treatise of *The Redeemer's Dominion over the Invisible World*, and uttering an indignant protest against "Hell" being confused in all instances with "Hades," the invisible world, and Christ consequently "represented as the Jailor of Devils." Let every refinement be employed about "Hades," there are yet three undoubted passages, according to Dr. Farrar's enumeration, in which "Hades is used for a place of torment," and why not in these use the appropriate English word?

Equally successful is Canon Farrar in obscuring the position of αἰώνιος in the argument. His main strength is spent in proving what no intelligent exponent of "the popular view" denies, that αἰών and its derivative αἰώνιος are used again and again of limited periods. But Canon Farrar fails to add that in many of those cases—as with our own words *ever* and *never*—it is also undeniable that no idea of limitation is at the time present to the mind of the speaker or writer. While the words do not necessarily express, they do not necessarily exclude, unlimited duration. Such instances prepare αἰώνιος for its higher applications, in which Canon Farrar admits that it is used of what is essentially endless, though not of itself connoting endlessness. Without insisting upon the strong presumption in this admission, it is enough for conviction that it is beyond dispute that the word is employed when no end is in view. The whole burden of proof that there is an end ever attainable in the duration of the misery of lost souls, therefore, falls upon the Canon, and he must make his case good without this word, seeing it reveals no end.

Canon Farrar therefore must show, for instance, that at the final scene in the last act of Earth's tearful tragedy,—when, according to his own statement, the Angel shall with uplifted hand have sworn that time shall have ceased to be, and the wicked shall from the face of the Judge of All go away into banishment from bliss, the duration of which is unmarked by time's pauses,—that then αἰώνιος, which is applied to that banishment beyond the cycles of time, most *necessarily* contain a hope of release and of return. Until this be done, and the tremendous doubt lifted from that scene, does not every instinct of tenderness, of philanthropy, demand that men should be warned of the overwhelming peril of an irreversible exclusion from the "face of God and of the Lamb"?

That Canon Farrar has not, even to his own satisfaction, mastered every doubt is very broadly written upon his volume. He is timid about putting his views into the articles of his Creed, contenting himself with calling them allowable "opinions." It is true something more is intended by the glittering legend—Eternal Hope—being inscribed on every leaf of the book. Yet I must confess that, as I perceive too on almost every page surmises, guesses, questionable postulates, "most lame and impotent conclusions," and ever and anon glance up at the firm and stable superscription, it seems to me that a certain subtle irony runs through the production and awakens in the soul something more of the nature of chagrin than of "eternal hope." Surely if there be an "eternal hope," it must have a better basis.

Some grains of consolation are scattered to "willing" and "wilful" sinners by Canon Farrar's eloquent scorn of the dogma that probation is bounded by the grave, but who dare venture to pick up these grains while he is at the same time told that it may "be awfully true that our millenniums depend upon our moments"? A fitful gleam is thrown across the dread apprehensions of present rejecters of God by the assurance that "the path of repentance may never be closed to us;" but in what a "horror of darkness" does it die away when there is set upon every sinner's track a "Sacred Nemesis," "with leaden footstep, and gathering form, and towering over you," which "smites you at last with the iron hand of its own revenge"! Timorous souls may perchance heave a sigh of relief as Canon Farrar buries beneath the heavy adjectives of his scathing invectives the whole imagery of the "terrible and the awful," as orthodox divines were wont to set it in array against impenitent sinners; but in a moment he himself fills to the brim the cup of trembling by his own "terrible and awful" picture of "the heavy wrath of God." "It is," says he, "but as if I plucked one leaf and showed it you as a specimen of the boundless forest; it is but as if I showed you one little wave and told you that a whole ocean was behind." In vain Canon Farrar practises metaphysical refinements and asserts that the Lawgiver is all mercy and love, while His just Law utters the apocalyptic cry, " Woe to the inhabitants of the earth!" The conscience of mankind will evermore apprehend the Lawgiver in His Law. When at last Canon Farrar conducts us to his haven of "Eternal Hope,"—the *limbo* upon which he has happened on the worm-eaten charts which some of the early Fathers drew of the unseen world,—his words of cheer are by no means those of Dante's guide :—

"' Fear not,' my master cried,
'Assured we are at happy point. Thy strength
Shrink not, but rise dilated. Thou art come
To purgatory now.'"

"Shrinking" considerably on arriving at purgatory instead of "dilating," as Canon Farrar elsewhere in many passages does, upon the æonian fire of God's love into which sinners shall be plunged at death, he is obliged to confess, "I see nothing to prove the distinctive belief attached to the word Purgatory; I cannot accept the spreading doctrine of Conditional Immortality; I cannot preach the certainty of

Universalism." Even the fond dream of Purgatory, then, with its hither side of æonian fire, its yonder side of refined purity, here joined to earth, there bordering upon heaven and issuing in its bliss, must pass away as the baseless fabric of a vision. The one dread certainty remains, which the honesty of Canon Farrar will not dissemble, from which his quick tenderness of soul recoils, which his faithfulness yet obliges him to shadow forth as a hell so dark, so deep, that from thence the miserable inmates never catch a glimpse of the golden pinions of hope even fitfully fluttering over the abyss.

Thus, while Canon Farrar casts down the theological structure of his opponents, he re-erects their scaffolding. While pleading with men to keep in the middle way of piety, he shows that the avenues of virtue are all fenced by an endless contiguity of shade. Is his "Eternal Hope" but the changing of the names of unchangeable certainties? What avails it that "damnation," "hell," and "everlasting" are expunged from the Bible, if while these *umbræ nominum* are gone the dire realities remain? What boots it that where once I read "Hell," I am now to read Gehenna, Tartarus, or Hades, if there still may lurk darkling under any of these terms, in the working out of sin's bitter course, a deep, a still lower deep, a fire that never may be quenched, and a condition never amended? And is it with this message that ministers of consolation are to be furnished in repairing to the home of the bereaved, or to the bedside of the dying, as a balm for every wound, and a cordial for every fear, of sin? The very question lays bare to every thoughtful man the keen mockery of such a ministry to "a mind diseased" with sin's hot fever, the ghastly travesty and revolting burlesque so enacted of the glad tidings of *salvation* through faith in the Lord Jesus Christ. More consonant by far, surely, with the whole consensus of the Gospel, is the message of those who hold the "popular teachings," which tones not down the "terrors of the Lord," nor abridges nor postpones His mercies, but, with the tender pity of the Word of God, puts the question, "How can we escape if we neglect so great a salvation?" yet affirms, that ere we leave this world, "the blood of Jesus Christ cleanses us from all sin," that "he that believeth is not condemned," and cries even to the would-be suicide and murderer, "Believe on the Lord Jesus Christ, and thou shalt be saved." Here is "strong consolation." But the hope whose flickering rays dimly fall upon us from the incalculable distance of millenniums, which can be realised only after passing through æons of agonizing fire, is not of a nature to support a life of chequered suffering, or to soothe a dying pillow.

XV.

By the late A. J. B. BERESFORD HOPE.

It is without doubt laudable to be angry in the cause of that which appears to be truth and mercy; but the preacher who engages in a voluntary controversy, and who elects to conduct it with the weapons of invective, is bound to regulate his most impassioned flights by the spirit of forethought and moderation. I cannot quite allow that Canon Farrar's *Eternal Hope* complies with this counsel of prudence. The Canon, it seems, had for all his thinking life borne the burden of a fierce indignation against the "coarse terrorism" of the "popular" view of man's hereafter, especially on the punitive side; and at last, having the opportunity of a commanding position, he flashed his protest upon the world in a course of sermons cast in his characteristic style of torrent-like eloquence. This was a mistake when the subject-matter of his polemics was a question at once so momentous and so mysterious. The politician must deal with the changeful vicissitudes of the day, however pregnant of permanent results, by way of speeches, and the preacher who is called upon to draw the passing lesson from the tempest of events will naturally seek his pulpit; but when he is the originator of his own question, that being a question of speculative thought—with eternity for its subject-matter—he will most wisely consult not only for being immediately understood, but for the ultimate success of his views—supposing them to have vital energy—by thinking his theory out in all its extent, and under all its aspects, and then embodying his conclusions in the calm and logical language of a scientific treatise. When he has done this, he has qualified himself as the champion of a principle, and he may then without fear offer battle for his conclusions in the pulpit or the rostrum, with a perpetual appeal to the enduring record of his formalised system. Canon Farrar has chosen the less excellent way of marshalling his rhetoric in the foreground, while he slowly and, as I shall attempt to show, imperfectly brings up his reserves of reasoning. The result is a failure on his part to deal with one element of the question which must, under any theory of the Christian dispensation which recognises its historical presentment, be of transcendent importance. I take Canon Farrar's own definition of his intentions. The main scope of his sermons is to array the religious sympathies of his countrymen against what he terms the " common " idea (1) that the future of the soul is immediately and irreversibly settled at the moment of death, and (2) that for the majority of souls this future will be one of endless torment. I must in passing observe that it seems a little arbitrary on his part to couple the beliefs in the immediateness and irreversibility of the doom with the statistics, so to speak, of salvation, as if there were a necessary connection between the two opinions, although no doubt they are, practically speaking, very much held together. Canon Farrar is not so precise in explaining what he does as what he does not hold. However, we have some statements of a positive character. In the first rank is his confession—which might with advantage have been somewhat amplified —" I am not a Universalist." It is beyond controversy, that while the debates over the comparative numbers of the saved and of the lost, and over the lowest limits of eternal happiness or eternal pain, are such as do not necessarily appeal to first principles, the distinction between Universalist and non-Universalist is fundamental. Each appellation respectively excludes the other. When, therefore, Canon Farrar, in a very solemn treatise, makes the unequivocal statement, "I am not a Universalist," I am bound to take him as meaning what he says, and thereby ranking himself—however idiosyncratic he may be upon special points—among the believers in the older and more generally accepted system of the hereafter. The phrase in the mouth of a less self-respecting man might mean, "I do not know whether I am a Universalist or not;" but it is impossible to suppose Canon Farrar can have put his pen to paper in the controversy until he had ascertained his own mind on a question which lies at its threshold. On the other hand, he repudiates the fancy of "Conditional Immortality," and, in distinctly rejecting the Roman doctrine of Purgatory, he makes the progressive discipline of the soul in the after-life the pivot upon which he bids his only half-developed theory to revolve. I pass over the vehement pages in which he argues that the pains of "Gehenna" must be moral and not material, for in spite of the stress which he lays upon the consideration, it is surely but a detail by the side of what he unaccountably overlooks. How often would any of us choose the most racking toothache as a merciful substitute for some abiding heartache!

The great omission of the whole book, which I attribute to the rhetorical fervour with which it was thrown off, is that from one end to the other of this system of eschatology, no attempt is made to give its place to that unique break in the flow of time—that "one supreme Divine event to which creation moves"—upon which Scripture is so precise and so emphatic, and to which in its various phases it so eagerly reverts, the principal among them being the Second Advent, the Resurrection of the body, and the General Judgment. Inferentially Canon Farrar recognises it, as elsewhere, so in the passage which refers approvingly to Martensen's expression, "a realm of progressive development in which souls are prepared and matured for the final judgment." But it never seems to have occurred to him, not only that neglecting to face the consideration deprives his treatise of its claim to philosophical completeness, but that some of the strongest arguments for the positions which he most dearly prizes are to be found in its acceptance. When he desired to arraign the idea of the "doom passed irreversibly at the moment of death on all who die in a state of sin," he might have pleaded that this theory in its naked completeness reduced the General Judgment in the case of all those lost ones to a ghastly but empty "march-past," and in the case of the redeemed to a "march-past" as truly unreal—though joyful and triumphant. Let us, however, hold the faith of Scripture and the Universal Church, that at some totally uncertain — and as I believe still indefinitely far-off — day, the whole human race will recommence existence under new conditions of endlessness, and of "spiritual" embodiment, and that this will be the date at which the doom will be recorded; then the mode and the time of that gradual discipline of the sin-stained soul on which Canon Farrar so eagerly dwells assumes a definite and intelligible place in the economy of the Divine order. Among the fallacies of the popular theology which are intimately connected with those which he denounces, although unnoticed by him, is the crassness which refuses to see that the conditions of the disembodied soul before the Resurrection, and of the soul reunited to the "spiritual body" after that event, must be generically different.

Whatever the characteristics either of "Paradise" or Heaven may be—whatever may be those of the 'prison" or of the "lake of fire" —it is clear that the respective differences between the members of either pair must be as substantive as their resemblance can be, or else the "Resurrection" as a fact is eliminated. Canon Farrar himself gives unconscious evidence of a similar confusion by the way in which he distributes the after-death probation by reserving that of the intermediate state to the "imperfect souls who die in a state unfit for heaven," while he co-ordinates more punitive sufferings with his idea of hell. Sufficient attention has hardly been directed to the circumstance that the mutual operation of the hard materialistic doctrine of Purgatory which has obtained in the Roman Church, and of its theory of canonization, combine to produce a confusion between the intermediate state of the disembodied soul and the Heaven of the risen "spiritual" man, similar to that which has been engendered amongst ourselves by the savage theology of the Calvinist terrorist. By the Roman system the "Saint"— the being capable of invocation and the causer of miracles—is, in the pre-resurrection αἰών, in "Heaven," enjoying the Beatific Vision —that is, he occupies the position which Scripture assigns in virtue of the Resurrection to the risen denizen of that Heavenly Jerusalem which has yet to be revealed. A familiar and recent illustration of this confusion is afforded by a hymn written by a most determined Romanist, but widely popular among religionists of very different schools—Faber's "O Paradise." Nothing can be more evident than that the holy enjoyment which the poet yearns after in "Paradise" is in truth the consummated "rapture" of the "New Jerusalem."

I may be allowed to deviate for a few moments from the direct discussion to suggest that in any exhaustive treatise on the subject the relation of scientific discovery and of the revealed deposit of doctrine must be faced. In itself I welcome science, for—as I am unable to conceive two antagonistic systems of truths—I believe that scientific discovery and revelation must be identical, and that the apparent discrepancy proceeds from the pride or the stupidity of those who strive to make a quarrel where God intended harmony. In this particular relation of the intermediate state it is undoubted that a long term before the Judgment-day makes the παίδευσις of the better, and the punitive anguish of the worse, soul more easy of comprehension than it would be in the opinion of those who sum up the history of the human race in an arbitrary four thousand years before the Incarnation and of perhaps an almost exhausted two thousand years afterwards. It may be urged against this suggestion that, after all, the period before the Judgment must resemble a terminable annuity, and end in a vanishing value. But if we are to believe the intimations given of the condition of the latter times, virtue then will be so heroic in its sufferings, and vice so flagrant in its enormities, that a very short period, materially considered, will be sufficient to sum up far-reaching results. I may be pardoned for referring to one fact strongly insisted upon by anthropologists on considerations which, to an outsider, seem irrefragable, and which, I venture to think, comes to the succour of revelation where the popular chronology appears least able to help. Arguments seem wanting to establish any theological value attaching to the physical length of the "days" of the Creation, however long or however short might be the space of time which that word indicated. But the received doctrine of Adam's fall and Christ's redemption, as revealed to us in Scripture, involves an hereditary and not a tribal connection of the human race with the first man. Now no candid student can deny that it is at least very difficult to reconcile the descent of all mankind, as past history and contemporaneous ethnology reveal it, from one couple, according to the Ussherian chronology. But once the "antiquity" of the human race is granted, this difficulty vanishes. Again, to recur to the resurrection. The popular pre-scientific idea of the world's history is, roughly, that a chaos retrospectively infinite was followed by a short-lived "kosmos," in which no great changes have occurred, or will occur, until it shall come to an abrupt end, and be succeeded by a very different "new creation." The appeal to mankind to believe the latter fact rested, according to this hypothesis, on no scientific analogy, and the sceptic could plausibly urge that the burden of proof lay against it. This he can no longer do in the light of modern science, which has revealed the mysterious working through bewilderingly protracted ages of physical and chemical mysteries to which the ostensible "face of nature" gives hardly any clue. The appearance—according to some law which is not less natural because fore-ordained and predicted—

at some indefinitely future period of cosmic life of "spiritual" bodies, which shall bear to actual man an analogy which St. Paul explained by the figure of grain and of the mature wheat plant, can no longer be scouted as *à priori* unscientific. The worst which any votary of "evolution," who may at the same time be a freethinker, can, if he be consistent, say of it, is that it is unproven.

I must conclude these remarks, which are, it will be seen, in the nature of a demurrer. It is impossible now for Canon Farrar to withdraw his eloquent but incomplete and emotional exposition of an arbitrarily chosen fragment of a complex mystery. But it is equally impossible that he can, in the hours of analytical retrospect, be content to leave the question of man's eternal hereafter in a condition in which, so far as he has made it his own, so much has been unsettled in proportion to that which has been settled. Discussion must follow, nay, it has already begun, and among the various topics which will force themselves upon public attention, a foremost place will certainly be given to the contrast of the intermediate state as the abode of the disembodied soul, and of the "heaven" and the "hell" which will be the lot of the "spiritual" man. This is a truth very plainly stamped upon Scripture, and signified in the Creeds, although most strangely neglected in the narrow systems of modern popular religionism. The Church of England, I believe, from the prudent moderation of its dogmatic statements, enjoys an advantage in reconciling ancient formularies and modern thought which other communities have let slip by the harsh rigour of their traditionary pronouncements. When holy and humble men of heart have appreciated in reality, and not as a mere phrase of decorous formalism, that the world, both seen and unseen, is together God's one perfect creation, and that all reason, all experience, all Scripture, unite in the teaching that the Divine work of discipline goes on behind as well as before the veil, they will then be able to accept, not as the vindictive menace of intolerant cruelty, but as the yearning monition of solicitous love, that voice of our fathers in the faith which comes to us across the centuries, realising Christ "with" us "upon all the days, even to the completion of this finite term," sympathising with the soul's continuous training in life and in the after-life, clinging to the judgment-seat, coupling, in the name of God, good faith and good works as the way of life :—

"Quicunque vult salvus esse, ante omnia opus est ut teneat Catholicam Fidem : quam nisi quisque integram inviolatamque servaverit, absque dubio in æternum peribit.

"Ad Cujus adventum omnes homines resurgere habent cum corporibus suis ; et reddituri sunt de factis propriis rationem. Et qui bona egerunt, ibunt in vitam æternam : qui vero mala in ignem æternum."

XVI.

BY A LAYMAN (THE LATE W. B. RANDS, AUTHOR OF "LILLIPUT LEVEE," ETC.)

UP to this point the subject of the discussion has been, I think, exclusively in the hands of clergymen. But the everlasting condition of half the men, women, and children that have been born since Adam, and that will be born till the stars fall like untimely figs—a few hundreds of millions or so every generation—can hardly be an ecclesiastical preserve. There is even a point of view from which a problem so tremendous, so appalling, may make a simple man rather impatient of the sight of a learned professor setting himself to grind the solution out of a revised text, with Liddell and Scott at his elbow, and Tillotson and Tertullian somewhere handy. It is not a topic to be handled irreverently; but if ever there was a question on which every possible window of criticism, from natural religion, from the deeper humour of the heart, and even its despised "sentiment," should be frankly—*and fearlessly*—

opened, this is such a question. I will attempt to open one or two of such windows.

One of the things which we must make up our minds upon is this—namely, that the difficulties about the "Infinite," the "Absolute," the relativity or non-relativity of all human knowledge—all difficulties, indeed, which refer themselves to metaphysical Ultimates — are to be cancelled on both sides of the question, if cancelled on either. We must not, for example, having laid it down that God is just and good, ride off from a moral difficulty on the back of the remark that we do not know what forms justice and goodness might take in an Infinite Being. Many a time have I heard from the pulpit, or read in tracts, the remark that "sin, being commited against an infinitely holy Being, hath in it a kind of infinity." It is not rude to say that the man who is capable of *that* hath in him a kind of stupidity. But it is very rare indeed to see a discussion of this subject in which difficulties of the order above specified are not called in or turned out at random, just as the case may seem to require. This is forbidden. Let us clearly understand that we have to deal with this question "in terms of the moral system" (to use Mr Mansel's phrase); and, having said that, let

us stick to it. This alone will, I am bold to
say, erase three-fourths of our trouble, and of
the writing on the subject. Are we to speak
of a Governor, a Father, who can be displeased,
who can change the front He shows to us, whom
we can obey or disobey, to whom we are
related as living in time and space, and so
on and on? Be it so—let us remember it.
Upon this footing we may legitimately say
(for one instance) that the child or the subject
must not at all times think he is completely
able to judge of the procedure of the Father
or the Ruler; but we are shut up from drag-
ging in "the Infinite" to help us out of a
difficulty.

We must take care, also, not to use moral
terms fetichistically. Now this is constantly
done. I think there is many a reader of these
lines who will find, upon introspection, that he
uses such terms as "the Divine holiness," the
"Divine justice," with a haze around them
which is purely fetichistic. But, when all is
done, we can say no more, we can *mean* no
more, we *want* no more than this—that God
is wholly good. To the nature of the Divine
disapprobation of wrong we have no clue but
what we find in our own bosoms when we are
at our best. A good man's disapprobation of

wrong varies in height, depth, and otherwise; but if complete, it would be the disapprobation felt by holiness. When I think of the milky way, or the stormy sea, or am thrilled by love or grief, *any* feeling of mine may become more lofty or more intense—may touch what we call "the bounds of the Infinite"—but it does not change its nature. Nor can the addition of the word "Infinite" change its nature—or its function either.

The word "sin" too often is used as if there were something fetich about it. Now sin is wrong-doing considered or felt by me as between me and God—that is to say, as interfering with the love, trust, and reverence which are normal as between my Father and Ruler and myself. Yet there is, I think, in most minds, a sort of feeling connected with the word "sin" which it is difficult to describe except by some such phrase as academic superstition. I have, indeed, hesitated to use the title Ruler by the side of Father, because there seems to be a kind of superstition hanging about its ordinary use in theology. As if God, considered from our moral relations, were our governor in some (what shall I say?) occult, iron, adamantine, or inflexible sense. All these superstitions must be removed from the mind, if we would see our way clearly through this subject. There is nothing (as all historic observation proves, and as introspection will confirm) which the Academic Mind, especially if Theological also, is not equal to. " Enter Ens, the father of the ten Predicaments, whereof the eldest stands for Substance, with his canons; the next, Quantity and Quality; then Relation is called by his name." Let your seraphic doctor once get his tools about him; he will then oppose Justice and Mercy and Sin and Holiness in purely academic " predicaments" which can have no counterparts in morals; and though he would not in his own person hurt a fly, he will in his commentaries proceed to roast the universe in the Phalaris' bull of his own intellectual consistency without a halfpennyworth of compunction.

Difficulties connected with " the Infinite" and " the Absolute"—difficulties which refer themselves to metaphysical Ultimates—creep into our arguments unawares, unless we keep our eyes very wide open indeed. The origin of evil, for example. Now, we have no business with this matter here. It is a form of the problem of the One and the Many, and take it up by which handle we please, it cuts all ways—may be used equally against any theory. We must shut it out then, and adhere strenuously to those terms of the moral system in which alone we can discuss the subject. We are told that the real difficulty is the *existence* of evil, and that we must solve that problem before we deny its "right" to continue. But I deny this—it is plainly wrong. In "terms of the moral system," we can only conceive of evil as a thing which is willed to cease. So long as we continue withinside of our "terms of the moral system," we are shut up to the Evanescence of Evil; and it is a mere juggle to tell us that the case is just the same whether pain and wrong last in such and such instances of conscious being, for suppose, ten æons, or whether they last for ever in the same instances. We are in time and space, and are dealing with things that have "limits," and no others—for we must conceive God Himself as "limited," if we conceive Him as a Father or Governor, we ourselves having free-will. Περὶ δὲ τῶν ἀϊδίων οὐδεὶς βουλεύεται, οἷον περὶ τοῦ κόσμου, ἢ τῆς διαμέτρου καὶ τῆς πλευρᾶς, ὅτι ἀσύμμετροι—a well-known sentence of the third book of the Nicomachean Ethics, which might have been written for the occasion. We start with no theory at all—with no abstractions of Good and Evil. We simply take things as they are, and proceed to deal with cases. Where is Man? I never saw him. John I know, and Thomas I know. John and Thomas both do wrong. Will John and Thomas suffer such and such things at the hands of their Maker— or in consequence of any arrangement of their Maker— for ever and ever? That is the question.

Upon the only hypothesis admissible "in terms of the moral system," we cannot, I say, conceive of good except as that which is to supersede evil. In other words, evil cannot last for ever. But if we push the matter further,—if we cross the boundaries which have been systematically crossed on all sides in these discussions,—we are still, and equally, shut up from believing in sharp lines between "heaven" and "hell." We can then only conceive of the relation of good and evil in a never-ending series of pulsations or moments, in which good conquers evil. On the one hand, we perceive that finites may be added together (we have now, it will be understood, passed the boundary) to all eternity without coming any nearer to infinity; and that moral quality without resistance presupposed is impossible in a finite creature; on the other, that, *even apart from that*, we could not avoid the difficulty by putting heaven on one side and hell on the other (for the sake of an absolute ideal substratum); because the question we started with was the question of the *separate* ledger account of *each* separate creature with the Creator.

There is, to my mind, something almost grotesque in one of the arguments of the "Catholic priest," quoted by Mr. Plumptre— but it is, after all, only one shape or side of an argument which has been used by some of the disputants. *Question* put—If death does not close the era of moral uncertainty or effort, what are we to preach to saints or to sinners concerning the life to come? would it be fair to the much-tried saint, whom we now teach that in death his trial is over, at least so far as this, that his condition is finally settled,— would it be fair to him to let the sinner have a chance too? And if we take this view of the matter, what becomes of pulpit edification? How are we to preach to the stupid or the impudent? These are questions indeed! I hardly know how to feel serious about them. (See Matt. xx. 15.)

We cannot help thinking and speaking of death as the gate of rest; and we know not but that it is actually so. The more serious and pathetic poetry of all peoples has made it so. But poetry has had another word to say upon this subject. Mr. Tennyson sings of Virtue—

> "She desires no isles of the blest, no quiet seats of the just,
> To rest in a golden grove, or to bask in a summer sky:
> Give her the wages of going on, and not to die;"

and a definitely Christian poet—

> ".... that Joy is never higher
> Than when love worships its Desire
> Far off. ...... After all
> Hope's mere reversal may befall
> The partners of his glories who
> Daily is crucified anew:
> Splendid privations, martyrdoms,
> To which no weak remission comes,
> Perpetual passion for the good
> Of them that feel no gratitude,
> Far circlings, as of planets' fires,
> Round never-to-be-reached desires,
> Whatever rapturously sighs
> That life is love, love sacrifice;
> All I am sure of heaven is this,
> Howe'er the mode, I shall not miss
> One true delight which I have known."

And when we closely catechise our own hearts at their best—in the moods which make this reconciliation of the calm and rest of the beatific vision with effort and self-sacrifice a possible thing—in these moods what do our hearts tell us? Why, the moment we lose the view—from the heights of poor human love—of the shepherd seeking the lost with the will to save them, that moment we have parted with the vision or the "faith," without which no bright hope for ourselves is *fairly* possible to us. Looking at this from the other side, we find (and the fact can easily be verified) that when a given soul has started with a traditionary belief in final heaven and hell, with sharp lines between them, excluding progress from below, then, in proportion as that soul scales now and again the heights of love and trust, in that proportion it, under Divine compulsion, as it were, widens the "continent marge" of what it calls "charity" till heaven and hell melt into each other on the map. Such a soul may, and often does, out of what it calls "reverence," retain the traditional formula; but if you watch it, take the human cases one by one, you will find that the spirit of sacred love cannot, and does not, face the thought of endless banishment from God in any one of such cases. The mind may say, "I believe it," may believe it even, but, in doing so, it has declined into a colder and cloudier region, and scarcely holds the hem of the Divine garment.

In vain will you claim that this is mere sentiment. When the heart pronounces concerning an act of ingratitude or treachery, the emotion is not "mere sentiment" (so long as there is no error in the facts); it is a moral judgment delivered in emotive form. And so is the verdict in the other case. Let us test this matter. You are satisfied, we will assume, of the perfect goodness of Christ. Now, how do you get at that *rationally?* You cannot. You must first be infallible as a moral judge, and you must then have absolutely infallible knowledge of every word, deed, and thought of Christ. You will, in fact, easily find, upon self-examination, that your verdict is of the nature of what you coolly exclude as " sentiment " when it suits your purpose. And so all round these and similar fields of inquiry.

Here is the question " in terms of the moral system :" *Is any man, the basest worm that ever crawled, to be punished by endless suffering immediately inflicted by the hand of my Father and Ruler?* Now, my answer is that the moral presumption against the affirmative is immeasurably too great to be overcome by any amount of " evidence " for it.

But let us take one step more. You object to what you politely call the "coarser forms" of the doctrine. You tell me, in elegant and reserved language, that my heavenly Father simply leaves the man to the natural consequences of his own sin, for ever—having given him a probation of thirty, fifty, seventy years. To this I answer, you would have improved your position dialectically if religion, in any high or living sense, were reconcilable with the conception of a God who could, so to speak, abstract Himself from the moral life of any creature of His own making, so as to be and continue wholly outside of it. But the highest and most living religion is *not* reconcilable with that supposition. Suppose a creature, whose birth in this world was for the time hypothetical, were called into one moment of ante-natal existence, shown the "orthodox" conditions of the future life, and then asked whether he would choose to pass on to post-natal life, or to be at once recalled into the unconscious abyss,—there is not, never was, never could be, a soul capable of understanding the problem (and what other could be morally responsible?) who would not at once shrink back, appalled, into nihility.

If we pass beyond the limits set by "terms

of the moral system," we too easily dash against questions of another order. But some very important points are hybrid,—you may take them on one side or the other of the line. For instance,—is not every possible form of moral quality in finite natures fluxional by necessity, — evil containing possibilities of ascent towards good; good, possibilities of declination upon evil? In other words,— whether we presuppose a "scheme of redemption" or not, and whatever we may in the one case affirm of "faith" or "free grace,"— is it abstractly conceivable that the qualitative and the quantitative should not run into each other indefinitely all the way up and down the scale? I have always failed, year after year, to find this any more thinkable than a triangle of which one side should be as long as the two others. But if this be so, how is a sharp line possible between the most eminent saint and the vilest sinner? And again: Can an Infinite Moral Being, absolutely Supreme, "upholding all things by the word of His power,"—as He must for ever, if "things" are to be at all,—*can* such a Being exist without incessant moral relations with all His moral creatures; such relations involving moral fluxion? This also, year after year, I have found unthinkable, on abstract grounds.

There would not be room to debate these matters with such persons as fancy they are got rid of by any doctrines concerning a Fall, or concerning Grace or Faith, or Redemption. Nor is it necessary. Such persons, if any, may be left to find out for themselves that the introduction of these terms *cannot* alter the problem. A very little reflection will make that plain. Hence, the introduction—a "scheme of Redemption" being supposed—of any doctrine of "latent faith," or the like, throws the whole case into irretrievable fluxion. The confusion becomes endless. As I read the letters of the "Catholic priest" (pp. 131 to 137), I had (who could escape it?) this thought among others — Is the condition of those who are adjudged to have had saving faith to exclude moral progress or not? If not (which is likely to be the answer), of course there must be free-will. And if there is free-will, why should there not be the possibility of declension, even to the uttermost? If you say that the Lord has so set the conditions as to make this impossible, I have two more questions—first, What then becomes of the free-will? and, second, If the Lord, as it appears, *can* so set the conditions, what awful thing shall we have to say of His goodness when we turn our eyes towards the pit?

In all that goes before, it will be seen that I have assumed (what the majority of thinking men admit as even axiomatic), namely, that no "revelation" can be established upon such evidence that it shall not be afterwards open to fatal attack upon intrinsic grounds. Holding this to be axiomatic, I do not argue it, but will put the case—a part of it, rather—upon lower grounds:—

You, the anti-Universalists, have been arguing, page after page, about the rendering of a Greek adjective, and the reading of certain sentences in certain ancient writings. Now, I will ask you, not as commentators or as clergymen, but simply as honest men, who would not cheat me in a bargain, or tell me an untruth,—do you really dare to look me in the face and tell me that you think the evidence for the claims of those documents to decide the question will bear that strain? *Do you?* Will you maintain this—to men who have thought for themselves, after Lessing and Baur and Keim, and the greater French and English critics on the negative side? Never mind whether they are right or wrong, my question is, whether evidence which *can* be so " shaken in cross-examination" will bear that strain ? Pick out of the foulest kennel of history the most malodorous wretch ; lift up Cæsar Borgia, with all his stench about him ; strip him, poor worm! of his illusions; conceive his soul naked to the heavenly glory, and quick with sense of doom. How many thousand years of writhing in remorse would *you* allow to pass before you would be ready to die to help him ? You do not know. Did you ever have an hour's real remorse yourself? Nay, did you ever see a dog crushed by a cartwheel ? Oh, wait ! wait! till your next hour of agony for sin, and *then* pause in your pain to recall what it is you ask me, upon such evidence, to believe of that awful Being who made mother's milk and mother's love as well as the bands of Orion.

But as you may not unfairly ask me what I think is to be found in the New Testament upon this topic, I will venture upon some hints in that direction. I take it, then, for as nearly demonstrable as anything in that kind can be, that there is *no* doctrine clearly delivered in the New Testament upon the ultimate fate of all souls ; nor anything in any way bearing upon final moral classification which must

not be read with large allowance for differences
of moral and intellectual dialect, differences
between the psychology of the first century
and that of this, differences between the
Semitic and the Aryan usage in matters of
symbol,—and otherwise. A great deal both
in the Gospels and Epistles which refers purely
to the Messianic hypothesis of the time and
the next or Messianic "æon" *only* (see, *e.g.*,
Matt. xii. 31, 32) has been read as if it referred
to questions which were not present to the
minds of the speakers or writers *at all*. I
think, however, that the largely prevailing
symbolic *suggestion* is that of the destruction
of "the wicked." There are occasional gleams
of universal immortality; but these are few
and doubtful. So far, I hold Mr White to
have the truth. But I am careful to say, *so
far*, and there I stop with regard to the textual
question. And I ought to add that I have
read no book specially addressed to the subject for twenty years past. Two "practical"
remarks remain. First, the number of those
who even profess to believe in any form of
everlasting hell is small. Hell always has
been, and still is, the standing joke of the
multitude. Second, I have been a little (not
much) surprised to note the hold which the

"first fallacy" of Protestantism still has upon people's minds. You will find, among educated and thoughtful persons, a few here and there who cannot at once see, or will not admit, that the idea of an infallible Book is as absurd as that of an infallible Pope; but, as a general rule, an educated man *does* see, when it is once put to him, that he can get no more authority out of a book than he has put into it; and then all you have to do is to remind him that he is himself fallible. I did once, indeed, meet an educated man—a clergyman and a graduate—who, when I had driven him into a corner, said, contentedly, "You may arrive at a reasonable belief of the infallibility of a book," and then, when I laughed and said, "You have thrown up your brief, the Court will enter a nonsuit," was very angry, not understanding the meaning of his own language. But able men and women usually see their way at once. The difficulty is to break down the conspiracy of silence on this subject —under cover of which the *less* able preachers and teachers do what they like with the multitude by quoting the old texts, and interpreting them just as if they had been written yesterday, and were simply to be read by the rules of modern grammar and psychology in the West. Now, to those who help to keep up this conspiracy of silence, I would dare to hint that they lose more than they gain; for perhaps those to whom my first practical remark applies might be reached by "the goodness and severity of God" put before them in terms which were just and frank, however vague; whereas now the whole doctrine of distributive justice hereafter misses any hold of them.

XVII.

BY THE REV. PROFESSOR MAYOR.

THE question of general interest in the present discussion is not whether this or that writer is too rhetorical, but whether any, and if so what, alteration is needed in the view of future punishment which is received as orthodox among Protestants; that view being, that the present life settles finally and irrevocably for each human being whether the whole of the endless existence which follows is to be spent in sin and misery, or in virtue and happiness : to which is usually added as a corollary, that the great majority of the human race belong to the former category. The difference between this and the ordinary Roman Catholic view is that the latter postpones the happiness of the saved (except in cases of pre-eminent holiness) until they have passed through the torments of purgatory, which, if we may trust the assertions of Aquinas and Bellarmine, far exceed in intensity any pains which can be experienced on earth.

After having been accepted without misgiving for hundreds of years, this view has of late come to be felt a terrible burden and difficulty by many orthodox believers, of whom we may take Professor Birks as an example, when he tells us (p. 197) that the thought of the future lot of mankind caused him months of "almost intolerable anguish," until he was led to see that the received doctrine rested upon no warranty of Scripture, and was not really a part of revealed truth.

On comparing the positions of the various writers, I find that all but two, Mr. Arthur and Professor Gracey, express themselves in favour of some modification of the traditional view. Many expressly challenge its authority either as resting on a wrong interpretation of isolated texts without regard to the antagonistic bearing of other texts, or to the general tenor of revelation, or as not being authorised by the Catholic Church, or as condemned by the voice of reason and conscience, which they hold to be the ultimate court of appeal in the matter. One of the strongest assertions of the authority of conscience comes from Dr. Allon, who in practice attaches more weight to the letter of Scripture than many others, as, for instance, in regard to the probability of a continuance of probation in the next life. He says (I quote with slight abbreviations), "To a man's own moral consciousness all teachings of religion must appeal." "When we are exercising our holiest thoughts about God, we may safely say that whatever broadly contradicts them, and compels us to qualify our ideas of God's holiness and love, must be untrue. That the mediæval conception of future punishment contradicts such elementary feelings is fully conceded. Good men have had forcibly to subdue this feeling, to reason it down by logic, or to determine to believe in spite of it, because they deemed it authoritatively taught; but this is both a wrong to the moral nature, and a spurious homage to revelation"[1] (pp. 166, 167).

---

[1] The same view (that it is wrong to stifle doubt) is forcibly expressed in Mr. David Vaughan's thoughtful volume, *The Present Trial of Faith*, where he quotes and comments on Bishop Callaway's words, "As surely as men stifle doubts and crush them blindly out, so surely will they rise up again to haunt them" (p. 295). It is instructive to compare the view of a liberal Churchman of the last generation on the same point: see *Arnold's Life*, Letter cvii.: "All speculations on such points [as the continued existence of moral evil] should be repressed by the will, and if they continue to haunt us, they must be prayed against, and silently endured as a trial."

The modifications proposed are, as might be expected, very various, it being always more easy to see the objections to an existing system or view than to agree upon one which should take its place: and if this is found to be the case in matters of ordinary human experience, so that it takes many years to elaborate a satisfactory scheme even for so comparatively simple a thing as university or municipal reform, how much more in a question which transcends experience in so many points, while it is at the same time so intimately bound up with our experience that we find it impossible to keep our thoughts from it, or to refrain from endeavouring to harmonise the conclusions to which they naturally lead us?

If we start with the suggestion already alluded to, of a probation continued after this life, we find many different shades of opinion included under this head, some holding that such extended probation is only exceptional, being limited to those who have never had any real probation on earth; while others look forward to an indefinite series of probationary states, issuing in the final salvation and happiness of all mankind. Dr. Rigg may be named as a representative of the former view, Professor Plumptre of the latter, which we ought rather to call a hope, as he distinctly refuses to dogmatise in the matter. While strongly condemning Universalism, Dr. Rigg speaks in high terms of what Professors Plumptre and Birks have written on the Intermediate State, and thinks that, though the suggestions made by them are unsuited for practical teaching, they may be of great value for removing the speculative difficulties connected with the future of infants, heathens, and ignorant persons generally (pp. 187, 188). If we turn to the papers written by the two Professors, we find Professor Birks saying (p. 209) that "besides the Church of the Firstborn, saved out of the trials of this world, and heirs of a special dignity, there will be countless and growing myriads of redeemed men in the generations of the world to come;"[1] and Professor

---

[1] On further consideration, I am inclined to think, after comparing this passage with other writings of Professor Birks, that he is not here speaking of myriads restored in some future stage after failure in this stage, but of a new race of men born under happier conditions in some millennium to come. Such a hope must commend itself in some form or other to all who cherish the belief in human progress, but to my mind the gloom of earth is only deepened by the contrast with the assured blessedness which is to follow, if the suffering generations of the present epoch, the forlorn hope of humanity as we may call them, are destined for the most part to final

Plumptre (p. 139) that "as this life is a probation for the next stage of our being, so that, in its turn, may be a trial-time also, and the 'lowest place' will differ from the highest, as the result of the total aggregate of the past; and so the belief in an universal restoration is compatible with a belief also in the eternity of punishment." Of all the writers, Dr. Allon is, I think, the only one, except Mr. Arthur and Professor Gracey, who regards the suggestion of a continued probation in any form as inadmissible, "notwithstanding the strongest predisposition to optimist views."

Passing on from the various modifications of the received doctrine which turn upon this idea of extended probation, we come to two

---

ruin. In this world of failure there may be parents who could find an adequate consolation for the disgrace of a daughter or the criminality of a son, in the thought that the rest of the family had turned out respectably; but it is indeed a strange conception that the heavenly Father, whose responsibility for each of His children so infinitely transcends that of earthly parents, could ever comfort Himself under their loss by fresh exertions of creative power. It is not the ninety and nine just persons who need no repentance that are nearest to the heart of the Good Shepherd, but the one lost sheep which He seeks until He finds it, and brings it home rejoicing.

With regard to the question of continued probation, Professor Birks leaves no doubt as to his dislike of Universalism, but I cannot find any distinct statement of the position he would take in reference to a milder form of the doctrine.

others which may be held either apart from it or in connection with it. The first identifies the second death with annihilation; the second, while assenting to the ordinary view, in so far as it condemns the lost to endless existence in hell, yet holds such an existence to be not incompatible with what, judged by the standard of earth, may be considered a high degree of virtue and happiness. Mr. White combines the doctrine of Annihilationism with that of extended probation, holding that, " after the exhaustion of all redemptive processes on earth, and in some cases in Hades," the "unrepenting remnant of God-rejecting men" will be finally destroyed by "the operation of the law of their nature" (p. 113); Dr. Allon, while he considers that the "finality of moral condition" is established by the testimony both of Scripture and of the moral judgment, says that this need not imply unending being, and that what "seems the most plausible suggestion is the ending of sin and of sinful being by the natural cessation of the latter." The idea of a softened or virtuous hell is represented by Professor Birks, but it is unfortunately only alluded to, without any clear or full explanation. I believe his view will be found not to differ materially from that put forward in Mr. E. H. Bickersteth's poem, *Yesterday, To-day, and for Ever*, which was analysed in the *Contemporary Review* for May 1876. According to the summary there given, not only is there no actual sin in the final state of the lost, but there is no sinful desire: it is only the germ of sin which is supposed to be ineradicable, and liable to break out if restraint is removed. On the other hand, there is resignation to the Divine will, there is self-condemnation and self-distrust, and, instead of the despairing envy which would seem so natural under the circumstances, there is positive delight in the happiness and holiness of the blessed in heaven, from whom they are for ever separated. There is something very noble in this view, and those who will read Professor Birks' treatise on the subject will be surprised to find how much there is in the language of Scripture which accords with it; but logically, I confess, it seems to me to lead up to the doctrine of universal restoration. Can we suppose a process of reformation carried so far, only to stop short here? If by God's grace these lost souls have been raised to a pitch of unselfish virtue beyond anything which has ever been realised by the greatest saint on earth, must they not still continue to grow from grace to grace? Must not the confirmed habit of virtue be gradually formed within them as they persevere in the exercise of virtuous acts and feelings?

If I may be allowed, after the fashion of the ancients, to introduce into our discussion a nameless *umbra*, I should like to compare here the view given by a writer in the *Church Quarterly* for April. The extremely conservative character of that Review, and the somewhat *banal* and *borné* tone of the writer, seem to me to give special importance to the article, considered as a sign of the times. He begins by telling us that the difficulties felt in connection with the doctrine of eternal punishment are owing entirely to the Calvinistic system; if viewed from the High Church side, the doctrine emerges in harmony with the conscience of mankind and the goodness of God. The Catholic theory is that the separation between lost and saved is determined by the impression produced upon the soul at its entrance into the intermediate state. If it is attracted by the light, if it is capable of love, it is saved; if repelled, it is lost; but we may safely indulge the hope that by far the majority belong to the former class. Many may have to undergo a long course of discipline, but their final happiness is assured. On the other hand, the damned are those who have lived so as to be incapable of love; damnation consists in their being formed into a society outside the kingdom of Christ, governed, as human society now is, on the principle of κόλασις, not on the principle of love. After the penalty of past sin has been paid in the fire, coercive discipline is not resorted to except in cases of insubordination. "There may be penal settlements, so to speak, in which the wicked are finally fixed in evil, but in the higher societies we conceive there would be degrees of the moral state very much as now." "So far as natural appliances are concerned, the life of hell might be an advance upon the present. It might have a higher and more perfect civilisation." "There is nothing to show but that God may do for the damned the very best of which they are susceptible. It is true they are deprived of supernatural good, but there is the whole field of natural good which may be awarded to them in proportion to their deserts."

So far the writer would seem to agree with Dr. Allon as regards "moral finality," but further on he refers to the Greek Church as having always maintained that it is just possible for a soul in the intermediate state to pass from the lost to the saved; and he is himself inclined to put the possibility of such a change on the same level with that of a deathbed repentance. It may be worth while to add that he takes, what Dr. Hunt tells us is Hobbes' view of the use of the word αἰώνιος, as referring to the fire itself, not to the sufferings of those exposed to it. He ends by claiming for his view, which leaves the lost soul in peace in hell at last, a superiority in mercifulness over "the cruel theory" which supposes it driven to heaven by a succession of probationary states, each more severe than the preceding.

It is hard to believe that this grotesque imagination is seriously put forward as a portion of the sober Anglican Creed; yet the writer is professedly urging it upon the younger clergy as a safeguard against the growing danger of Universalism. I can only afford space for one or two remarks upon it. Hell, it appears, in its final state, is to be very much a repetition of the present life, with a higher civilisation and a good average morality in the best societies : though the inhabitants are debarred from supernatural good, they will be rewarded for their orderly conduct with any amount of natural good, and they may look forward to enjoying this throughout eternity. In the first place, is this prospect calculated to be a deterrent to worldly men in this present life? In the next place, what is meant by the opposition of natural to supernatural good, in a world where all is supernatural? Thirdly, how is the high tone of morality to be kept up? Here, we know it is by the unceasing prayers and struggles of the more aspiring part of humanity, but these have all been drafted off. Are we to suppose a fresh nucleus of holy aspiration springing up under the new circumstances? But then arises the difficulty already mentioned in reference to Professor Birks's theory: How can this be without supernatural grace, more especially when we remember that the lost are *ex hypothesi* incapable of love? And then again, if there is real goodness, how can it fail to grow; and what else is heaven but a state of goodness ever growing under the Divine influence? But we need not proceed; the idea of beings incapable of love, but capable of morality and happiness, is self-contradictory. Whatever modification is needed in the ordinary doctrine, this at least we may pronounce to be impossible.

To turn now to an examination of some of the arguments employed in the course of the discussion: one which is most frequently and most confidently urged against Universalism is that which may be stated in the words of Dr. Rigg (pp. 177, 178): "Universalism implies fatalism. It makes sin to be nothing else but inconvenience or misfortune; it gives the lie to conscience, and declares the unrighteousness of all punishment whether by divine or human law." And so Dr. Littledale (p. 97): "It militates against the existence of free-will, and the consequent possibility of a volition of evil through eternity."

What first occurs to one on reading such passages is that they attempt to settle *obscurum per obscurius*. It is hard enough to reconcile our experience here with the assumption of free-will; to take it as our starting-point for speculations as to the unknown future does not seem a very hopeful proceeding. To refuse to discuss the possibility of future repentance, because it militates against some theory of free-will, is precisely on a par with the conduct of the Epicureans of old who denied the law of the Excluded Middle in logic for fear of committing themselves to the principle of Necessity. In reality, it seems to me that there is just as much, or as little, infringement of free-will in affirming that "there are some men who will not be saved" as in affirming its contradictory, "it is untrue that there are some men who will not be saved." Further, it is to be noted that, in the particular case at issue between, say Dr. Rigg and Canon Farrar or Mr. Baldwin Brown, the latter affirmation is not put in this positive form, but merely as a hope, "we hope it may not be true that there are some who will not be saved." It is plain that in this case it is Dr. Rigg, and not his opponents, who limits the action of free-will. Dr. Rigg's assertion, in fact, comes to this, there is a property in human nature called free-will, which prevents men from being similarly actuated by the same motives, and therefore makes it impossible to predict any course of action common to the race. I should say that our experience proves the contrary: the freer a man's will, the more we can count on his being sensitive to right motives to action; so that if a burnt child does *not* shrink from the fire, or if a child trained up in the way he should go *does* depart from it when he is old, we have to account for such an unnatural development either by discovering fresh counteracting motives, or by denying the exercise of free-will, as in cases of insanity. Many orthodox Christians are of opinion that the future salvation of all men is declared in our Lord's words, "I, if I be lifted up, will draw all men unto Me;" and in St. Paul's words, "The last enemy that shall be destroyed is death;" "In Christ shall all be made alive." Others, of course, explain them differently; but I cannot see that the former interpretation is more opposed to any intelligible doctrine of free-will than is any other prophecy involving a reference to action or conduct. Surely it is conceivably within the power of God to present to the mind such constraining motives as infallibly to engage man's will on the side of right. If we do not admit this, I cannot understand what sense we give to the words of the collect: "O Almighty God, Who alone canst order the unruly wills of sinful men, grant unto Thy people that they may love the thing which Thou commandest, and desire that which Thou dost promise." If we do admit it, then the supposition of all men finally choosing the right is not *à priori* contrary to free-will. Whether there is any ground for believing that such will be the case in fact, is a different question which will be considered immediately.

Again, it is allowed by all, as has been stated above, that sin cannot be forgiven till it is repented of; repentance is an exercise of free-will; Canon Farrar expresses the hope that this exercise of free-will may be possible in the case of every human soul after this life, as well as during it; Dr. Rigg denies this. Which of the two, I ask again, limits free-will? But, it may be said, you hold it possible that in the end the various wills of men may all determine in one direction. We do, because we know that the mightiest forces and the permanent motives are all at work to draw him in that direction, and to fix him in it when drawn there, those forces and motives which we believe to have fixed for ever the wills of the redeemed in heaven; and this being the case, even if we were to look upon man's free-will as entirely unmoral, a mere chance oscillation between conflicting motives, which seems to supply the extreme of unaccountable and unpredictable action, yet even on this doctrine of chances each of these human atoms must, in the endless ages, eventually be caught up and made to take its place in the universal order. How much more, if we think of man as a being made in the image of God, gifted with what we loosely call the faculties of reason, will, and conscience, for this very purpose that he may know and do what is pleasing to God?

Dr. Rigg thinks that, if we accept this conclusion, we do away with guilt, and punishment becomes unrighteous. Why so? The guilt consists in resisting the better motives and yielding to the worse. The punishment is the employment, in each successive stage of probation, of stronger motives where weaker ones have failed. Since some natures are more readily susceptible to good influences than others, the less susceptible have to be placed under a sterner discipline for their own sake as much as for the sake of others, both in this life and in the next life. Where is the unrighteousness? As Plato said long ago, punishment, corrective discipline, is that which is really good for the sinner. It is only when punishment degenerates into a gratification of the desire of vengeance that it becomes unrighteous.

Passing on from the abstract question of free-will and moral responsibility, have we any ground for supposing that the moral condition of the lost after this life will, as a fact, be such as to admit of improvement, or that the circumstances in which they will then be placed will be more effective in influencing them for good than the circumstances of their life on earth have been? "The essential tendency of evil," says Principal Tulloch, "is to intensify its own misery." "The idea that all men shall become good at last is opposed by the course of experience here" (p. 47). "There are some," says Professor Salmon, "who have died to all appearance irreformably wicked, and if they then enter on a life which is anything like a continuation of the present one, they must do so under conditions infinitely less favourable than those under which they started here." So Dr. Allon, "The odds against the moral renovation hereafter of a man who here has sinned away his moral sensitiveness are overwhelming" (p. 172); and Dr. Rigg (p. 191), "It is presumptuous to imagine that more powerful motives to repentance may be applied in another world than are offered (here) to the hearers of Christ's gospel."

As to all this matter I think there is one thing which is generally agreed to, and that is, that the immense majority of grown men and women, whether called good or bad, whatever progress they may be making in particular directions, have certain faults of character which do not seem to get less under the discipline of this present life ; and yet we believe that in many instances, at any rate, these faults of character will be cured in the next life, which shows that, however we may talk, we do ascribe to the next life a greater reforming power than we find to be at work here. In the next place, when we speak of "irreformable wickedness," we use a very bold phrase. Will any one point to a single character either in history or in his own personal experience, of which he would venture to say that it defied every possible moral engine which it is in the power even of man to employ? We are accustomed to look upon Judas Iscariot as the worst character brought before us in the Bible, and yet what a vast reserve of moral feeling is shown in the words, " I have sinned in that I have betrayed innocent blood," and in the desperate act by which, apparently without waiting for the last scene on Calvary, he tried to atone for his crime ! If we may venture for a moment to carry on our thoughts to the meeting in Hades between the betrayer and the Betrayed ; if we may presume to imagine the penetrating yet compassionate gaze—not less compassionate, surely, nor less love-compelling, than that which melted the heart of another less sorely wounded by Satan—is it not a moral certainty, from all we know of the laws of human nature, that out of the midst of that agony of shame and remorse there must have sprung up the consciousness of a love inexhaustible and invincible, which would make even the terrors of "his own place" not only endurable but most welcome to the sufferer when they were looked upon as the appointed remedy of his sin, the token of a Father's forgiveness to him who rightly received them? And yet, though we may see reason to believe that the sin of Judas has been forgiven, we shall not think the language of Eastern hyperbole overstrained when it says of one whose name was destined to be synonymous with traitor till the end of time, "It were better for him if he had never been born."

I have slightly digressed, because the history of Judas is often insisted upon in opposition to the idea of final restoration. Supposing, however, that there are cases in which the moral sensitiveness seems really sinned away, or supposing there are cases in which we not only find ourselves practically powerless to promote any amendment, but in which, as far as we can see, there has been every advantage of education and circumstances, so that we cannot even imagine any improvement in the external influences which have been brought to bear; does it follow, as Professor Salmon appears to think, that such a life has been merely wasted, and that the next stage of being must commence under infinitely worse conditions than the present? It appears to me that not only is such a supposition irreconcilable with the Christian idea of God, but that it is even possible for us to see how the contrary may be the case. How often has a badly spent youth been the prelude to a deeply penitent and earnest manhood? What ground have we for assuming that the sin of this infinitesimal moment of time, which we call life, will remain necessarily ingrained in the character through eternity? May not rather the experience here gained of the weakness of our nature, the miserable effects of sin, and the contrast presented by the rewards of righteousness, now at last appreciated,—may not all this supply in the second course of probation a stimulus which was wanting in the first? And if to us men reformation appears impossible, does that prove that the Divine resources also have come to an end? What happens to such a man at death? Principal Tulloch would seem to say that we can only suppose a continued process of hardening. If so, I would say that there must be a special miracle to effect it; that is, supposing death is what we believe it to be, the separation of soul from body, the removal of the veil between illusion and truth, between the temporal and the eternal. I will not repeat what I have said upon a former occasion as to the altered aspect in which sensual indulgence, the lust of the flesh, the lust of the eye, and the pride of life, must present itself to the disembodied spirit; but may we not fairly apply our Lord's words here, "Thomas, because thou hast seen Me, thou hast believed: blessed are they that have not seen and yet have believed." Those who in this world of confusion and darkness have believed in the light, rise, as it were, by a natural selection to special blessing in the life to come; those who have failed to believe here will see and believe there. The parable of Lazarus may serve to illustrate the power of the new influences under which the soul is brought at death. On opening his eyes in Hades the rich man is filled with deep anxiety not only for himself but for others, in place of the easy indifference which seems to have characterised him before.

The next argument I will examine is, that the endless duration of moral evil is no greater difficulty than the palpable fact of its present existence. We find this urged by Dr. Allon (p. 169), though his practice is hardly consistent with his theory, as he adopts the principle of annihilationism in order to avoid the eternity of evil. Professor Salmon gives an ingenious turn to the argument by the suggestion that at any given time hereafter it is credible there may be other worlds in the same state of development as ours is now, so that even if we suppose evil finite in the individual it may be endless in the universe (p. 119). There is a difficulty in meeting the argument, because, to me and, I should think, to most people, finite evil and infinite evil, evil vanquished and evil victorious, are such totally incommensurate ideas that if any one says he perceives no difference between them, one hardly sees what there is left to appeal to. All that I can do is to draw out the two hypotheses side by side. According to the one, it is the Divine plan to raise humanity by slow and gradual steps from the level of the brutes into a moral conformity with the image of Christ. As a part of the process of this development, came the struggle between the higher and lower nature, the possibility and the consciousness of sin; but this is merely a transitional state intended to prepare the way for the reception of the higher divine life which will in the end be manifested in every child of man. According to the other, God, the All-holy and All-good, created man immortal, knowing that many, if not most, of the species would, after a moment of doubtful happiness and chequered goodness here, be doomed to an eternity of uniform sin and misery. Nor does the supposition of successive worlds following the same course of development make any difference. To Him who sees the end from the beginning, who sees the Christ already formed in hearts which to men may appear desperately hardened, the passing shadow of sin is lost in the succeeding blaze of light; or rather, for to Him there is no succession, it is already swallowed up in the glory of the eternal day. When Professor Salmon further says (p. 119), "We lose all explanation why God should have made us exposed to temptation here, if we think it possible that He can hereafter ordain a constitution of things in which the inducements to well-doing shall be so overpowering that wrong-doing shall be impossible," he seems to me just to reverse the truth. It is the imperfection of this world, viewed in the light of our own moral instincts, which makes it necessary for us to believe in another world where all is perfect. It is the faith and hope in that other world which makes this world endurable, and enables us to retain our belief in Righteousness as the supreme law of the universe.

I should like, in conclusion, to say one word as to the contrast drawn by Miss Wedgwood, in her late interesting article on William Law,[1] between what she characterises as "the comfortable assurance (of our times) that everybody will come right at last" and Law's "awe-struck sense of a holiness that would not be satisfied till it had communicated itself to every spirit, how lost, guilty, and degraded soever." No doubt, on this as on most subjects, there is a vast difference between the pre-revolutionary and the post-revolutionary modes of thought. The Revolution may be said to have performed for Christianity the same service which Socrates performed for philosophy—brought it down to earth from heaven. That God is no respecter of persons, that He is able of these stones to raise up children to Abraham, that when He corrects us it is that we may *live*, that it is our duty to love our

---

[1] See *Contemporary Review* for December 1877, p. 98.

neighbour as ourselves, that we are all members one of another, that election, whether of nation, or class, or individual, is not for the sake of the chosen seed exclusively or principally, but to the end that, in and through it, all families of the earth may be blessed,—these are no longer mere texts for sermons, but are echoed back by the *vox populi* in strange-sounding phrases of "fraternity" and "solidarity," which make the hearts of nations vibrate. And this inarticulate religion of the *vox populi* reacts again on articulate religion, and is making itself felt everywhere as a *vox Dei*, confirming the whispers of reason and conscience in the individual man. It is impossible for one who has learned that the end of punishment, when it passes beyond the elementary stage of self-preservation, is not revenge, but reformation, to believe that Divine punishment can be conducted on lower principles than we men have attained to; it is impossible for one who has learned that goodness cannot be happy in presence of the vice or misery of others, except in so far as it may hope to convert the vicious and to comfort the miserable,—it is impossible for such a one to believe in the happiness of heaven co-existing with the sin and misery of hell.

In this sense, then, Miss Wedgwood is right in contrasting our age with Law's. Law stood almost alone in upholding a truth which is rapidly becoming the all but universal belief among thoughtful Christian men. It required great faith *then* to do what requires little faith *now*. Yet the change has been brought about within very few years; would Miss Wedgwood deny to him who, more than any one man, was the cause of it, Frederick Denison Maurice, "the awestruck sense of a holiness which would not be satisfied till it had communicated itself to every spirit"? On the contrary, it would be difficult to find words which would more exactly convey to a stranger the impression left by his memory in the minds of all who knew him. Is then the converse proposition true? Have the recent opposers of the established doctrine attacked it simply on the easy Epicurean grounds attributed to them by Miss Wedgwood? We are tolerably familiar with this literature, and cannot call to mind a single book of which this could be truly stated. What we do know is that the generation which has now reached middle age, and which was brought up on the usual orthodox traditions, has had to pass through a struggle of the most painful kind, leading in some cases to insanity, in some cases to atheism, but on the whole resulting in that truer and higher view of the Fatherhood of God, which we would desire to leave as our best heirloom to the generation which succeeds us.

ETERNAL HOPE

XVIII.

ETERNAL HOPE.

(*Reply* BY ARCHDEACON FARRAR.)

My immediate task is to answer the objections which have been urged by writers in this *Review* against my treatment of that solemn topic which has lately awaked so much eager controversy in England and America. I would gladly offer towards the decision of the question a contribution far more exhaustive than the sermons which have been subjected to so fierce a criticism, and the notes which I threw together in their support. At present this is not possible; but this at least I can say, that I have read with respectful consideration, and with a mind entirely open to conviction, a great deal which has been urged in opposition to my views, and that I have not met with one argument to which I was unable to offer what appeared to me, and to others wiser and more learned than myself, a perfectly serious and perfectly conclusive answer. Let me, in the fewest words, get rid of all that is personal in this controversy.

To the larger number of the well-known writers and theologians who have expressed their opinions upon the subject treated in my "Eternal Hope," I owe my grateful thanks for their candour and courtesy. But some of them have overlooked, and one of them at least has ungenerously ignored, the circumstances under which the book was published. I explained, as fully as I could, that it could not profess to be a formal treatise. The main part of it consisted of sermons, written, I may fairly say, under the difficulty of interrupted leisure and uninterrupted anxieties; written a day or two before they were delivered; written to be addressed to large miscellaneous audiences; written lastly under the influence of emotions which had been deeply stirred by circumstances, and had taken the strongest possible hold of my imagination and memory. While I was musing, the fire burned, and it was only at the last that I spake with my tongue. It is not thus that I should have addressed a small audience of learned theologians. It is not thus that I should have addressed *any* audience but one which for the time being I could regard as my own. Expressing the same convictions I should have formulated them with more deliberate completeness. " Every one," says Dr Newman, "preaches according to his frame of mind at the time of preaching."[1] If he have a firm grasp upon the truths which he is uttering, surely it is neither possible nor desirable for him so utterly to repress his own individuality as to exclude his feelings from waking some echo in the words which he employs. I have been rebuked, I know not how often, for my "rhetoric." If by the word "rhetoric" be meant the natural language of strong emotion, I do not see why it should involve a reproach. If by rhetoric be meant a style *artificially* elaborate, *intentionally* vehement, *deliberately* ornate, I can boldly plead not guilty. No one, I think, has ever intended to charge me with that pompous inflation and sophistical insincerity which is attached to the ordinary conception of a rhetorical style. I can only express myself in such words and images as first present themselves, and I have always desired to say what I have to say in the manner in which it comes to me most naturally to say it. It may be that in some instances my very " defects " may

---

[1] Apologia, Appendix, p. 15.

have been rendered "effective" for good purposes; and if so, I am content; but at any rate, let the supremely unimportant question of my style be eliminated from the serious discussion of the truths which I have endeavoured, at any rate without any ambiguity, and I trust without any want of courage, to express and to defend.[1]

But it has been objected that on a subject which is supposed to belong to the domain of theology, I ought to have spoken otherwise, or at any rate ought not to have published my sermons. I reply that whether the question of "endless torments" belongs to theology or not, it is one which possesses a very practical and a very terrific interest for many myriads of living men and women. I appeal to any parochial clergyman who reads these pages, whether he does not know people, and especially women, who, though they are not flagrant

---

[1] Thus Mr. Beresford Hope will see how far I was from having sought an opportunity to give vent to my feelings from a special vantage-ground. Let me take the opportunity of saying that Mr. Beresford Hope rightly points out that I was guilty of an omission in not dwelling *more prominently* on the forgotten, though clearly-revealed doctrine of an Intermediate State—Hades not Gehenna. I was, indeed, dealing with a vaster question, but Mr. Beresford Hope has rendered a very important service by dwelling on this truth.

sinners, are yet conscious of grievous imperfections, and on whom the popular doctrine rests with agonising incidence, not as a deterrent from sin but as an incentive to despair? Whether they have not met with men of intellect, and men of science, who reject all religion because they hold it to be bound up with a belief against which their moral sense revolts? Whether they have not known hearts made sad which God had not made sad, by the awful dread lest those who were dearest to them should have passed, and passed irrevocably, into those blistering flames and diabolical complications of unending torture, where the popular Nonconformist preacher tells them "that the damned for ever jingle the burning irons of their torment"? It only needs a glance at our recent literature to see that Atheism has made its very stronghold in the indignant sense of pity which repudiates a Gospel which it identifies with images of endless despair and hideous torment. I believe that the faith of Christ will gain an incomparable force—I believe that it will reassert its waning empire over the prevalence of scepticism, when noble and earnest-minded men shall see that the Judge of all the earth will do *right;* and that neither in Scripture nor in the

Catholic faith is there anything which excludes —while alike in Scripture and in the Catholic faith there is very much that encourages—the doctrine of Eternal Hope; the doctrine (that is) that, even if in the short span of human life the soul have been not yet weaned from sin, there may be, for some at any rate, a hope of recovery, a possibility of amendment, if not after the Last Judgment, at least in some disembodied condition beyond the grave.

On every ground, therefore, I held it to be a duty not to refuse to face the solemn question I had in nowise sought, but which had been brought before me in the ordinary course of my ministrations. It was, however, no part of my duty to publish what I had said. While utterly despising what "A Layman" calls the "conspiracy of silence," I have never been eager to plunge into controversy. During a ministry of more than twenty years, though I have never taught what I did not believe, and though in my published sermons I have alluded quite distinctly to the hope which I have ever held, I have been almost invariably content to dwell on those vast truths respecting which all Christians are heartily agreed; and I would earnestly advise our younger clergy to do the same. I refused multitudes of requests to publish these sermons, simply because I had no wish to subject to the fierce glare of minute and most hostile criticism opinions which, in an ordinary sermon, it was impossible to formulate with the rigid and exhaustive accuracy of a formal treatise, or to defend with a complete array of authorities and arguments. But this matter was not left to my own decision. The sermons had been taken down in shorthand, and were published against my will and without my knowledge, and were being sold by tens of thousands in unauthorised and incorrect forms, of which I had never seen a single copy. I was therefore driven at last to show what I had said, in order to defend myself against a deluge of misrepresentations; and in the notes and preface I mentioned, at the shortest possible notice, some of the reasons on which my views were founded. If these facts had been borne in mind, my severest critics would, I think, have been led to write in a different and a fairer tone.

Once more, then, I would ask, What is it that I have advocated? What is it that I have impugned?

I have advocated the ancient and Scriptural doctrine of an interval between death and doom, during which state—whether it be regarded as purgatorial, as disciplinary, as probational, or as retributive—whether the æon to which it belongs be long or short—we see no Scriptural or other reason to deny the possible continuance of God's gracious work of redemption and sanctification for the souls of men; and I have added that I can find nothing in Scripture, or elsewhere, to prove that the ways of God's salvation necessarily terminate with earthly life. I have never denied—nay, I have endeavoured to support and illustrate—the doctrine of Retribution both in this life and the life to come. I have never said—as I am slanderously reported to have said—that there is no "Hell," but only (and surely this should have been regarded as a self-evident proposition) that "Hell" must mean what those words mean of which it is the professed translation; and that those words—Hades, Gehenna, Tartarus—mean something much less inconceivable, much less horribly hopeless, than what "Hell" originally meant, and than what it has come to connote in current religious teaching. I have not maintained Universalism, in spite of much apparent sanction for such a hope in the unlimited language of St. Paul, because I did not wish to dogmatise respecting things uncertain, and because I wished to give full weight to every serious consideration which may be urged against the acceptance of such a hope. I have earnestly maintained that no soul can be saved while it continues in sin; or saved by any means except the efficacy of Christ's redemption. So far from derogating from the necessity of that awful sacrifice,—as has been so often and so strangely asserted,— I know of literally nothing which is so infinitely calculated to enhance our sense of its blessedness, or our love to Him who made it, as the hope that its power will be unexhausted even beyond the grave. And it is monstrous to represent this hope as a modern novelty. To speak of it as a "new theology" is to speak with complete ignorance. I have shown,—and, so far as I am aware, no sort of attempt has been made to set aside my proofs,—that it is far more primitive and far more catholic than the darker Creed by which in the last three centuries it has been superseded;[1] that it was held in the very earliest ages of the Church;[2] that it has been in every age of the Church demonstrably permissible;[3] that it has been held by some of the Church's greatest teachers

---

[1] Eternal Hope, 9th Ed. pp. 154-169.
[2] See the *Pastor of Hermas*, iii. 278, and p. 155.
[3] *Ibid.* pp. 159-167.

and holiest saints;[1] that, though eagerly debated and widely prevalent, it was not condemned by any decree of the four first œcumenical councils;[2] that it has never been condemned by any article of any universal Creed or by any decree of any œcumenical council;[3] that in some form or other it enters into the faith of by far the greatest part of Christendom;[4] and that even St. Augustine, and St. Jerome, and Luther himself,—though from them mainly, in ancient and modern times, the popular teaching is supposed to be derived,—use language far more accordant with man's instinctive sense of God's mercy, love, and justice than is heard in the majority of modern pulpits. For even St. Augustine believed in a sort of purgatory,[5] and wrote, "Neque hoc dixerim ut diligentiorem tractationem videar ademisse de pœnis peccatorum *quomodo in Scripturis dicuntur æternæ.*"[6] And St. Jerome held that Christians at any rate would be saved after a future punishment;[7] and even Luther wrote, "God forbid that I should limit the time of acquiring

---

[1] See the *Pastor of Hermas*, iii. pp. 156-183.   [2] *Ibid.* p. 167.
[3] Eternal Hope, p. 159.   [4] *Ibid.* p. 180, *seq.*
[5] Aug. De Civ. Dei, xxi. 24.   [6] In Matt. xxv. 26.
[7] See references to St. Jerome's opinions, *Eternal Hope,* p. 166.

faith to the present life! In the depths of Divine mercy there may be opportunity to win it in the future state."[1] But what have I impugned? Not the humble and awful dread, not the trembling and sensitive submission of pure and loving Christian souls, but that hard, exaggerated, and damnatory literalism,—that unreasonable insistence on admitted metaphors and emotional appeals—that interpretation of words in senses which they will not bear,—that hideous play of the imagination employed for the ignoble purpose of promoting virtue by stimulating a sense of abject terror, of which some religious writers have been so dangerously guilty. Principal Tulloch says with perfect truth that " a Christian theology must not be made responsible for these lurid pictures ;" but my very object was to show that they form no true part of Christian theology at all, and ought to be eliminated from popular teaching as dangerous to faith and dishonouring to God. It is on these accretions alone that my so-called invectives fell, and not on the more sober teaching of thousands of holy and loving ministers of the Gospel, whose hearts will not allow them to indulge in such language as led to

---

[1] Letter to Hansen von Rechenberg, 1522.

the celebrated exclamation, "*Oh Dr. Emmons! Dr. Emmons! has God then no mercy at all?*" But many are *now* anxious to repudiate as at all expressive of their views such amplifications as those of Mr. Spurgeon on the parable of Dives:[1] "*See how his tongue hangs from between his blistered lips! How it excoriates and burns the roof of his mouth as if it were a firebrand!*" But, however much it may now be rejected, it certainly *was*, and *is*, a fair representation of much that is still uttered by Christian ministers, and endured by Christian congregations. "What do the wicked do for ever in Hell?" is the question of a once celebrated catechism, which many of my readers must have learned in their childhood. "*They roar, curse, and blaspheme God.*" Where has this teaching been repudiated? When, and where, and by whom, until within the last month or two, has there been a distinct refusal by teachers of this school to endorse the sentiments of the frightful sermon of Jonathan Edwards, entitled "Sinners in

---

[1] Who, be it observed in passing, was not in Gehenna at all, but in Hades, the intermediate state; whom Abraham still addresses as son; and who can speak, and speak words of sympathy and affection, in pite of his burning and excoriated tongue.

the hands of an angry God"? "*The God that holds you over the pit of hell, much in the same way as one holds a spider or some loathsome insect over the fire, abhors you and is dreadfully provoked.*" Apart from the metaphor, is this to be regarded as orthodox teaching or not? Is this the God who has bidden us love our enemies? Is this the God of whom we are taught that His love is deeper than that of a mother, and that His tender mercies are over all His works? Is this the God who says that He will not cast off for ever? Is this the God who "pardoneth iniquity," who "retaineth not His anger for ever, because He delighteth in mercy"? If language, such as I have quoted, be utterly reprehensible, if it be an unconscious blasphemy against the love and pity of our Father in Heaven, why have my sermons been so vehemently attacked? I have received so many letters on the subject, from all sorts of strangers in England and America, that few living men are, I suppose, better able to estimate the character of the extreme popular view, or the hardening, embittering, inquisitorial, Pharisaical, depraving, pride-and-hatred-engendering influence, which it exercises on the minds — not, of course, of all—but of too many who hold it.

This was the doctrine that produced the Torquemadas, the Arnolds of Citeaux, the Sprengels of the Middle Ages. This is the doctrine which often makes the so-called religious character so little lovely and so little religious. This is the doctrine which to this day produces the dull and obstinate fanaticism of many whom we would fain win to a diviner charity. The Bishop of St. Andrews, having recently written a letter on the war question, received the next day the following post-card: "Your letter . . . is quite a scandal. . . . *Why, you make Christian people rejoice that there is in God's providence a place of retribution for workers of evil like you.*" I can only say, "Legant, erubescant, horrescant, Christiani. *Perpendant, perhorrescant!*"

Undoubtedly this vindictively remorseless style of dwelling upon the "*horribile decretum,*" though, as I have experienced, far from extinct, is being gradually modified, and is inevitably doomed to pass away. Professor Birks, in his somewhat acrid paper, complains of my "loose massing of authorities" against the popular view, because many of these authorities differ widely from each other. To me it seems that their very divergence in other matters adds almost indefinite weight to their unanimity in this. I will not mention the many names of the illustrious dead, from Hermas down to Archbishop Tillotson, from Origen down to Archbishop Whately, from St. Gregory of Nyssa down to Bishop Ewing of Argyle, from Johannes Scotus Erigena down to Professor F. D. Maurice, from Clement of Alexandria down to Canon Kingsley and Dr. Norman M'Leod; but if men, otherwise so dissimilar in their views as Dr. Littledale and Mr. Llewelyn Davies, the Dean of Westminster and Archdeacon Reichel, Mr. T. J. Rowsell and Mr. Jukes, Bishop Moorhouse and Mr. S. Cox, Professor Jellett and Mr. J. Baldwin Brown, Professor Plumptre and Mr. E. White, Mr. H. N. Oxenham, and Professor Birks himself—to mention but a few out of hundreds of living divines, of all schools, ranks, and degrees of learning, in the Protestant Churches of England, Sweden, Germany, and France—are agreed in rejecting the doctrine of endless torment in the form in which it has been preached even recently, in all its undisturbed horror, by many preachers, then this fact alone is a very decisive proof that such a doctrine cannot at any rate be regarded as indisputably Scriptural. Controversialists of the type of those who are contented with Horbery's "hundred and three texts on his side" (!) or with the assertion that eternal torments are "*indisputably* taught in twenty-six passages of the New Testament," might have thought themselves justified in using such language fifty years ago, but now simply put themselves out of court as having failed to comprehend the most elementary conditions of the controversy. Assertions of that type are simply a mark of incompetent provincialism, and they fall to the ground at once before the unbiassed remark of the devout, learned, and excellent Dr. Isaac Watts, that "for the doctrine of an immortality of endless torment he found in Scripture no warrant whatever." In the face of such facts, in the face of all Church history, in the face of the existing belief of the largest part of Christendom, how can any one, without condemning himself, venture to assert that the four accretions to the doctrine of future retribution which I rejected—viz., physical torture, necessarily endless duration, irreversibility after death, and the all but universality of the doom[1]—are undeniably parts of the

---

[1] They profess to found this doctrine on an entire misinterpretation of Matt. vii. 13, 14, which only conveys such a meaning when it has been tortured by a systematic and

Catholic verity? I have been anathematised by many who are innocent of the veriest rudiments of criticism; but is it not a significant fact that of the fifteen divines—Irish, Scotch, and English—who have been invited to criticise my sermons, all but two, as well as both the eminent laymen, agree with me in repudiating the *main* points which I have rejected; and that even the two who desire to defend the current opinion, make large concessions as to the untenable character of popular eschatology?

Having thus endeavoured to clear the ground, I will now glance with all possible brevity at the criticisms contained in these papers.

Professor Jellett, with a calmness and courtesy worthy of all praise, has defended the great canon of Bishop Butler on the relations of natural to revealed religion. Principal Tulloch also points out, with admirable force, the necessity of allowing weight to the moral intuitions of mankind. He urges against Universalism the Law of Continuity. I am not concerned to defend Universalism;

---

inferential literalism which would fill all Scripture with contradictions, and which is practically only tolerated in a few favourite texts.

but seeing that repentance is always possible in life—seeing that so long as life lasts any man *may* become good—the Law of Continuity was one of the very grounds on which I based the doctrine of Eternal Hope. If the greatness of God's mercies lasts till the grave, the Law of Continuity strengthens our hope that it will not be for ever cut short by the accident of death. If the efficacy of Christ's Atonement lasts till death, the Law of Continuity helps to strengthen our conviction, so well expressed in the eloquent and admirable paper of Mr. J. Baldwin Brown, that "the love of God cannot be the one Divine power in the universe which, for man at any rate, is paralyzed by the hand of Death."

With the greatest part of Dr. Hunt's able paper I entirely agree; but when he says that the doctrine of never-ending torments "has been believed by the majority of Christians in all ages, in all Churches," this belief must be most carefully distinguished from the post-Reformation dogma—a dogma which even Luther could not accept—of an all but universal, unmitigated, and irreversible doom to endless torments at the moment of death.

Mr. White thinks that the doctrine of Eternal Hope "gives to the generality of defiant men a cheerful and even hopeful view of their ultimate destiny, and that it differs *toto cælo* and even *toto inferno* from the fearful doctrine of Christ and the Apostles, and will be attended practically, as experience shows, by widely different results." I reply that (1) this is but an opinion; and (2) that if my view thus *appears* to differ from the *letter* of some of Christ's utterances, it agrees most absolutely with both the letter and the spirit of others; and Mr. White himself will hardly say that it differs *toto cælo* and *toto inferno* from the parables of the Lost Sheep and the Prodigal Son, and Christ's prayer for His murderers, and St. Paul's unlimited prophecies of the final Palingenesia. And (3) that we have nothing to do with *results*, but with truths. The doctrine of endless torments, being at any rate unknown to the Old Dispensation, cannot be necessary to deter from sin; and if the Gospel of Hope be wrested by some to their own destruction,—which I doubt, seeing that, in the words of St. Paul, "we are saved by hope,"—it certainly rescues others from despair. But in truth Mr. White is taking a wrong point of view when he talks of my holding out to defiant men a cheerful view of their future. To them we preach that so long as they are defiant, so long must they remain in that outer darkness which is alienation from God. We tell them that sin is loss and ruin, and must inevitably entail, both here and hereafter, that dread law of consequence in which they only refuse to believe when it is presented to them with impossible additions. We tell them that the longer and the more defiantly they continue in sin, the greater and the deadlier must be that loss, which, even if it do not assume the form of physical torment, may continue to be loss—a *pœno damni*—for ever. The hope of the *mitigatio*, the *refrigeria*, the remissions, which God may grant hereafter, the cessation of a maddening agony and a gnawing remorse, is surely a very different thing from the assertion that all sinners will ultimately be admitted to the beatitude of heaven—to those joys which eye hath not seen, nor ear heard, nor has it entered into the heart of man to conceive.[1]

I can only attribute much of Professor Salmon's paper to his having "skipped or

---

[1] Canon Ryle, and many others, fall into this misconception. I, at any rate, have never taught that "we shall somehow or other all get to heaven hereafter." In fact, nine-tenths of what has passed for triumphant refutation of what I have said is only triumphant in its refutation of what I never dreamt of saying at all.

skimmed many pages" of the book which he was professing to criticise. A less supercilious process might have shown him that my supposed horror of physical pain, as compared to mental remorse, is not due, as he hints, to personal pusillanimity, but to my belief that the physical pain of which I was speaking—material fire and material worms—could only be inflicted by arbitrary external acts, the supposition of which degrades our conception of God. Professor Salmon entirely fails to see that I regard vindictive and purposeless inflictions not as " too *dreadful*" to believe, but as too contrary to my faith in God's love ; too impossible to reconcile with the declaration that He punishes " not willingly but for our profit, that we may be partakers of His grace."

Dr. Littledale's paper calls for no notice at my hands. I regret, but shall not imitate, the arrogant discourtesy by which it is characterised. Let others decide whether the tone which he sees fit to adopt is justifiable or becoming.

I have no such grounds of complaint against Mr. Arthur. And yet I am simply amazed at his statements that I found my opinion on two texts; that I do not refer to history and experience; that I suppose the world to be governed on the painless principle; that I assume that the Ruler of the Universe could never inflict pain; and that, on this subject, I do not seek guidance in the rules maintained amongst us on this side the grave. I could almost suppose—were it not that it would have been unworthy of his seriousness—that Mr. Arthur had adopted the "skipping and skimming" methods of Professor Salmon. If it were respectful to Mr. Arthur, I could only vent my astonishment by several notes of admiration: as it is, I will simply refer to the pages of my book, literally from end to end, in direct refutation of every one of his assertions. One indeed of his allegations is perfectly correct—that I have not alluded to "the procedure in the case of angels." I have not done so, because, apart from Scholasticism and Milton, we know so very little about it, and are so entirely unable to estimate the analogies to the destiny of man which it may or may not present. I do not hold, as Mr. Arthur thinks, either that all who repent in Hades "pass to heaven," or that sin is put away by pain. I fear that Mr. Arthur will be —but he ought not to be—surprised when I entirely agree with him in saying that Christ taught that "they who will not repent will suffer an endless penalty;" but I instantly part company with him if he makes the unwarrantable addition, "they who will not repent *in this life*," since my whole book is a statement of the reasons why I venture to hope that the gates of mercy are not finally closed after the brief span of earthly existence. Again, I hold with Mr. Arthur that if "God's severity is all love," so God's love is sometimes manifested by severity, and that punishment does not necessarily imply cruelty. But *endless* punishment—billions of millenniums of unutterable and flaming agony for each tenth part of a second of sin—has Mr. Arthur faced what that means? Protection, as Mr. Arthur says, may require punishment, but can he prove that it requires *endless torments?* And if in all my "impetuous flights" I "barely graze the surface of the mystery of suffering, like a bird skimming over a still but unfathomable deep," what human writer has ever done more? Not even the eagle-wing of the logical and theological can do more, much less "smooth, gliding swallows, and noisy, impudent tomtits"—

"Quales ego vel Cluvienus."

Mr. Arthur writes like a high-minded and earnest man, but I would respectfully submit that, so far as I am concerned, his paper, from beginning to end, is a good illustration of what is meant by *Ignoratio Elenchi.*

I now proceed to make a few remarks on the second series of papers.

My friend, Dr. Plumptre, quotes some remarkable letters from a Catholic priest. I have not been told who he is, but it is not very difficult to conjecture, and, at any rate, his letters are sufficient to show that he speaks with authority. How very remarkable, then, is his statement—how deeply ought that statement to be weighed by the multitudes who have so blindly asserted that my view has in all ages been condemned by the Church—that "there is nothing incompatible with the faith of Catholics" in the view that vast multitudes who have popularly been considered to fall under the awful doom of everlasting punishment, may be withdrawn from it by substituting the notion of a purgatorial punishment in its place. How remarkable, again, is the statement that Catholics may hold "that there are innumerable degrees of grace and sanctity among the saved, and that those who go to purgatory, however many, die, one and all with the presence of God's grace and the earnest of eternal life, however invisibly to man, already in their hearts," so that "faith and repentance may be believed to exist in many of those who die and make no sign." And if such an one—one who is so exceptionally high an authority on patristic literature—admits that this view was held " by several of the Fathers," what becomes of the reckless, cruel, and ignorant assertion that it is heretical, when it can be proved to every candid reader that, though thus held, and universally known to be thus held, by leaders of orthodoxy like the two Gregories, yet as a demonstrable, historical fact it has *never* been authoritatively condemned?

I quite agree with Dr. Allon, that the teaching of our Lord respecting a future life can hardly be settled by the philological analysis of one or two words. If I have adduced and examined those words with a view to prove that their true *sense* was misunderstood, it is because I was, for the time being, occupied with that element of the question which consists in showing that those words, especially "Gehenna" and "æonian," not only do not convey, but in my opinion distinctly *exclude*, the senses which have been popularly attached to them. The common interpretation of them has indeed been all but universal *since* the days of St. Augustine; but this general *consensus* is of little value if strong evidence can be adduced to prove that the original meaning had become gradually obscured, by uncritical ignorance, and yet that this original meaning continued to be maintained, not only by multitudes of simple Christians, but by some of the most profound and learned of Fathers during the earlier centuries. And surely when Dr. Allon says that our Lord "in the most absolute manner affirmed, and intended to affirm, the finality of religious conditions *after death*," he must mean (though he repeats the phrase several times) not "after death," but "*after the Day of Judgment.*" I agree with one of our most eminent and learned Bishops, who, in a letter on this subject, remarks how strange it is that any who profess to be guided by the Bible only should reject the primitive and catholic belief of an Intermediary State between death and judgment. If not one word which our Lord uttered can be perverted into any statement of a final decision *at the moment of death*, I should be quite content to leave untouched the much more tenable—though not, I think, at all demonstrable—conviction that He left no hope of alleviation for those who were finally doomed at the Last Assize. And if Dr. Allon holds it legitimate, nay, imperative, to introduce limitations into what he calls "rhetorical passages" of unlimited promise and hopefulness in St. Paul and St. John, must it not be far more admissible to refuse (if need be) a scholastically rigid acceptation to passages of professed parable and admitted metaphor? Again, Dr. Allon thinks that, after all, "finality of moral condition does not imply unending being, or unending consciousness of retribution." Yet surely this view is far more at variance with the *primâ facie* teachings of Scripture than one which mainly protests against attaching the conception of "endlessness" to a word which, by universal concession, does not necessarily or generally convey such a meaning?

Dr. Rigg is chiefly arguing against Universalism. Now I have said, and I repeat with all sincerity, that I am *not* a Universalist. I do not mean that I condemn the doctrine as heretical or untenable; or that I do not feel (can there be such a wretch as not to feel?) a longing, yearning *desire* that it might be true. But I dare not say that it *must* be true, because, as I intimated in my book, no man has ever explained the present existence of

x

evil, and no man has ever sounded or can know the abysmal deeps of personality or "the marvel of the everlasting will."

Dr. Rigg and others seem to fancy that I have overlooked this mystery of widespread evil as a factor in the final conclusion. I should have thought it stood out, terrible and palpable, on every page of the Fifth Sermon. The rebukes which bid me not to construct a God, or a Universe, after my own liking— even if that liking be guided by all that Scripture teaches us to regard as most Divine in the character of God—are to me quite needless. It is not I, but the maintainers of the popular opinion—with all those fearful accretions of it which I hope I shall have helped to sweep away—who are "wise above what is written." I take some of the books of God— Reason, Conscience, Nature, Experience, History; they reveal antinomies which I cannot solve, and apparent discords which I do not deny; but when I turn from them to Scripture, in which I believe that we hear *most* clearly the voice of God speaking through the mind of man, I find that we are there taught to trust in God, *in spite of* all that might seem at strife with the love and perfectness of His being; I find ample grounds for the hope that all apparent discords shall ultimately be harmonised in one vast concord; and I do *not* find one simple word which, when fairly examined, sanctions the hideous accumulation of dark human fancies which have gathered round the supposed data of a literalism which was at first inevitably ill-informed and then became inevitably traditional.[1] The mystery of the present evil is, indeed, insoluble; but does it not become transcendently *less* insoluble —does it not produce an infinitely less severe strain on man's faith in the merciful omnipotence of God—if we are entitled to, nay, encouraged in, the belief that Evil at last shall end, and God be πάντα ἐν πᾶσιν, *all things in all men?* "So at least thought St. Paul," says Archdeacon Reichel, "if his language means what it appears to mean. To him the whole Creation presents itself as travailing in the

---

[1] Since Dr. Rigg doubts my view of Canon Kingsley's opinions, I must reassert, on the highest authority, that they were as nearly as possible identical with my own. If any one desires to satisfy himself respecting that, let him consult his *Water of Life*, p. 76, *seq.*; his *Westminster Sermons*, and his *Life*, i. 318, 319, 371-375, 392-396, 469-471; ii. 41, 42, 207 395-397, 446. Whatever apparent contradictions on the subject may be found in his writings, as in those of Archbishop Tillotson, and some of the Fathers, I have the best reasons for positively affirming that Dr. Rigg is mistaken as to the opinion which he held to the very last.

birth-throes of something new and better, along with ourselves who are its highest part. . . . May not evil be likened to a discord or dissonance in the vast harmony of Creation, tolerable, even beautiful, if resolved into a concord; intolerable if taken by itself, or protracted for ever without such resolution?"[1]

Interpolation by the Editor.

[Here I slightly reduce the ARCHDEACON'S "Reply" from the original version. A paper by the Rev. S. Cox, D.D. (author of *Salvator Mundi*), which appeared in *The Contemporary Review*, came in at this point, and is not included in these reprints. The major part of the article was a *précis* of De Quincey's Essay, which is now given in full at the commencement of this volume. The writer terms it "one of the most characteristic and charming of his essays," and remarks that "as De Quincey is a scholar praised by scholars, it may be hoped that his authority, and still more his argument, which seems unanswerable, may tell for something, and even for much, in the present controversy."

Dr. Cox, before concluding, adverts to that part of Dr. Littledale's "thoughtful paper," in

---

[1] Sermon in St. Patrick's Cathedral, June 28, 1877.

which he remarks that no sufficient stress has been laid on the cardinal fact "that the Scriptures of the New Testament contain two parallel and often seemingly contradictory statements as to the Last Things, one of which, even after being jealously sifted by hostile criticism, does make for the popular theology, and another which more than implies a full restoration, and the final victory of good over evil."

. . . . .

The author of *Salvator Mundi* "would ask those who are thus perplexed in thought to consider whether their perplexity may not spring from a common, and perhaps necessary, feature in revelation of every kind? Do not the phenomena always, or almost always, point in one direction, and the underlying facts or realities in another? Is anything what it seems—even light, or sound, or heat? A single force vibrating in different ratios, and therefore manifesting itself in an incalculable variety of forms, may be our simplest and truest conception of the material universe ; but is it the first to present itself to our minds ?

. . . . .

"When, then, we find these conflicting currents of statement, whether in the Old

Testament or in the New, and are compelled to choose between them, or at least to subordinate the one to the other, what is the wiser and the better part? Surely it is to lean to the larger, the more generous and spiritual side of the alternative. If we believe that 'God is a Spirit,' and that 'God is Love,' what can we do? If the Jews would have done well had they committed themselves to the deeper current, the larger hope [the writer here refers to the spiritual reign of the Messiah], shall not we also do well if, of the two currents in the Scriptures of the New Testament, we commit ourselves to that which affirms or implies a full restoration, and the final victory of good over evil? Let those who demur to that course at least remember that if they were to treat the texts in the New Testament which relate to the Supper of the Lord as they treat the texts which relate to the future punishment of the wicked, they would infallibly find themselves landed in the doctrine of Transubstantiation; or, at the very lowest, in Luther's somewhat paltry evasion and substitution for it, the doctrine of Consubstantiation."
—J. H.]

Archdeacon Farrar then proceeds to observe

that De Quincey states, with clearness and
force, the fact which only prejudice can deny,
that the word *æonian* is always coloured by
the substantive to which it is joined. [Here
the "Reply" resumes.] Of all arguments on
this question, the one which appears to me the
most absolutely and hopelessly futile, is the
one in which so many seem to rest with entire
content; viz. that "eternal or *æonian* life"
must mean endless life, and therefore that
"*æonian* chastisement" must mean "endless
chastisement." This battered and aged argument, . . . if it had possessed a particle
of cogency, would not have been set aside as
entirely valueless by such minds as those of
Origen and the two Gregories in ancient
days, nor by multitudes in the days of St.
Augustine and St. Jerome, nor by the most
brilliant thinker among the schoolmen, nor by
many of our greatest living divines. . . .
No proposition is capable of more simple
proof than that *æonian* is *not* a synonym of
endless. It only means, or can mean, in its
primary sense, pertaining to an *æon*, and therefore "indefinite," since an *æon* may be either
long or short; and in its *secondary* sense
"spiritual," "pertaining to the unseen world,"
"an attribute of that which is above and

beyond time," an attribute expressive not of duration but of quality. Can such an explanation of the word be denied by any competent or thoughtful reader of John v. 39; vi. 54; xvii. 3; 1 John v. 13, 20? Would not the introduction of the word "endless" into those Divine utterances be an unspeakable degradation of their meaning? And as for the argument that the redeemed would thus lose their promised bliss, it is at once so unscriptural and so selfish that, after what Mr. Cox and others have said of it, one may hope that no one will ever be able to use it again without a blush. I cannot here diverge into a discussion with Bishop Wordsworth and Canon Ryle, whose sermons need some *adversaria* rather longer than I can here devote to them; but as they both dwell on the fact that people who spoke Greek interpreted αἰώνιος to mean endless, I reply that some of the greatest masters of Greek, both in classical times and among the Fathers, saw quite clearly that, though the word *might connote* endlessness by being attributively added to endless things, it had in itself no such meaning. I cannot conceive how any candid mind can deny the force of these considerations. If even Origenists would freely speak of future punishment as αἰώνιος but never as ἀτελεύτητος,[1]—if, as even these papers have shown, Plato uses the word as the *antithesis* of endlessness—if St. Gregory of Nyssa uses it as the epithet of "an interval"—if, as though to leave this Augustinian argument without the faintest shadow of a foundation, there are absolutely two passages of Scripture (Hab. iii. 6 and Rom. xvi. 25) where this very word occurs in two consecutive clauses, and is, in the second of the two clauses, applied to God, and yet is, in the first of the two clauses, applied to things which are temporary or terminated — what shall be said of disputants who still enlist the controversial services of a phantom which has been so often laid in the tomb from which it ought never again to emerge? How is it that not one out of the scores of writers who have animadverted on my book have so much as noticed the very remarkable fact to which I have called attention, that those who followed Origen in holding out a possible hope beyond the grave *founded their argument for the terminability of torments on the acknowledged sense of this very word*, and on the fact that other words and phrases which *do* unmistak-

---

[1] Not ἀτελεύταιος, a word known to Dr. Littledale, but not to the Greek language.

ably mean endless are used of the duration of good, but are *never* used of the duration of evil?[1]

Of the carping verbal criticism to which Professor Birks has descended, I take no notice. I have already alluded to what he says about my "loose massing of authorities," and to the entire misconception which he shares with Professor Salmon as to my *reason* for betraying "a dislike of any element of sensible pain in the punishment of the future." I am sorry that he should charge me with "vehement invective and gushes of indignant declamation against those simple believers in the Bible, who dare not give up any part of the creed of their childhood till they see surer grounds for rejecting it than the unwillingness of sinful hearts to believe anything so alarming, and an offered choice, in its stead, of three or four contradictory alternatives which exclude each other." I fear that this sentence proves that Professor Birks has not, even in the school of persecution, himself learned that "caution, and patience of thought, and exclusion of hasty speech," which he preaches to me. He will not find in my book a word of invective against

---

[1] Cæsarius, Dial. 3, in Huet's *Origeniana* (Opp. ed. Paris, iv. 233).

"simple believers," though he will find what he calls invective and declamation against errors which I believe to be at dangerous variance with that revelation which God has given us of Himself in His Son. On the contrary, he will find that, in order to represent the "*horribile decretum*" in its very best light, I gave it originally, not in the language of modern pulpiteers, but in the powerful images of men of splendid genius. No names could have been selected which lent more lustre to the false theology of revolting, vindictive, material torments than those of Dante, Shakspeare, Jeremy Taylor, and Milton; and no names certainly which I regard with a warmer love or a deeper reverence. And if *this* were not a sufficiently obvious proof that I did not dream of attacking those who held even the most abhorrent and the most unscriptural accretions to the belief in hell, I expressly said that I knew them to be held in deep sorrow by many good, holy, and loving Christians. I need not stoop to refute the uncharitable insinuations that I reject these inferences because I regard them as "alarming," or because I share the prevalent tendency to set aside the warnings of God. If my Fifth Sermon does not suffice to show the utter baselessness of such innuendoes, I am more than content to leave them unanswered. There are some criticisms which are sheltered from refutation by disdain. And yet how strange it is that Professor Birks, determined to use a two-edged sword, goes on to say that I myself adopt the very method of those whose terrible pictures I reprobate, when I speak of the horrors of that disease which is God's executioner on drunkenness. Well, but in the first place, the description is not mine at all! It is simply quoted from the pages of one whose name I purposely suppressed, because he has not only seen, but actually suffered from, this frightful retribution. Has Professor Birks never seen it? Alas! I have, and that in women! And did it never even occur to him that I at least was alluding to *facts* which no human being has ever dreamt of denying, while in my opinion Dante and Jeremy Taylor were alluding to the unwarranted and faith-destroying *fictions* of human fancy which are now rejected (as Professor Birks himself admits) by the almost unanimous conviction of mankind? "But," says Professor Birks, "the Scriptures give us no pattern of such 'ghastly' modes of impressing their warnings!" One might have read such a sentence without surprise had it been written by a sceptical layman, but it is very surprising indeed when written by a Cambridge theologian. Has Professor Birks never so much as read Deut. xxviii. 28-35, or Prov. xxiii. 26-35, or Isa. i. 4-6, or Isa. li. 17-20 ? Might not multitudes of such passages have recurred to his memory had he been less eager to find fault ?

I could adduce many more passages in which Professor Birks has not been just in his criticisms. At the close, for instance, of his paper he says that "the practical creed of millions is Universalism," and thinks that my involuntarily published volume will "give fresh currency to some of the worst elements of a widespread popular delusion"—that namely, which, under the name of religious consolation, tells sorrowing relatives that every one "except a few prodigious wretches," has gone straight to heaven. Now as to the fact here alluded to, it is indisputable, and it ought to demonstrate how utterly inoperative, how worse than useless, is the popular doctrine, because it is so often instinctively rejected at the very moment when it should have been most effective. But this is the very kind of hypocrisy which I abhor, and the very kind of consolation which I never use. When indeed I find a woman mourning for a drunkard, whom yet she loved,—and driven into wretchlessness by thinking that he is burning in endless flames,—although I should try to soften the agony of that hard despair by the gleam of possible ultimate hope which I think that God Himself has lighted in the mysterious gloom of the sinner's future, I should never dream of holding out any hope to her that he had gone to bliss. He had suffered retribution in this world—terrible retribution; and if that had failed to win him, he might have to suffer a continuance of that terrible retribution hereafter. But I should certainly not exclude a hope that at least in the Intermediate State God's love revealed in Christ *might* find him ere the last great day. And as for the common run of men—imperfect, faulty, not saints but sinners, yet with many possibilities of good—I should be content to say that wherever they were, and whatever might be the retribution which their sins had incurred, they were "taken to the mercy of the Merciful." I never met with any saying about death which seemed to me at once more tender and more reverent than that of F. W. Robertson : " He is gone. . . . Why should we have wished him to remain a little longer ? Better surely as it is. And as to the eternal question—we know of him all that we can ever know of any one removed beyond the veil which shelters the unseen from the pryings of curiosity— that he is in the hands of the wise and loving. Spirit has mingled with spirit. *A child, more or less erring, has gone home. Unloved by his Father? Believe it who may, that will not I."*

I come lastly to. Professor Gracey. He too indulges in verbal criticism, to which I have neither space nor inclination to reply, though I think I could give him a very satisfactory, and even important, explanation of some passages which he seems to regard as mere nonsense. When he thinks that he "understands my ignorance," he is only "ignorant of my understanding." But let me say in reply to his concluding page, that I am not at all ashamed of not having "mastered every doubt." I came with no compact system; no flawless theodicy. No such is to be had. My object was very different. It was to show that things which were taught as Scriptural were as unwarranted by Scripture as they were by the confession of even Calvin and Jonathan Edwards, agonizing to the conscience, abhorrent to the reason of mankind. Professor Gracey is not content with Hope. Does he then prefer Despair? He says that possible *æons* of retribution furnish a dismal look-out— a fearful looking-for. Undoubtedly it is so, and I do not think that God meant it to be otherwise. But does Professor Gracey think it *more* consoling to accept the retribution as *unending?* If not, his last eloquent sentences are to me entirely unintelligible. He thinks that I have offered but a weak basis for æonian Hope; but I need not surely remind him that hope is not certainty, is not even faith. "For we are saved by hope: but hope that is seen is not hope; for what a man seeth, why doth he yet hope for? But if we hope for that we see not, then do we with patience wait for it."

The three remaining papers powerfully support what I desired to maintain. Professor Mayor has written with the learning and thoughtfulness which we should have expected from him, and has dealt ably with points which I left untouched. Mr. Beresford Hope, alone of all my critics, points out a decided omission in my treatment of the subject, and I hail with deep thankfulness his declared belief that "all reason, all experience, all Scripture, unite in the teaching that the Divine work of discipline goes on behind as well as before the veil." The remarks of the Layman deserve the very earnest consideration of all who desire above all things to be faithful, honest, and true.

I have finished my task, and have not consciously left a single objection without reply. And now I ask, What have the writers who did not hold my opinion effected by their criticisms? Not one of them has touched, much less attempted to set aside, the proof which I adduced for my palmary argument, that we must mean by "hell" what our Lord meant by Gehenna, and that Gehenna did not mean endless torment. In spite of unfair depreciation, I venture to say that, hastily as my book was produced, no modern writer has furnished a fuller contribution from Jewish testimonies to the decision of this important question; and if this position cannot be shaken, how strongly does it tell in favour of Eternal Hope? Again, which of my critics has overthrown, or even attempted to overthrow, the various arguments founded on the uses of the words *Olam* and αἰών or αἰώνιος? And which of them has produced the article of Creed, or decree of Council, or decision of our Church, which diminishes the force of the distinct historic proof that this view, even when least popular, has never been considered as untenable? And which of them has attempted to disprove that the splendid name of Butler, so often invoked against us, is absolutely on our side? And which of them has weakened the testimony of the many distinct passages which favour, nay distinctly imply, an Eternal Hope? And which of them has even attempted to refute the exegesis which shows the πρῶτον ψεῦδος of post-Reformation traditionalism? It may comfort and harden those who love and cling to the current dogmatism on endless torments —it may effectually blind their eyes from any enlightenment as to the real meaning of Scripture—it may disastrously prevent them from having those noble thoughts of God and large hopes for redeemed humanity which seem to me to be of the essence of religion,—to be told that not we only, but also all the great saints and lofty souls who have believed in a salvation by faith and hope, have only repeated the lie of the old serpent, "Thou shalt not surely die;" or that we are robbing the blessed of their hope of bliss; or that Scripture *could not have used clearer language* (!) to express the endless duration of penal torments; or that the non-endlessness of punishment is (in spite of the highest decision to the contrary) irreconcilable with the language of the Prayer-book; or that God's justice is the *antithesis* of His love; or that His justice demands the *endlessness* of misery; or that we only reject endless torments because we do not like them; or "which of the two shall we believe—Satan the father of lies, or Jesus Christ, who is truth?" and so on, and so on. But all this is not argument. It is not even the shadow of argument. It may stereotype the bigotry of ignorance, and render impregnable the obstinacy of prepossession, but it will not have a feather's weight in the ultimate decision. "Believe me that there is nothing which *Satan* more desires than that we should believe that there is no such place as hell and no such thing as eternal torments. *He* whispers all this into our ears, and *he* exults when he hears a layman, and much more when he hears a clergyman, deny these things. *For then he hopes to make them and others his victims.*" So writes Bishop Wordsworth. "*Spectatum admissi* . . .?" Setting aside the excessively loose, inaccurate, and misleading statement of my opinions—if indeed (as I am informed) the sentence was meant for me,—one would have said, had the language been used by any one less to be honoured than so estimable and learned a prelate —one would have said—

> "Hic nigræ succus loliginis, hæc est
> Ærugo mera. Quod vitium procul afore chartis
> Atque animo prius, ut si quid promittere de me
> Possum aliud vere, promitto."

And when Canon Ryle says, " At the end of six thousand years the great enemy of mankind is still using his old weapon (the daring falsehood ' Ye shall not surely die ') to persuade men that they may live and die in sin, and yet at some distant period finally be saved ".—one would have said of so glaring an abuse of that text (which would tell equally against any who preached the Forgiveness of Sins), and of this attribution of a primitive Catholic opinion to the devil, and this identification of those who hold it (saints though many of them have been, in nowise inferior in holiness to Canon Ryle) with the devil's emissaries—one would have said of him who spoke thus, had he been a less excellent man than the vigorous and worthy Canon,

> "Hic niger est; hunc tu, Romane, caveto."

But it is more charitable to refuse to treat such remarks as serious. What would Canon Ryle say were I to charge *him* with repeating the devil's daring falsehood, when (as I suppose) he teaches that men may live in sin, *and yet not die*, but even on the bed of death be saved by repentance? I should be every whit as much justified in saying this to him, as he is in saying it to me; for he holds exactly what I hold, that men *may* be saved from death, upon repentance, by Christ's merits, even though they have sinned. But one is accustomed to this style of theological discussion, and one can make large allowance. One could hardly expect that eminent teachers should confess that they have been mistaken all their lives, and, abdicating the papacy of their infallible opinions, should go humbly back to ignorance again. Yet we all ought to do this if necessary. But let those who cannot accept our hope learn at least a deeper wisdom and a truer charity in the attempt to refute it. To go on repeating such arguments of the Dark Ages as those which I have quoted is to rely on bows and arrows in a battle-field swept over its whole surface from every point of vantage by the mighty artillery of modern war. They may identify us, if it so pleases them, with the emissaries of Satan; but certain passages of the Gospel in which the Pharisees were blasphemously guilty of a similar identification might make them pause and tremble, lest in so doing they should be guilty of a very frightful sin. But we shall not retaliate. Do they love God? So do we. Do they put their trust in Christ? So do we. But, let them denounce as they will, our hope for ourselves and our fellow-men proves this only—that our trust in the love of God is deeper, our faith in the efficacy of Christ's Redemption is stronger and larger, than is theirs.

ÆONIAN METEMPSYCHOSIS

XIX.

ÆONIAN METEMPSYCHOSIS.

(*Sequel*) BY FRANCIS PEEK.

WHATEVER may be the formal verdict passed by the religious world upon the controversy on Canon Farrar's book, we may safely predict one practical result from it, namely, that those grossly material views of the future state until lately so general, and which are still held by many persons who claim peculiar orthodoxy, will have received a further blow. If any proof were needed that the spirit of this theology still exists, not in one, but in many churches, it may be found in the extracts given by Mr. Jukes in his work, *The Restitution of all Things*. Some of the horrible details there cited are hardly, if at all, exceeded by the teaching of the Koran as to the future state; which, for example, says—"That unbelievers will be cast into a place of fire, where they will be burned for ever, and that, as fast as the old skin is consumed, God will provide them with another, in order that they may never cease to suffer the full intensity of the torment." Surely, in the face of the shocking beliefs often put forward publicly, it was high time for an authoritative discussion of the matter.

Before going further, it may be well to deal with a preliminary point. One of Canon Farrar's critics blames him because, while expressing himself so severely against the doctrine of future material torment, he does not show equal repugnance to the idea of future mental or spiritual suffering, the objector justly observing that this is really often more hard to bear than bodily pain. No one, we think, will deny this. It will be seen, however, on a little consideration, that we are here dealing with two ideas between which there is a vast difference. Let us look at the subject closer. According to the old orthodox view, every unconverted being becomes subject at death to "material" torture, and this for ever. There are, as respects the fate itself, no distinctions, no qualifications. The bright, kindly youth, the attractive, amiable girl, the noble-hearted patriot, the philanthropist, all, if not actually in the state of a true believer,

share the same fate with the worst of the race,
the only partial exception being those totally
ignorant of God's will. Stated nakedly, this
idea of God's character is so horrible, that, at
every step, we seem to want evidence of its
being really held by anybody; but those who
are conversant with the literature of a large
section of the religious world, know it is only
too prevalent. It is brought out with revolting
vividness in a little book published a few years
since, entitled *Grace and Truth*, the sale of
which is stated to have reached 115,000
copies.[1] The details given in its pages only

---

[1] The following extracts are from the above-named book, which is by W. P. Mackay, who describes himself as "a minister of the *Gospel:* "—

"You, educated, amiable lady, in God's sight, are just the same as the vilest profligate; just the same before God as that man you heard about who was hanged for murdering his wife. This is most terrible, but it is *true*" (page 4).

"If you had lived for fifty years without committing one sin or having one wrong wish or thought, and just then you had an evil thought, and afterwards lived another fifty years and died, aged one hundred, with only this one evil thought (not even a word or an action), when you came to stand before God in judgment, He would put you beside all the offscourings of the earth, men who for a hundred years never had a good thought, and He would say, '*There is no difference*'" (page 7).

"Your name may have been written on the communion-roll of any or all the Churches, or it may have been written in fall short of the culminating statement of the old Calvinistic preacher, who, carrying the doctrine to its logical conclusion, declared that there are in hell babes a span long.

No doubt, it would be admitted, even by such teachers as these, that there is some difference in the intensity of punishment; some being beaten with few, and others with many stripes. This mitigation, however, must not be pushed too far. To make the theory consistent, its upholders assume that the few stripes are simply less extreme punishment, but still eternal, only differing from the many stripes in that the latter are more severe.

Putting on one side, for the present, the question of duration, it will be found that as soon as the idea of material punishment is got rid of, and that of spiritual suffering, whether temporary or enduring, is substituted, we have, as above hinted, passed into another region. Our views as regards God's dealings with men become after that substitution altogether

---

the sheets of the Newgate conviction-book for murderers, but 'there is *no difference.*' The lake of fire levels all distinctions. In hell, and perhaps only there, for the first time, you will believe that 'there is *no difference.*' Every one believes it there" (page 13).

clearer. We are then able to realise that the punishment, in the very nature of it, rests upon the just principle of consequence, that the fruit is the result of the seed sown. The belief then becomes this, that evil deeds justly result in suffering exactly proportioned to the kind and the amount of guilt; and this truth, once grasped, throws a new light upon our life, both present and future. By its aid, we can even calmly contemplate the death of those whose life we cannot but acknowledge to have been a failure, since we know that the punishment they have brought upon themselves, being the exact outcome of their conduct, will be, both in kind and in amount, such as a most perfectly just, wise, and loving God approves—such, moreover, as the sufferer himself, could he be brought to see things in the light of Divine love and wisdom, would acknowledge to be necessary and entirely consistent with these qualities.

It is worthy of remark, incidentally, that a strange confusion prevails in the views of certain theologians regarding the qualities of justice and mercy. Statements are made as if it were possible that those qualities could in some way clash or be contrary to each other; but it must be admitted that as justice would cease to be perfect if *swayed* one hair's-breadth by mercy, so it equally would do if it yielded in the slightest degree to vindictiveness. Apply this reasoning to the case before us. Perfect justice in the Supreme Being must include what we call mercy, which, if rightly considered, is only the full recognition by omniscient love of every circumstance that can mitigate directly or indirectly the fault of the criminal, and it would be impossible for God to stop short of this without forfeiting all claim to be *perfectly* just. Indeed, the only true hope as well as the greatest comfort which man possesses, is his confidence in *this* perfect justice of his Creator, not a justice of a kind that we are unable in any sense to understand, but the quality as it is understood amongst men, and seen here to be enforced by the Divine law. Were God's justice in reference to the life hereafter different from that which He has held up for man's admiration and imitation in this world, the name and the attribute would be alike unintelligible to us.

Result of the Recent Controversy.

If we now go a step further, and pass from the consideration of views soon, it is to be hoped, doomed to become obsolete, and ask what light the recent controversy has thrown upon the actual state of belief in authoritative quarters to-day as to future punishment, we at once note that it is now acknowledged by most thoughtful men, that the final condition of individuals cannot always be justly determined in the brief time allotted to them on earth. To that view we ourselves at once adhere. It surely becomes a rational conclusion, when we bear in mind how comparatively few of the human race in each generation have any really adequate opportunity of attaining to that faith which is declared to be necessary to salvation, and even of those few who may be said to be within the sound and influence of the Gospel, a small proportion indeed attain in their character to that likeness to the spirit of Christ which the Scriptures declare is the only proof of an acceptable faith and an essential qualification for eternal life. Are not these the plain facts of the case? In the rest of mankind, we behold every variety of character, ranging from the kind-hearted unselfish man of the world—whom we must in so far admire, for his life displays in those respects the same spirit that was in Christ—down to the heartless, cruel sensualist, from whom those who know him best shrink in horror and aversion.

To maintain that these differing characters, and all others intervening between them, living for such different periods of time,—some cut off at the earliest dawn of responsibility, some dying in extreme old age,—share at death the same doom, is to shock every idea of righteousness and justice, and to set up the worship of a dreadful Moloch in the place of that of an equitable, loving God.

So far as to the general conclusion which the controvery has to our thinking clearly made out. But there are yet the details. Among the many theories which have been suggested trying to solve, by the supposition of an intermediate state, the difficulty of some men passing out of this world so imperfect, no mention was made of one which has nevertheless much to be said in its support, and which ought to be set forth, if the discussion is to have anything like completeness. But before stating it, a little clearing of the way is needful.

The Metaphors of Revelation.

The Bible revelation, it will be granted, is comparatively silent as regards eternity, either stretching back in the past or towards the future. In this it is in striking contrast to its teaching as to our present life and conduct, which is clear and precise. Certainly it gives us no clue by which to solve that greatest of all mysteries, the origin of evil, and in all that it says concerning the future existence, it speaks only in metaphor and parable. For example, we find it, when describing the abode and condition of the blest, speaking of a place of rest in which praise never ceases ; a Paradise where there is no death, and in which the Tree of Life grows abundantly on each side of a stream of living water for the healing of the nations; a golden City, the breadth and the length and the *height* of which are equal, protected by gates of pearl that are never shut by day, although there is no night there. Regarding the state and place of the unblessed dead, it tells of a *bottomless* pit, an eternal death, an awaking to shame and everlasting contempt, an everlasting destruction, a Gehenna of fire, where the refuse of Jerusalem is consumed with continual burning, of a field of carnage, such as followed the great battle of Gog and Magog in the prophetic vision, of a place where the *dead* bodies of the men who have offended are beheld undergoing perpetual consumption by the undying worm and the unquenchable fire. In reference to those who in life professed to know Christ, but who possessed so little of His Spirit, that they did not imitate Him in His sympathy with earthly suffering, and made no personal effort to administer to the hungry and thirsty, the sick and the prisoner, it speaks of a departure from Him into everlasting fire prepared for the devil and his angels. All this is very solemn in its significance. These are Figures indeed, but terrible ones, representing, as they must do, awful realities.

Definite Teachings of the Bible.

That is one side of the Scriptural presentation; there is another complementing it. Besides this symbolical teaching as to the future, there is the Divine revelation regarding the past of the race. The statements, as we have said, are not very full, but something is told us of what happened far back, as well as of the present spiritual condition of man, and the means needful for his salvation. It tells us of a Fall, resulting in hereditary corruption, a truth which finds confirmation in every good man's struggle with temptation, and is effectively illustrated in every bad man's history. It speaks of salvation from this corruption through spiritual union with One who is the Prince of Life—the Son of God—who has taken upon Himself the human form to save the human race. Through His lips it gives us, in one long, matchless sermon, a perfect moral code which, if only universally obeyed, would produce on earth a paradise of peace and happiness. It pictures—in colours so vivid that many an unbeliever in its contemplation has been compelled to bow his head in reverence—a human life admittedly too perfect for the human mind to have ever conceived—a Divine love so amazing that it forced the Apostle, who of all men most grasped its fulness, to sum up Christian perfection in the comprehension of the breadth and length and depth and height of the love of Christ, which passes knowledge! Whatever separate action of this recorded life we contemplate, we recognise in it perfection, absolute justice, fullest dignity, completest truth, and a love exhaustless, both in its human and Divine aspects. This amazing perfection was sufficiently tested. During thirty years of a life of trial and suffering we can discover no failure in it; and at the very close each attribute becomes intensified as He hangs upon a malefactor's cross, suffering every variety of pain, in order—as we believe—that the Divine Man might be able to rescue every soul that will accept Him from death, both temporal and eternal. This is the main Scriptural revelation by which all the details must be tried; and where the human heart is not altogether dead in selfishness, the proclamation of this cross of love has never failed to draw men to Christ. The record presents this picture to us, with the simple precept, Believe on Him, and life eternal is yours. Not indeed that it is offered as an arbitrary reward, but only as a consequence, since true belief involves, through daily struggle, a gradual conforming to His Spirit, and the union thence existing implies the destruction of selfishness or sin, which is death, and the beginning of righteousness, which is life. A soul once united by faith to the perfect Christ, and so made a partaker of His life, can never die. For it there can be no purgatorial pains, no re-incarnation is necessary. "Where Christ is, there shall His servant be," and, as the worn-out tenement of matter falls away, the real man must rise, deathless and immortal, to be "for ever with his Lord."

Such, freed from all excrescences, is, we hold, the ideal creed intended for the whole Catholic Church, but as we look away from its contemplation and gaze around, there are perplexities. How often must every thoughtful mind have felt almost crushed at the apparent inconsistency of the existence of such a world as this is under the dominion of such a God as the New Testament discloses? While pondering on the myriads who have already passed away even during the last eighteen centuries, to whom even the Name of Christ was never known; while viewing the apparent triumph everywhere of evil over good, the corruption, the baseness, and degradation everywhere abounding, the never-ceasing tales of innocence corrupted, of villany successful, the poor robbed, the weak oppressed, how can we keep thoughts and speculations from arising unbidden, as to how such a condition of things can be reconciled with the rule of an almighty and all-loving God? Pass through the lanes and alleys of our great cities and see the wretched children of profligate parents, half-clad, half-starved, covered with sores, foul both in body and mind, to whom the very Name of God is known only as an introduction to a fiercer curse, or a more cruel blow. Wander through the wards of such an asylum as Earlswood, and contemplate the forms of the drivelling idiots, sitting through life listlessly in chairs, from which they may never rise till their day of doom, and presenting human faces from which humanity is absent, yet who still are recognised as members of the human race, since otherwise they would have to be destroyed as useless and loathsome animals. Viewing such sights as these, we cannot but speculate and conjecture, as the disciples of old did when, looking upon the man who was born blind, and remembering that their Divine law declared that the sins of the fathers were visited upon the children, they asked, "Master, who did sin, this man or his parents, that he was born blind?" The reply of Christ to this question is not a little remarkable. He does not say, "Your question is foolish; how could the man have sinned before his birth?" but He replies, "Neither hath this man sinned, nor his parents, but that the works of God might be made manifest in him." This is a form of words which certainly permits the conjecture that, as some cases of suffering were undoubtedly caused by the parents' sin, so in reference to some others there might be such a thing as sin before birth visited by suffering from and after birth. On the other hand, Christ does not satisfy the curiosity of His inquirers, and therefore any speculations of this kind regarding the past or future must be held as conjectures only, although they may be to some extent of use, if they suggest a *possible* solution of some of the difficulties which trouble us in these matters; and with this view any theory may well be discussed.

Theory of an Intermediate State.

Among those holding the necessity for an intermediate state, it has for long been generally supposed that such a state must be spiritual, and therefore be under different conditions from those of the present world. But to this opinion forcible objections have been urged. For instance, it is said that for man, as we know him here, Christ took upon Himself a human form to die; and that there appears no reason why discipline in an intermediate state without a body should change the depravity of character which had been contracted in a physical frame. Or to use the words of Canon Ryle, as recently published :—

"There seems nothing in such an intermediate state to bridge the wide gulf between natural man and his perfect Maker, to effect the enormous spiritual change which every child of Adam must go through if he is to dwell for ever in God's presence; and there is an utter absence of any information in the Bible that this change can take place after death."

Metempsychosis.

The question is, whether there is not a mode of meeting these difficulties. Cannot the objections, regarded as intellectual ones only, be done away by giving to the supposed intermediary state an earthly location? It is not maintained that this theory will solve every difficulty, especially that fundamental one as to the origin of evil in eternity and its permitted *entrance* into this world; but if it is conceived that, not in another sphere, not as spirits only, but by re-incarnation in this very world, those who have failed in past lives may, again and again if need be, return to undergo æonian punishment on earth till the Gospel reaches their hearts, and sets them free for ever, the whole question takes on another aspect. The idea of metempsychosis contains nothing new. It is a dogma of many religions, and was once, in the early centuries, held in a certain form among Christians. The most remarkable view of it, of course, is the Buddhist doctrine, which teaches that all life is an evil, and that each individual at any stage of being is but the embodiment of the defects of his former existence; so that, when all defects of character have been overcome, there being nothing left upon which a new life can be formed, existence will cease for ever—the individual attaining Nirvana.

There is nothing inconsistent with natural or revealed religion in the mere idea of metempsychosis. As we have already shown, the words of Christ Himself, in one case at least, suggest its possibility, and the teachings of nature give many hints of the process of such a change as is involved in the idea. The elements of a tree, when the old body decays, return to their primary uses and form similar structures; and the chemist can point out numberless instances where elements that have become corrupted, and undergo the changes of death, return to form parts of similar bodies. There appears no reason, in the nature of the case, why the spirit of a man who has failed in one short period of existence should not return from Hades (or the place of departed spirits) to be incorporated once more at birth in an infantile body, under the decree of Divine justice, to suffer punishment in strict accordance with the character of a past life. On this hypothesis we should have a Dives entering into the body of a Lazarus, condemned to suffer the same poverty and wretchedness which he selfishly left unaided;—

the grand lord or lady who, amidst wealth and splendour, passed their time in frivolity and sin, in corrupting the innocent and increasing the misery of the world, would be re-born children of the vicious and profligate, justly obliged to suffer, in poverty, wretchedness, and woe, the penalty of their own past sins, while no less fulfilling that strange law of God's government, the visitation of the parents' sins upon their children. Carrying out the conception a stage further, it may be that, in looking upon the repulsive face of the drivelling idiot, we may be beholding the re-incarnation of one who, like Byron, abused his glorious gift of genius to corrupt and degrade mankind.

At any rate,—and it is this which gives to the speculation a chief part of its intellectual interest,—this theory offers a seeming explanation of the extraordinary inequalities which meet us every day, not only in adults, but in the condition and even in the character of infants and very young children. Take the latter point. In the same family we see the strangest differences. Some of the children are born apparently more or less of a cruel and malignant disposition; others at the earliest tage show themselves most amiable, unselfish, and affectionate. Again, some children are born in homes of vice and profligacy where it would seem nothing short of a miracle could save them from degradation, while others are born to happiness and prosperity, in Christian families where every influence is beneficial. In this way, too, an explanation seems to be offered of the instinctive desire for children, which, on any technical theological view—at any rate, any of those held among Christians who believe that the great majority are born to everlasting suffering—is inexplicable. If it is not necessarily a new spirit that comes into the world, to run the risk of defilement through a life which both Christians and unbelievers unite in describing as almost universally involving more suffering than joy, and often meaning intense misery, but, instead, may be the re-incarnation of a spirit that has previously failed (perhaps of one already loved and wept over as lost), and which has now another opportunity, through the ministry of the Gospel, of being brought into communion with Christ, and thus escaping for ever from this world and entering the joy of heaven—then every Christian would indeed desire the possession of children. And if we push the hypothesis to its extreme, it may be to what may seem it's grotesque limit, it might account for the extraordinary disappearance of the aborigines before the advance of higher types of humanity; the aborigines gradually disappearing in order to be re-incarnated, and thus gradually to advance, through contact with Christianity, to a higher life. It would also throw light upon the chief mystery which must have sorely puzzled every thoughtful mind, the long-continued existence of this evil and suffering world, explaining how, notwithstanding all the evil and all the suffering which have since occurred, the Bible speaks of the salvation of Noah in the ark as an act of mercy, whereas if the orthodox view is correct, it has been the cause of endless misery to countless millions of human beings.

Mysterious History of the Jewish People.

Further, it accounts for the mysterious history of the Jewish people. Eighteen centuries ago they invoked the curse of the innocent blood of Christ on themselves and on their children; and they have, ever since, suffered its awful punishment, being for long ages objects of cruel oppression among all nations, and still continuing so in some regions, although in intellectual power and most moral qualities the Jews are inferior to no people. Can it be that in this case the proverb that Ezekiel so indignantly repudiated on God's behalf is true, and that, because eighteen hundred years ago the fathers ate sour grapes, the children's teeth have ever since been set on edge, or is it possible that during all these generations the very men who rejected their Saviour have been suffering æonian retribution for their crime ? When perfect virtue appeared in human form they hated it and crucified it, and, according to the principle of this speculation, they would justly, age after age, suffer in every form of cruel oppression from the spirit of that robber whom they preferred to Christ, and will be still condemned thus to suffer, with only such modifications as God's providence sees wise, till the veil is taken away and the last time comes, once dimly foreseen by the Apostle, when in prophetic rapture he exclaimed : " If the casting away of them be the reconciling of the world, what shall the receiving of them be, but life from the dead ? . . . And so all Israel shall be saved. . . . For God hath concluded them all in unbelief that He might have mercy upon all." This stupendous statement would seem far too large to apply only to that insignificant number of

Jews who may be alive at the time of the restoration, but rather to point to some grander exhibition of the mercy of God, of which, indeed, the Apostle seems to have caught one dazzling glimpse as the prophetic vision faded from his view, and left him with the exclamation on his lips : " Oh the depth of the riches both of the wisdom and knowledge of God ; how unsearchable are His judgments, and His ways past finding out !"

Predictions as to the End of the World.

This theory of metempsychosis would make it easier to understand those mysterious statements found scattered throughout the inspired book, which seem to foretell a great increase in wickedness as the end of the world approaches—predicting that, instead of progressing in virtue, as might be expected, it shall wax worse and worse till, like Sodom and Gomorrah, few, if any, righteous can be found in it—and also throw light on that saying of our Lord regarding the time of the end, which He declares shall be when the Gospel shall have been preached to every nation. It would also make plainer St. Paul's statement regarding the development of the mystery of iniquity, which it is declared shall be destroyed by the brightness of the Lord at His Second Coming. The explanation which is pointed to is that when every soul has had every possible opportunity which perfect love and justice can afford, the world and all that remains in it would be burnt up. May not this include the obstinate and impenitent who have resisted through ages every painful discipline and every presentation of the Gospel of love, and of whom, indeed, it may then be well said, " It were good for such that they had never been born"? Here we stop, having no intention to push the matter further than the statement of it as an intellectual speculation bearing on this controversy.

Conversion.

Perhaps some may be prepared to raise the objection that there is no reason for supposing that a man who has failed in one life will repent and attain salvation in another. But a little thought will show that this objection does not apply. Hundreds and thousands of our best men have only become Christians comparatively late in life—often after many years of thoughtlessness and sin. Had these been cut off in youth or early manhood, as many millions of others less guilty than themselves were, they would, according to the orthodox view, be now in endless, hopeless torment; the mere fact that their lives were preserved for a few years having, if the old view be supposed true, made for them the awful difference between endless bliss and endless torture. But the matter may be stated more widely than this. Who can deny that the salvation of each soul has some reference to the circumstances in which it is placed, when, as the Apostle declares, none can "believe in him of whom they have not heard"? This, be it remembered, includes a far greater multitude, even in this Christian land, than is generally supposed. The idea that this one life decides eternity, whether such life be cut off in the first dawn of responsibility, or prolonged to old age, is only consistent with the strictest Calvinistic doctrines of Election and Reprobation and the awful logical conclusion of "babes in hell a span long!"

Again, it may be urged that the character of the new life at its commencement must be exactly that which existed at the termination of the old one, and the position therefore be less advantageous, and more certain to result in failure. But there is something to be said in answer to this. Conversion is often seen to take place in this world after many years of sin in connection with some mere hap of circumstance—it may be sickness or the being brought under the ministry of some good man. There are, so to speak, violent interruptions shown, not a level of continuity. Moreover, the objection takes no account of the influence that the body has upon the spirit. How much better would even the best be, could they in mature life get rid of their bodies, with all the habits and physical tendencies to evil which repeated departures from right have made, as it were, part of their bodily nature, and which often prove too strong for their utmost efforts to resist. Suppose, for example, the spirit of one of those amiable characters who, through the influence of bad examples and bad companions, has been seduced to habits of drunkenness, from which vice, when once it has taken possession of a man, escape is almost impossible, —suppose it freed from the body, which has become thus degraded, and consequently liberated from the cravings which the bodily appetite has contracted, and that such spirit be re-born in a family where all are temperate —how naturally should we then expect a better life for it; while, at the same time, how just it would be that such a life should begin in a condition of suffering—the natural fruit which former vice had produced in the old body. By such an application of this theory, you may hypothetically account, indeed, for those numberless instances of sufferers whose presence in a family is a source of exquisite pain of a certain sort to others of the circle, and which nevertheless becomes, from the way in which the sufferers themselves bear their trial, in other modes an unspeakable blessing to all about them. Moreover, and this is the strong point of the case in this particular aspect of it, each fresh incarnation would give a new opportunity for the revelation to the soul of Christ, so often rejected in health, but, at last, accepted in suffering.

Individuality not Dependent on Memory.

Now we come to the final objection to the hypothesis which will probably be the one most urged, namely :—That, inasmuch as the remembrance of the past is blotted out, the new existence would, practically, involve a new individuality. In the first place, it seems necessary that there should be this forgetfulness, if life here is to be a state of moral probation. If all was remembered, the punishment would tend to take a mechanical effect. But it is obvious that this objection is founded upon the belief that the memory of the past is necessary for the continuance of personal identity. But is this made out? It is stated authoritatively that in some diseases the memory of a portion of the past life is entirely erased, although the effect that that past life has had upon the self remains, and the fact that the past is forgotten in no way diminishes its practical effect upon the individual. For example, let any one imagine twelve months of his own life to be altogether forgotten, is he not forced to believe that his character will still remain very different from what it would have been had those twelve months never been lived? Indeed, it may be held reasonably made out that personal identity has no absolute connection either with recollection or with sameness of the body. This latter point is amply proved by our experience in this world. Take the case of a child who in a fit of passion injures itself. Through life he or she suffers the effect of that injury, though no memory of the childish passion remains, and though, as years pass on, the very body in which that passion was experienced has become changed more than once in the process of natural growth. Probably most persons in later life suffer from the effects of indiscretions or sins of which the remembrance has become quite obliterated. From all these instances we see that, even in this world, though the remembrance has ceased and the body become changed, yet personal identity remains. It, therefore, violates no natural, nor any Divine law, to extend this reasoning, and suppose in a sufficient number of cases to cover the puzzling difficulties of the world that, as a spirit enters a new-born babe, it may come, not from the void, but from the place of departed spirits, to begin, in a state more or less happy, more or less suffering, the just æonian punishment for the past, but finding in it a merciful opportunity for the future. Let us restate the practical application of the theory. It is that, according to this view, selfish men of wealth may be re-born as the despised pauper, — that the sensualist and profligate may be re-born a child of profligate parents, inheriting the fruits of their vice, and the punishment of his own sin, not knowing, it is true, why he suffers, but being in these indirect ways prepared by the effects of that suffering to apprehend the true nature of sin, and the acceptance of the Gospel, and through it, by the ministry of Christ's people, to be brought to that union with Christ which is immortal life.

Hell on Earth.

One last possible objection suggests itself—the amount of the penalty. If any one concludes that there is not sufficient possibility of punishment in such a re-incarnation, let him consider the depth of the wretchedness which is the fate of so many—a misery so bitter that it leads some even to face, by self-destruction, hell itself, as represented in the pictured material horrors still believed in, rather than endure this world's sufferings.

Certain Hope.

To some these, or any other speculative conjectures, may appear mere dreams. Be it so, but even dreams, if they are hopeful ones, are sweet. They will from others have a welcome, if by their shadowy flittings they suggest even a possibility of some solution of a mystery so painful as this one is. We are but as

"An infant crying in the night,
An infant crying for the light,
And with no language but a cry;"

and we are assured that such conjectures have relieved the distressing strain which all must more or less experience who realise the extent of the woe and misery prevailing in the world. But beyond all such speculations we have a surer source of comfort in the certainty, that, whether such notions contain a truth or not, we know that though clouds and darkness are round about Him, "justice and mercy are the habitation of God's throne," and therefore we are not left without gleams of light. Walking through the streets of our large towns, saddened by painful sights, by discordant sounds, and wondering how such a degradation can be permitted of those beings God once made in His own image, it is some relief to realise the fact that saddest suffering in this world *is* consistent with God's laws of government. As we raise our eyes to the church spires which offer us a glimpse, far up, of the emblem of that cross upon which the incarnate God once suffered for man, we go on our way in the light of His cross, comforted with the sure conviction that by and by it will be seen that not one of the pangs suffered on earth has been unnecessary, and if, unhappily, *one* soul is doomed to suffer eternal woe, it can only be after every effort possible to infinite love,— every means that infinite wisdom can put forth to save it,—shall have been tried and tried in vain.

MERCY AND JUDGMENT

XX.[1]

MERCY AND JUDGMENT.

BY ARCHDEACON FARRAR.

"We know our place and our portion : To give a witness and to be condemned ; to be ill-used and to succeed. Such is the law which God has annexed to the promulgation of the truth : its preachers suffer, but its cause prevails."—DR. NEWMAN, *Tracts for the Times*, iv. p. ix.

AGAIN and again it has been asserted or implied—even by those whose character and position should have made them more careful in their statements—that I deny the eternity of punishment.

Once more, and once for all, I desire to render such false witness inexcusable by saying on the very first page of this book that I have never denied, and do not now deny, the eternity of punishment. And, to avoid any possible mistake, I repeat once more, that though I understand the word eternity in a sense far higher than can be degraded into the

---

[1] This Section consists of the "PREFATORY AND PERSONAL" opening to Archdeacon FARRAR's *Mercy and Judgment*, published in 1881.—J. H.

vulgar meaning of endlessness, I have never even denied, and do not now deny, even the possible endlessness of punishment. In proof of which, I need only refer to the pages of my own book—*Eternal Hope*—standing as they do unaltered from the very first.

In the month of November 1877, during my ordinary course of residence as a canon, I preached a sermon in Westminster Abbey on 1 Peter iv. 6, "For for this cause was the Gospel preached also to them that are dead." At that time there had been some discussions both on the nature of Eternal Happiness, and on the question, "Is life worth living?" Accordingly, on October 14 I had preached on "What Heaven is;" and on November 4 upon the value and preciousness of human life. But since I desire always and above all things to be truthful and honest, it was impossible for me to attempt the refutation of that cynical pessimism which treats human life as a curse and as a mistake, without entering into the awful question of future retribution. While in common with all Christians I believed that there would be a future punishment of unrepented sin, and even that it might continue without any revealed termination so long as impenitence continued, it appeared to me that, on that subject, many of the conceptions constantly kept alive by current teaching were derived only from mistaken interpretations of isolated texts, and were alien from the general tenor of Divine revelation. I knew it to be the popular belief, sanctioned by ordinary sermons, that the vast majority of living men would pass from the sorrows, miseries, and failures of our mortal life into inconceivable, hopeless, and everlasting agonies. I gave some specimens of that teaching, and in order not to prejudge it, those specimens were chosen, not from the writings of the vulgar and the ignorant, but from the pages of great men whom I love and reverence—from Dante and Milton, and Jeremy Taylor and Henry Smith. I endeavoured to show, as far as could be shown in the narrow limits of a sermon addressed to a mixed multitude, that much which had been said on this subject was unscriptural and untenable. In that sermon, and in one delivered on November 18 upon the question, "Are there few that be saved?" it was my object to prove that the current belief went far beyond what was written, and tended to force upon men's minds a view of God's dealings with the human race which it was almost, if not utterly, impossible to reconcile with all that is revealed to us of His mercy and of His justice, and with the whole meaning of the Gospel of Salvation.

I venture to think that such subjects should not frequently be treated in the pulpit, because the field of undisputed and essential truth is so large as to supply the amplest materials for moral and spiritual edification, without forcing us to dwell upon controverted questions. I have always acted upon this conviction. During twenty-five years I have scarcely ever done more than refer to the speculative question as to the nature and duration of future punishment. In six volumes [1] of school, university, parochial, and cathedral sermons, the reader will scarcely find any allusion to the controversy. I have held it sufficient to dwell on the certain and awful truth that, both in this world and the next, God punishes sin; that without repentance sin cannot be for-

---

[1] *The Fall of Man, and other Sermons;* 4th Thousand. *The Witness of History to Christ.* Hulsean Lectures for 1870; 7th Thousand. *The Silence and Voices of God.* University and other Sermons; 6th Thousand. *In the Days of thy Youth.* Practical Sermons at Marlborough College, 1871-1876; 7th Thousand. *Saintly Workers.* Lent Addresses at St. Andrew's, Holborn, 1879; 4th Thousand. *Ephphatha; or, The Amelioration of the World.* Westminster Abbey Sermons, 1880; 3rd Thousand.

given ; that without holiness no man shall see
the Lord ; that by the death of Christ and the
gift of the Spirit the love of our Father in
Heaven has provided us with the means of
redemption and given us the grace which leads
to sanctification. But there would be no chance
of religious sincerity or of spiritual progress,
if we were never to enter a protest against
the tyranny of human error when it encroaches
upon the domain of faith and teaches for
doctrine the mistakes and traditions of men.
The pulpit of a metropolitan cathedral has
always been considered a legitimate place for
the treatment of questions which are not so
well suited for ordinary parochial teaching;
nor do I see any reason why Westminster
Abbey, with its large and mingled congregations, should not occasionally be used for
purposes analogous to those which made the
pulpit of St. Paul's Cross so powerful in the
days of the Reformation. Those who during
the last four years have heard my sermons
in the Abbey know full well that, there
as well as at St. Margaret's, in ninety-
nine instances out of a hundred, my aim
is entirely practical, and my subjects chosen
from the wide realm of those truths respecting which all Christians are agreed.

But I am not at all ashamed, nor do I in the least regret, that, when I was naturally led to deal with a question in which the popular theology goes far beyond the Catholic faith, I did not hesitate to express my strong conviction that the opinions traditionally accepted by the majority of those who have never seriously thought of them, are unwarranted and are dangerously wrong. To believe with awful reverence in Eternal Judgment is a very different thing from believing in the utter distortion and perversion of the language and metaphors of Scripture which ignorance and tradition, working hand in hand for centuries, have degraded into what a deeply religious modern poet has characterised as "obscene threats of a bodily hell."

It has been laid to my charge almost as if it were a grave fault that in those sermons I adopted a vehement tone. Is it a sin to feel strongly and to speak strongly? Are the Prophets and the Psalmists never vehement? Is St. Paul never vehement? Are St. Peter and St. James and St. John never vehement? As for "adopting a vehement tone," my reply is that I never "adopt" any tone at all, but speak as it is given me to speak, and only use such language as most spontaneously and naturally expresses the thoughts and feelings with which I write. " Every one," says Dr. Newman,[1] " preaches according to his frame of mind at the time of preaching;" and it is quite true that at the time when I preached those sermons my feelings had been stirred to their inmost depths. I am not in the least ashamed of the "excitement" at which party newspapers and reviews have sneered. I do not blush for the moral indignation which most of what has since been written on this subject shows to have been intensely needful. In the ordinary course of parochial work I had stood by deathbeds of men and women which had left on my mind an indelible impression I had become aware that the minds of many of the living were hopelessly harassed and—I can use no other word—*devastated* by the horror with which they brooded over the fate of the dead. The happiness of their lives was shattered, the peace of their souls destroyed, not by the sense of earthly bereavement, but by the terrible belief that brother, or son, or wife, or husband had passed away into physical anguish and physical torment, endless, and beyond all utterance excruciating. Such

---

[1] Apologia, Appendix, p. 15.

thoughts did not trouble the careless or the brutal, who might be supposed to need them. They troubled only the tender-hearted and the sincere. They were the direct result of the religious teaching which they had received from their earliest years. To the irreligious poor the common presentment of "endless torment" was a mere stumbling-block; to the best of the religious it was a permanent misery. The irreligious are driven to disbelieve in any punishment, because they have heard the punishment with which they are threatened described in such a way as to be utterly unbelievable; the religious accept these coarse pictures, and are either hardened by them into lovelessness or crushed into despair. Pharisaism and Infidelity are the twin children of every form of theology which obscures the tenderness of revelation, and belies the love of God.

Now to me it seemed that the Gospel of the grace of God ought to have in it at least *some* message of consolation for more than that mere handful of the bereaved who can feel sure that those whom they love are saved; and not for these only, but for all whose imagination is strong enough to realise what words mean, whose candour is sufficient to make them face the real significance of what they profess to maintain. For, if the common language of preachers on these subjects be true, there seems to be no escape from the logical conclusion that those who are saved are few indeed. Popular teachers still continue to argue, with no semblance of anguish or of horror, that the majority of the millions of mankind whom we daily see are perishing; that they are not walking in those paths which alone lead to heaven; that, to all human appearance, they die as they lived; and that, if those who have lived sinful lives, and brought forth no fruits of amendment, and not even given any visible indication of repentance, cannot enter into heaven, then all but a fraction of mankind are doomed to hell. Now to the mass of ignorant Christians the words "to be doomed to hell" have no other meaning than to be doomed to agonies in which sinners will burn to endless ages in torments to which all the racks and wheels and flames of the Inquisition—as religious writers again and again have told us—are as nothing; doomed to torments which exceed beyond all conception the deadliest agony which the mortal body can endure on earth.

I have been sometimes gravely warned not

to attempt to be wise " above what is written."
It was precisely because I feel the wisdom of
such advice that I wished to sweep away the
cruel dogmas and ghastly fancies which, pre
tending to represent "what is written," horribly distort it,—add to it and take away from
it, and entomb its pure words in inverted
pyramids of fallible inference,—and by so
doing furnish sad instances of being *unwise*
above what is written. I obeyed the precept
by pointing to the errors of that self-styled
orthodoxy by which it has been so habitually
and so grievously transgressed.

Already I observe among the better sort of
those from whose previous writings no other
conclusion than the popular one could logically
have been drawn, an anxiety to back out of
these conclusions; a tendency to explain them
away; an effort to repudiate them. They are
now trying to soften down all those parts of
their dogma against which the heart and conscience of man cannot but indignantly revolt,
because we should otherwise be driven to
admit that the life which has come to men,
without their seeking, is and must be to all but
the chosen few, no blessing, but an awful, intolerable, and inextinguishable curse. In the
following pages I shall prove, as I have proved

before, that the errors which I repudiate *have*, to their fullest extent, been the teachings of a majority of preachers, and even of theologians. It was my express object to show that they were *not* the teachings of Scripture when rightly interpreted, and *not* the teachings of the Church as decided by the decrees of her four great Councils, and by the authentic creeds and formularies of her faith.

Before proceeding, I should like to say one word on a very common charge which has been made against the opinions expressed in my *Eternal Hope*. It is that they were "inconsistent;" "that it was difficult to make out what I did exactly believe;" "that I adopted Universalist arguments while I repudiated Universalist conclusions." I reply that it was not my immediate aim to be constructive or positive; I desired to get rid of what I believed to be false, not to lay down fresh dogmas as to what I believed to be true. It is painful to me to have to repeat once more that the publication of my book was forced on me by shorthand reporters who published my sermons against my will; and that the sermons, though they expressed beliefs which I had held for years, were everyday sermons written in a few hours, not elaborate theological treatises prepared during long leisure. But further, I believe that in all arguments upon the details of this solemn subject it is very desirable that *no* systematic dogmas should be laid down. The Church herself has carefully abstained from laying down such dogmas; she has only sketched a few great limits, " *Quos ultra citraque nequit consistere rectum.*" I accept sincerely all that the Church of England has required us to believe concerning hell. What I repudiate is that which she has never required. And the reason why neither the Catholic Church, nor the English branch of it, has ever defined the precise beliefs which have been taught by hundreds of individual preachers, is because Scriptural teaching on this subject has left room for very wide diversities of opinion. If I gave their due weight to what are called "Universalist" arguments, it is because they ought to have their due weight side by side with the arguments which prevent most Christians from entirely adopting them. And we ought to distinguish between that which is permissible *as a hope* and that which is tenable *as a doctrine.* Is there any human being to whom it would not be an infamy to confess that he did not *wish* that it were true that all men might be ultimately saved, as it is God's will (1 Tim. ii. 4) that they should be saved? We are taught to pray : "That it may please Thee to have mercy upon all men." We pray for this. Would it not cause us the deepest joy if we could be fully persuaded in our own minds that our prayer can be granted? Do we *wish* that any soul of man should suffer endless torments? If not, we are surely permitted to pay respectful attention to the arguments of those who think themselves entitled by Scripture to believe that which *we* too desire, but scarcely even dare to hope. Those arguments may offer some relief to us even when we cannot affirm their absolute validity. They may cast some gleam upon a horror of great darkness, even if they do not enable us to enjoy the boundless day. God has given us natures disposed to love. He has bidden us to forgive and love our enemies. He has told us that His Name is Love. " I must believe," said a devout and learned writer nearly two hundred years ago, " that Thy grace will sooner or later superabound where sin hath most abounded, till I can think a little Drop of Being, and but one remove from Nothing, can excel in goodness that Ocean of Goodness which hath neither shore, bottom, nor surface.

Thou art Goodness itself in the abstract, in its first spring, in its supreme and universal form and spirit. We must believe Thee to be infinitely good; to be good without any measure or bound; to be good beyond all expression and conception of all creatures, or we must give over thinking of Thee at all. All the goodness which is anywhere to be found scattered among the creatures is sent forth from Thee, the fountain, the sea of all goodness. Into this sea of all goodness I deliver myself and all my fellow creatures. Thou art Love, and canst no more cease to be so than to be Thyself: take Thy own methods with us, and submit us to them. Well may we do so, in the assurance that the beginning, the way, and the end of them all is love."[1]—Is there anything wrong in such sentiments? Is it not well for the world that all which can be said in their favour should be fairly and kindly considered, even if they point to conclusions too bright and too vague to be formulated into our Articles of Faith?

There were, however, in my little volume some expressions which, to my great surprise,

---

[1] *The Restoration of All Things*, Jer. White, Chaplain to Oliver Cromwell, A.D. 1712.

caused ambiguity in the minds of readers.
When those terms are explained in the sense
in which alone I used them, it will become
even more clear than it has already become
to the minds of all candid theologians, that my
views are in the strictest accordance with all
that is required by the Catholic Church. I
assert fearlessly that they were, and are, in
far deeper accordance with "what is of faith,"
than the current errors which they were
intended to repudiate, or the bitter assertions
which have been urged in their supposed
refutation.

I. The first of these expressions was the
word "*eternal.*" By "eternal" I never meant
"endless;" by "eternity" I never meant
"endlessness." I do not exclude the connotation of endlessness from certain uses of the
word, but those uses are the accidents of its
meaning, not its essence. I use, and always
shall use, the word "eternal" in the sense of
the word *aionios*, and especially in St. John's
sense of that word. By "*Eternal Hope*"—
a title not of my own choosing—I meant
"*hope as regards the world to come*"
(just as in our form of the Nicene Creed,
"eternal life" is "the life of the world to

come ").[1] I used this word in what I conceive to be its true and not its vulgar sense, which I thought that I could do safely, because much of my book was devoted to establishing that true meaning. But I have evidently underrated the fatal force and fascination of words long used in inaccurate senses, " which, as a Tartar's bow, do shoot back upon the understanding of the wisest, and mightily entangle and pervert the judgment." In the following pages I ask the reader to observe that though the writers

---

[1] This clause is not in the genuine Creed of Nicæa, in which "I believe in the Holy Ghost" is followed by an anathema. In the "Constantinopolitan" Creed, or Revised Creed of Jerusalem, first occurs καὶ ζωὴν τοῦ μέλλοντος αἰῶνος; but in the Creed of Cappadocia now used by the Armenian Church, in the Revised Creed of Antioch, in the Creed of Mesopotamia now used by the Nestorian Churches, and in the Creed of Philadelphia as recited by Charisius at Ephesus, we have εἰς ζωὴν αἰώνιον. Nothing then can be more clear than that "aeonian life," in the Niceno-Constantinopolitan Creed, was regarded as the equivalent of "the life of the age to come." Now this latter phrase is very far indeed from a necessary implication of endlessness, for ὁ μέλλων αἰών is the "olam habba" of the Jews, and this future Age is in Scripture expressly regarded as only one step towards a final consummation (1 Cor. xv. 24). "Aeon," says Theodoret (*Haer.* v. 6), is "*an interval indicative of time.*" On the light thrown upon the meaning of the phrase by the fact that St. Gregory of Nyssa was not unconcerned in its admission into the Creed (Nicephorus H. E. xii. 13) I shall touch later on (p. 261). See Dr. Hort's *Two Dissertations*, pp. 106, 138-147.

whom I quote often use the word "eternal" when they mean endless, the word never has that meaning with me.

II. On the other hand, I generally used the word "*hell*" in its popular, and not in its theological sense. In current religious phraseology nothing is more common than the phrase "to die and to go to hell." Strictly speaking, such language is in every case inaccurate, for "hell," in the sense of "endless torments," as apart from the retribution of the intermediate state, is a condition which, in its final stage, does not begin till the Resurrection and the Judgment Day. When, therefore, I spoke of "hell" not being endless for all who incur it, I meant to indicate the doctrine which has now once more been brought into far greater prominence by English Churchmen than it had been for many previous years, viz., that a soul may pass hence into a retribution and punishment, which is yet not an endless hell, but is that intermediate state of purification which may be metaphorically included in the term "aeonian fire."

III. Lastly, by dying "*in a state of sin*" I meant dying without any *visible* repentance and amendment; in such a state of sin as—so far as human judgment is concerned—would render the soul unfit for heaven. Such being the case, I find, with deep thankfulness, that between Dr. Pusey's views and my own there is not a single point of difference as regards any matters of faith;—that there was no material difference between my views and those of many of our most learned living bishops and theologians I had already been assured.

IV. Further than this, the reason for some apparent contradictions was explained in many passages of the book itself. It was due to what, for want of a better word, I must call the "antinomies" of Scripture. By antinomies I do not mean absolute contradictions, but— partly adopting the sense in which Kant used the word—I mean that semblance of contradiction which results from the law of reason, when, passing the limits of experience, we seek to know the absolute;—I mean, in fact, truths which (so far as Scripture is concerned) may be maintained by opposing arguments of almost equal validity. There are some passages of Scripture which, if understood in their literal meaning, seem to teach a final restitution of all things, a final triumph of absolute blessedness, a final immanence of God in all things.[1] There are others which, taken in their literal meaning, seem to point to the final annihilation of the wicked.[2] There are again others which hold out no definite hope of alleviation to the doom of the finally impenitent.[3] There are others, again, which seem to point to some temporary punishment, some purifying discipline through which men must pass, but from which they may be saved.[4] It is in some form of the last aspect of the subject that I see the most probable solution to our difficulties and perplexities. In the doctrine of the Intermediate State, and of such changes in the condition of the dead as are implied in the ancient practice of prayers for the dead; in that "probatory fire" of the day of judgment, which the Fathers almost unanimously deduced from 1 Cor. iii. 13; in the doctrine of Christ's descent into hell; in the

---

[1] Luke ix. 56; John i. 29; iii. 17; xii. 32; Acts iii. 21; Rom. iv. 13; v. 15, 18, 19; xi. 26, 32; 1 Cor. xv. 22-28, 55; 2 Cor. v. 19; Eph. i. 10; Phil. ii. 9, 10; Col. i. 20; 1 Tim. ii. 4; iv. 10; Tit. ii. 11; Heb. ii. 14; 1 John ii. 2; iii. 8; Mic. vii. 9; Isa. xii. 1, etc.

[2] Matt. iii. 12; v. 30; x. 28; Luke xiii. 1-5; xx. 18, 35; Acts iii. 23; Rom. vi. 23; viii. 13; Heb. x. 26-31; Rev. xx. 14; xxi. 8, etc.

[3] Matt. xiii. 49, 50; xvi. 27; xxv. 46; Mark iii. 29; ix. 44-50; Rev. xiv. 10; xx. 10; xxi. 8.

[4] Matt. v. 26; Luke xii. 59; 1 Cor. iii. 13, 15.

doctrine of the "*pain of loss*" as containing the essence of future retribution; and in all these doctrines taken in connection with those conclusions which we cannot but form from the infinitude of God's mercy and the universal efficacy of Christ's Atonement, I see the dawn of a "hope for the world to come," and the emancipation of the human heart from the terrible pressure of teachings which not a few of God's saints have found it all but impossible to reconcile with His Name of Love.

But I have never pretended to have any ready-made rigid scholastic dogma on the subject. My object was to repudiate what I regarded as unscriptural, not to attempt the impossible task of formulating a dogma more definite than any which the Church has laid down as to what is true. It is doubtless because of those very antinomies which I have mentioned, which are perhaps inseparable from the nature of the subject, that the Church has left such large latitude to individual opinion.

"This alone," says Perrone, "is matter of faith that there is a hell."[1] The Church of England has not even condemned Universalism; she rejected the Forty-second Article,

---

[1] *De Deo Creatore*, iii. 6, § 3 (in Dr. Pusey's *What is of Faith?* p. 19).

which was aimed against it; and she has no
utterance in any of her formularies so distinct
"as to require us to condemn as penal the
expression of hope by a clergyman that even
the ultimate pardon of the wicked, who are
condemned in the Day of Judgment, may be
consonant with the will of God."[1] Knowing,
therefore, as I do, how many there are of the
highest intellect—especially among the laity
and among our most eminent literary and
scientific men—who regard the popular teaching respecting ". endless torments" as one of
their most insuperable difficulties in the way of
accepting the Christian faith, I still think it my
duty to show that those torments have been de-

---

[1] Privy Council judgment, Wilson v. Fendall. As regards
three or four expressions in the Prayer Book, such as "everlasting damnation" (an expression unknown to Scripture, in
which no such word as "damnation" in its popular sense
occurs), in the Litany, and "perish everlastingly" in the
Athanasian hymn, and "eternal death" (an expression
unknown to Scripture) in the Burial Service, I may observe
that—(1) the possibility of that awful doom is denied by
Universalists alone, and not by me; and (2) those phrases can,
in any case, only mean what is meant by their Scripture
equivalents; and (3) they do not exclude the sense of
"extinction of being," which is, at any rate, the very antithesis to endless torments. There is not a single word on the
subject of endless torments in all the Thirty-nine Articles, and
the Forty-second Article, which forbade Universalism, was
struck out in 1562.

scribed in a manner unauthorised by Scripture, and that their "endlessness" is not so distinctly revealed as not to admit of being regarded in an aspect less appalling to the heart and more reconcilable with all which our Lord has taught us of our Father in Heaven, than that in which it has been presented in popular teaching.

But while, in form, this book is a reply to Dr. Pusey, in reality my conclusions are almost identical with his, except on minor points of history and criticism. And though I may be met again by refutations, triumphant only in refuting what I have never said, I am not discouraged. The book will at least find *some* serious, candid, and high-minded readers. On these this mass of evidence will not be without weight. That which is true makes its way in time even into the minds of those who persuade themselves that they have rejected it. What is said of an individual matters nothing; but truth and justice ultimately prevail. "He that judgeth me is the Lord." To Him, humbly, yet with glad and perfect confidence, I trust the cause which I maintain. If what I have written be condemned on earth, I say with Pascal that what I here repudiate is condemned in heaven. *Ad tuum, Domine Jesu, tribunal appello.*

XXI.[1]

By Archdeacon FARRAR.

"So runs my creed : but what am I
An infant crying in the night :
An infant crying for the light :
And with no language but a cry."—TENNYSON.

"And Thou, O God, by whom are seen
All creatures as they be,
Forgive me, if too close I lean
My human heart on Thee."—WHITTIER.

BUT to conclude : If, as I have shown, the ultimate extinction of the being of sinners appears to be taught by the literal meaning of many passages of Scripture ; and if the final restoration of all mankind appears also to be taught in many passages of Scripture ; and if the popular conception of endless torments for the vast majority is nowhere indisputably taught in Scripture ; and if it is only by inference we are led to the fear that any souls may be finally excluded from the presence of

---

[1] This Section contains the "CONCLUSION" of Archdeacon FARRAR'S *Mercy and Judgment*, published in 1881.—J. H.

God at the end of the ages ;—if, I say, these are the conclusions to which Scripture alone has led us, what is it that on this subject I finally believe?

It will be seen at once that I propound no "Optimist theory" (as it has been called), "that all men will be saved;" though since the suppression of the old Forty-second Article that view is nowhere declared to be untenable in our formularies as interpreted by the highest authority. Still less do I teach that all men will attain to everlasting felicity, or that—to refer to the coarse instance selected by Jerome —a Jezebel will be at last as a Virgin Mary. Nay, I do not even say that some men may not for ever suffer from the consequences of their sins, and from impenitence respecting them, dearly as I wish that it were possible for us to believe in final universal felicity as a glorious triumph of the love of God and the cross of Christ. But I think that even if some portion of the "pain of loss" may continue for ever, there is nothing to sanction the assertion that such hopes as sinners may here embrace may not also be open to them, at least until the great Judgment, in the Intermediate State beyond the grave. The death of the soul shall last as long as its willing sinfulness lasts, and its "hell" burn as long as its enmity to God continues. The only hope is that from this sin and this enmity it may at last—far off—before the end of the ages—possibly be saved. Hell and death are endless conditions so long as there is persistent impenitence. They cease when the soul repents, but not till then. But who shall say that when the moment of death is over there can be no further answer to the sinner's cry, "Will the Lord cast off for ever, and will He be favourable no more? Is His mercy clean gone for ever? Doth His promise fail for evermore? Hath God forgotten to be gracious? Hath He shut up His lovingkindness in displeasure?"

But it is due to my readers that I should try to express this in language as clear as the subject admits, not by way of laying down a dogma or of giving expression to a novelty, but by stating what I hold to be the teaching —not of sects or of individuals, or even of majorities,—but of the Catholic Church, of which I am, and ever have been, a loyal and faithful, though most humble and most unworthy son.

In accordance, then, with what the Church has ever held—adding nothing to that Catholic creed, and subtracting nothing from it,

2 c

I believe that on the subject of man's future it has been God's will to leave us uninstructed in details, and that He has vouchsafed to us only so much light as may serve to guide our lives.

I believe in God the Father, the Creator; in God the Son, the Redeemer; in God the Holy Ghost, the Comforter.

I believe that God is Love.

I believe that God willeth all men to be saved.

I believe that God has given to all men the gift of immortality, and that the gifts of God are without repentance.

I believe that every man shall stand before the Judgment-seat of Christ, and shall be judged according to his deeds.

I believe that He who shall be our Judge is He who died for the sins of the whole world.

I believe that "if any man sin, we have an Advocate with the Father, Jesus Christ the Righteous, and He is the Propitiation for our sins."

I believe in the forgiveness of sins.

I believe that all who are saved are saved only by grace through faith; and that not of ourselves; it is the gift of God.

I believe that every penitent and pardoned

soul will pass from this life into a condition of hope, blessedness, and peace.

I believe that man's destiny stops not at the grave, and that many who knew not Christ here will know Him there.

I believe that "in the depths of the Divine compassion there may be opportunity to win faith in the future state."

I believe that hereafter—whether by means of the "almost-sacrament of death" or in other ways unknown to us—God's mercy may reach many who, to all earthly appearance, might seem to us to die in a lost and unregenerate state.

I believe that as unrepented sin is punished here, so also it is punished beyond the grave.

I believe that the punishment is effected, not by arbitrary inflictions, but by natural and inevitable consequences, and therefore that the expressions which have been interpreted to mean physical and material agonies by worm and flame are metaphors for a state of remorse and alienation from God.

I see reasons to hope that these agonies may be so tempered by the mercy of God that the soul may hereafter find some measure of peace and patience, even if it be not admitted into His vision and His Sabbath.

I believe that among the punishments of the world to come there are "few stripes" as well as "many stripes," and I do not see how any fair interpretation of the metaphor, "few stripes," can be made to involve the conception of endlessness for all who incur future retribution.

I believe that Christ went and preached to the spirits in prison, and I see reasons to hope that since the Gospel was thus once preached "to them that were dead," the offers of God's mercy may in some form be extended to the soul, even after death.

I believe that there is an Intermediate State of the soul, and that the great separation of souls into two classes will not take place until the final judgment.

I believe that we are permitted to hope that, whether by a process of discipline, or enlightenment, or purification, or punishment, or by the special mercy of God in Christ, or in consequence of prayer, the state of many souls may be one of progress and diminishing sorrow, and of advancing happiness in the Intermediate State.

I believe that there will be degrees of blessedness and degrees of punishment or deprivation, and I see reasons to hope that there may be gradual mitigations of penal doom to all souls that accept the Will of God respecting them.

I believe, as Christ has said, that "all manner of sin shall be forgiven unto men, and their blasphemies, however greatly they shall blaspheme;" and that as there is but one sin of which He said that it should be forgiven neither in this aeon nor in the next, there must be some sins which will be forgiven in the next as well as in this.

I believe that without holiness no man can see the Lord, and that no sinner can be pardoned or accepted till he has repented, and till his free will is in unison with the Will of God; and I cannot tell whether some souls may not resist God for ever, and therefore may not be for ever shut out from His presence.

And I believe that to be without God is "hell;" and that in this sense there is a hell beyond the grave; and that for any soul to fall even for a time into this condition, though it be through its own hardened impenitence and resistance of God's grace, is a very awful and terrible prospect; and that in this sense there may be for some souls an endless hell. But I see reason to hope that through God's mercy, and through the merits of Christ's sacrifice, the great majority of mankind may be delivered from this awful doom. For, according to the Scriptures, though, I know not what its nature will be or how it will be effected.

I believe in the restitution of all things; and

I believe in the coming of that time when —though in what sense I cannot pretend to explain or to fathom—

GOD WILL BE ALL IN ALL.

Δόξα τῷ Θεῷ.

RECENT WORKS ON ESCHATOLOGY

CONTAINED IN

THE LIBRARY OF THE BRITISH MUSEUM,

WITH

THE CATALOGUE MARKS ATTACHED.

ESCHATOLOGY.

GENERAL.

BUTLER, J. (Bishop of Durham). B.'s Analogy. Part I. The Introduction, and A Future Life. London, 1879. 8vo.   4018. a. 11.

NORDHOFF, C. God and the Future Life. pp. 228. London, 1884. 8vo.   4018. aa. 29.

HARRIS, H. Death and Resurrection. pp. 180. London, 1880. 8vo.   4257. h. 19.

F., H. O. The Hour of Death and the Invisible World. pp. 148. London, 1882. 8vo.   4257. g. 12.

LAWRENCE, L. A. "Do they love us yet?" pp. 234. New York, 1879. 8vo.   4257. cc. 15.

DORNER, I. A. The Future State. pp. 155. New York, 1883. 8vo.   4257. h. 30.

ADKINS, E. The Ages to Come. pp. 336. New York, 1880. 8vo.   4257. i. 17.

DANA, A. H. Enigmas of the Future State. pp. 250. New York, 1882. 12mo.   4018. g. 11.

ALGER, W. R. Destiny of the Soul. pp. 913. New York, 1878. 8vo. 4257. m. 2.

MEAD, C. M. The Soul Here and Hereafter. pp. 462. Boston [1879]. 8vo. 4257. h. 14.

FOSTER, R. S. (Bishop of the Methodist Episcopal Church). Beyond the Grave. pp. 269. New York, 1879. 8vo. 4257. aa. 2.

PETTINGELL, J. H. The Theological Trilemma. pp. 285. New York, 1878. 8vo. 4257. h. 13.

—— Bible Terminology relative to a Future Life. pp. 276. Philadelphia, 1881. 8vo. 4257. h. 26.

—— The Life Everlasting. pp. 762. Philadelphia, 1882. 8vo. 4257. i. 28.

LAYMAN. Good the Final Goal of Ill. pp. 140. London, 1883. 8vo. 4257. h. 29.

RUSSELL, P. "After this Life—what next?" pp. 157. London [1882]. 8vo. 4257. h. 25.

FECHNER, G. T. On Life after Death. pp. 95. London, 1882. 8vo. 4379. b. 17.

WEBB, A. B. (Bishop of Bloemfontein). Life in Paradise, and Life after the Resurrection. Tewkesbury, 1879. 8vo. 4478. c. 88. (22.)

PIKE, G. H. The Heavenly World. pp. 328. London, 1880. 8vo. 4257. cc. 17.

BOUDREAUX, F. J. Happiness of Heaven. pp. 192. London, 1881. 16mo. 4400. h. 10.

HARRISON, F. The Soul and Future Life. 1878, etc. 8vo. 12273. f.

HOPPS, J. P. Scientific Basis of Belief in a Future Life. pp. 34. London [1880]. 8vo. 4372. f. 6. (15.)

BIBLE—Appendix. To Be, or not to Be? pp. 30. London, 1883. 8vo. 4372. f. 11. (7.)

KARSLAKE, W. H. Intimations of Holy Scripture as to the State after Death. London, 1879. 8vo. 4257. d. 3.

TAYLOR, N. Eternal Life. pp. 247. Edinburgh, 1884. 8vo. 4257. k. 28.
BIBLE—Appendix. Eternal Purpose. pp. 325. Philadelphia, 1881. 8vo. 4255. aaaa. 31.
NOEL, Hon. R. B. W. Philosophy of Immortality. pp. 202. London, 1882. 8vo. 4255. aaaa. 32.
CHALLIS, J. Scriptural Doctrine of Immortality. pp. 135. London, 1880. 8vo. 4257. h. 16.
KER, W. Immortality. pp. 167. London, 1880. 8vo. 4372. de. 19. (10.)
RYLE, J. C. (Bishop of Liverpool). Thoughts on Immortality. pp. 86. London, 1883. 16mo. 257. e. 5.
CAIRD, J. Corporate Immortality. 1880. 8vo. Scotch Sermons. 4464. i. 2.
HENN, S. Truth set Free; or, A View of Immortality. pp. 82. London [1880]. 8vo. 4372. df. 7. (9.)
DOWNES, R. P. Man's Immortality. London [1878]. 8vo. 4372. g. 11. (14.)
BIBLE.—Concordances. Eternity; what does the Bible say? pp. 96. London [1880]. 8vo. 4257. h. 10.
BANKER. Eternity; what is it? pp. 45. London [1882]. 8vo. 4257. a. 12.
WHITE, E. The Endless Life. pp. 48. London [1882]. 8vo. 4478. e. 92. (8.)
HARRISON, J. The Everlasting Kingdom. pp. 56. London, 1880. 8vo. 4372. f. 6. (14.)
HENRY, C. S. The Endless Future. pp. 75. New York, 1879. 12mo. 4257. h. 12.
SCHAARSCHMIDT, C. Uber den Unsterblichkeitsglauben. 1883. 8vo. 12208. e.
KATTENBUSCH, F. Der Christliche Unsterblichkeitsglaube. pp. 31. Darmstadt, 1881. 8vo. 4372. h. 13. (7.)
EBRARD, J. H. A. Der Zustand des Christen nach dem Tode. pp. 32. Erlangen, 1879. 8vo.
4427. e. 3. (17.)
UNSTERBLICHKEITSFRAGE. Die Unsterblichkeitsfrage im

Lichte des Materialismus. pp. 53. St. Gallen,
1881. 8vo. 8463. df. 27. (4.)
MEYER, L. Ueber das Leben nach dem Tode. pp. 21.
Dorpat, 1882. 8vo. 8463. df. 26. (14.)
STADE, B. Über die alttestamentlichen. Vorstellungen
vom Zustande nach dem Tode. pp. 36. Leipzig,
1877. 8vo. 4372. g. 15. (10.)
BRENTANO, F. Brief an Herrn E. Zeller, aus Anlass
seiner Schrift über die Lehre des Aristoteles von der
Ewigkeit des Geistes. pp. 36. Leipzig, 1883. 8vo.
8463. df. 28. (9.)
PILATI DE CORNELIO, G. V. La rincarnazione. pp. 46.
Roma, 1882. 8vo. 4257. k. 22.
PERUJO, N. A. Narraciones de la eternidad. pp. 381.
Madrid, 1882. 8vo. 4257. k. 23.

CONDITIONAL IMMORTALITY.

HUNTINGDON, W. R. Conditional Immortality. pp. 202.
New York, 1878. 12mo. 4487. de. 3.
LAYMAN. Report of Conference on Conditional Immor-
tality. London [1876]. 8vo. 4257. k. 5.
GIRDLESTONE, R. B. Conditional Immortality tested by
Scripture. pp. 22. London, 1883. 8vo.
4372. h. 19. (8.)
A., M. Conditional Immortality. Liverpool, 1879. 8vo.
4372. g. 12. (18.)
ARGUMENT. Argument in Support of the Final Destruc-
tion of the Lost. London, 1880. 8vo.
4372. de. 19. (8.)
See also supra, GENERAL.

EVERLASTING PUNISHMENT.

GOULBURN, E. M. Everlasting Punishment. pp. 191.
London, 1880. 8vo. 4257. i. 9.
PUSEY, E. B. What is of Faith as to Everlasting Punish-
ment? pp. 290. Oxford, 1880. 8vo. 2206. c.

APPENDIX. 413

FARRAR, F. W. Mercy and Judgment. pp. 485. 1881.
8vo. 2206. a.
OXENHAM, F. N. What is the Truth as to Everlasting
Punishment? pp. 208. London, 1881. 8vo.
4255. aaaa. 29.
GRIFFITH, W. Evidence of the Evangelists and Apostles
on Future Punishment. pp. 364. London, 1882.
8vo. 4257. i. 24.
WOOD, T. The Doctrines of Annihilation and Universalism. pp. 203. London, 1881. 8vo.
4257. cc. 21.
REIMENSNYDER, J. B. Doom Eternal. pp. 384. Philadelphia, 1880. 12mo. 4257. i. 14.
UNDERWOOD, A. Future Punishment. pp. 204. New
York, 1878. 8vo. 4257. h. 9.
HALEY, J. W. "Supplicium Æternum." pp. 152.
Andover [U.S.], 1881. 8vo. 4255. aaaa. 30.
MERRILL, S. M. The New Testament Idea of Hell.
pp. 276. Cincinnati [1878]. 8vo. 4257. g. 4.
BARROWS, S. J. The Doom of the Majority of Mankind.
pp. 154. Boston, 1883. 8vo. 4257. k. 26.
MACKIM, R. H. Future Punishment. pp. 114. New
York, 1883. 8vo. 4257. k. 27.
ADAMS, N. Endless Punishment. pp. 168. Boston
[Mass., 1878]. 8vo. · 4257. h. 11.
WORD. The Latest Word of Universalism. pp. 277.
Boston [Mass.], 1878. 8vo. 4257. g. 5.
MACDONALD, T. M. Universalism. pp. 47. London,
1883. 8vo. 4372. df. 13. (5.)
TUCKER, W. G. An Eternity of Punishment. London
[1878]. 8vo. 4478. e. 88. (6.)
CLEMANCE, C. Future Punishment. pp. 88. London,
1880. 8vo. 4257. h. 20.
PERIODICAL PUBLICATIONS.—London.—*Fortnightly Review.*
Divine Veracity and Divine Justice. pp. 28. London,
1880. 8vo. 4372. g. 18. (12.)

HITCHENS, J. H. The Penalty. pp. 48. London [1882].
8vo. 4373. de 14. (2.)
STRICKLAND, J. Is Punishment Eternal? [1882.] 8vo.
—HANDCOCK, W. Burning Questions of the Day.
4466. h. 13.
TINLING, J. F. B. Doctrine of Everlasting Punishment.
pp. 87. London, 1881. 8vo. 4257. cc. 20.
HARRISON, J. Vicar of Jesmond and Eternal Punishment.
pp. 18. London, 1881. 8vo. 4372. f. 10. (10.)
TYLER, W. S. Teaching of Christ respecting Future Punishment. New York, 1878. 8vo. 4257. h. 7.
BIBLE.—Appendix. Scriptural Doctrine of Eternal Judgment. pp. 32. London, 1883. 8vo.
4372. h. 20. (5.)
SYMES, J. Methodist Conference and Eternal Punishment. London [1877]. 8vo. 4018. aa. 2. (1.)
INGERSOLL, R. G. "Hell." pp. 32. London, 1883.
8vo. 4081. aaa. 19. (11.)
BEEBY, C. E. Woes of the Gospel. pp. 62. London, 1884. 8vo. 4372. df. 17. (8.)
SYMES, J. Universal Despair. pp. 16. London, 1883.
8vo. 4018. aaa. 19. (13.)
BAUTZ, J. Die Hölle. pp. 210. Mainz, 1882. 8vo.
4257. k. 20.
DIRCKINCK-HOLMFELD, C. P. H. M. W. VON, Baron. Das Dogma ewiger Verdammniss widerlegt. pp. 32. Hamburgh [1876]. 8vo. 4372. g. 15. (4.)

INTERMEDIATE STATE.

PLUMPTRE, E. H. Spirits in Prison. pp. 416. London, 1884. 8vo. 4257. l. 10.
LUCKOCK, H. M. After Death. London, 1879. 8vo.
4257. cc. 11.
—— Second Edition. pp. 271. London, 1880. 8vo.
4257. i. 8.

LUCKOCK, H. M. Third Edition. pp. 271. London, 1881. 8vo. 4257. h. 21.
—— Fourth Edition. pp. 271. London, 1882. 8vo. 4257. i. 25.
SAVAGE, W. R. The Souls of the Righteous. pp. 248. London, 1881. 8vo. 4257. i. 20.
WORDSWORTH, C. (Bishop of Lincoln). Intermediate State of the Soul. pp. 32. London, 1885. 16mo. 4466. e. 18.
ALFORD, H. State of the Blessed Dead. pp. 96. London, 1882. 16mo. 4400. e. 17.
TOWNSEND, L. T. The Intermediate World. Boston, 1878. 8vo. 4257. h. 8.
PARADISE. First Day in Paradise. pp. 20. London, 1882. 16mo. 4422. b. 18. (8.)

ESCHATOLOGY.

NEANDER, HERMANN. The Gospel of Gehenna Fire in its Relation to the Cross, etc. pp. 180. Whiting & Co.: London, 1885. 8vo. 4257. h. 36.
POWELL, ARTHUR HERBERT. Our Eternal Life here pp. xii. 129. T. V. Wood: London [1885]. 8vo. 4257. g. 23.
OLIPHANT-FERGUSON, G. H. H. Man's Departure and the Invisible World: A Collection of Opinions and Facts . . . Second Edition. pp. viii. 240. J. Nisbet & Co.: London; Edinburgh [printed], 1885 [84]. 8vo. 4257. h. 35.
BENSON, RICHARD MEUX. The Life beyond the Grave. A Series of Meditations upon the Resurrection and Ascension of Our Lord Jesus Christ. pp. xxiii. 682. J. T. Hayes: London, 1885. 8vo. 4257. bbb. 13.
STRAUB, JACOB. The Consolations of Science; or, Contributions from Science to the Hope of Immortality.

... With an Introduction by Hiram W. Thomas, etc. pp. 435. The Colegrove Book Co.: Chicago, 1884. 8vo. 4257. m. 3.

QUESTION. A Question. What is the Future of the Lost? pp. 22. W. Skeffington: London, 1885. 8vo.
4257. g. 26. (8.)

PEILL, GEORGE. The Threefold Basis of Universal Restitution. ... Second Edition. pp. xliv. 156. Williams and Norgate: London; Glasgow [printed], 1885. 8vo. 4227. b. 27.

BABCOCK, M. The Religion of Humanity better than Eternal Punishment. pp. 36. Truth Seeker Co.: New York [1885]. 8vo. 4257. g. 26. (4.)

PULSFORD, JOHN. Our Deathless Hope. A Series of Discourses. pp. xi. 289. Hamilton, Adams, & Co.: London; Edinburgh [printed], 1885. 8vo.
4372. c. 24.

BROOKE, STOPFORD AUGUSTUS. Eternal Punishment: A Sermon [on Gal. vi. 7, 8], etc.—The Resurrection of Jesus: A Sermon [on 1 Cor. xv. 3-8], etc. [1883.] *See* SERMONS. Modern Sermons. Vol. I. [1883, etc.] 8vo. 4466 k.

IMMORTALITY. Immortality. A Clerical Symposium on what are the Foundations of the Belief in the Immortality of Man. By ... Canon Knox-Little, ... Hermann Adler, ... G. G. Stokes, ... and others. pp. vi. 259. J. Nisbet & Co.: London, 1885. 8vo.
4374. cc. 17.

LUZ, GEORG. Der Tod des Leibes und das Fortleben der Seele. Ein Blick über's Grab. pp. 111. Bernburg, Wittenberg [printed], 1884. 8vo. 4257. l. 12. (4.)

BAXTER, ANDREW J. Life, Death, and Immortality: or, The Human Soul and its Destiny, "according to the Scriptures," etc. pp. 72. Houlston & Sons: London [1885?] 8vo. 4257. l. 12. (5.)

ROBERTS, ROBERT (Christadelphian). Everlasting Punish-

ment not "Eternal Torments." . . . A Reply to
. . . J. Angus, etc. pp. 36. R. Roberts: Birmingham, 1883. 8vo.   4257. l. 12. (3.)
RYAN, T. Conditional Immortality and Unconditional Immortality: An A B C Dialogue. pp. 16. G. Herbert: Dublin, 1883. 8vo.   4257. g. 26. (1.)
LUCKOCK, HERBERT MORTIMER. After Death. . . . Fifth Edition. pp. xv. 271. Rivingtons: London; Edinburgh [printed], 1886 [1885]. 8vo.   4257. cc. 25.
ERLES, JOHANNES. Der Unsterblichkeitsglaube belegt mit geschichtlichen, philosophischen und biblischen Zeugnissen. pp. 96. Karlsruhe, 1885. 8vo.
4372. f. 13. (7.)
INGRAM, GEORGE S. A Letter in Answer to the Inquiry: "Do the Scriptures warrant a Belief in the Wicked being finally rescued from Perdition and admitted into Heaven?" pp. 16. Drummond's Tract Depôt: Stirling [1884]. 16mo.   4372. a. 2. (1.)
KOEBNER, JULIUS. Die neue Erde. Eschatologische Studie. pp. 53. Elberfeld, 1883. 8vo. 4257. i. 32.
SCOTT, DAVID WARDLAW. The Purpose of the Ages; or, The Final Salvation of All. pp. 39. Elliot Stock: London, 1885. 8vo.   4257. l. 11. (6.)
SCHMICK, J. HEINRICH. Die Unsterblichkeit der Seele naturwissenschaftlich und philosophisch begründet. Zweite, wesentlich vermehrte Auflage der Schrift "Ein Wissen für einen Glauben." pp. viii. 207. Leipzig, 1886. 8vo.   8470. cc. 12.
HORDER, W. GARRETT. Is there a Future Life? Intimations of Immortality, etc. pp. xiii. 183. E. Stock: London [1886]. 8vo.   4257. g. 33.
U., C. C. The Gulf Bridged; or, "The Everlasting Gospel" in the World to Come. With a Note on the Creation of the Universe. [By C. C. U., i.e. Charles Craddock Underwood.] pp. iv. 76. Elliot Stock: London, 1885. 8vo.   4257. bb. 11.

FISCHER, E. (Pastor zu Bessingen). Der Glaube an die Unsterblichkeit nach seinem Einfluss auf das sittliche Leben, etc. pp. 93. Gotha, 1884. 8vo.
4372. f. 12. (10.)

ENGEL, MORITZ. Die Lösung der Paradiesfrage ... Mit einer Karte. pp. xii. 195. Leipzig, 1885. 8vo.
3155. cc. 1.

BRINCKMAN, ARTHUR. Love beyond the Grave. ... Third Edition. pp. 55. G. J. Palmer: London; Cambridge [printed], 1885. 16mo.
4422. aaa. 57. (5.)

BLAND, JOSEPH. The Keys of Hell: Who holds Them, and Why ... A Lecture ... setting forth the Bible Doctrine of Hell. As distinguished from the Superstitions set forth by the Religious Teachers of the Present Day. pp. 24. R. Roberts: Birmingham, 1884. 8vo. 4257. l. 11. (4.)

CREMER, HERMANN. Über den Zustand nach dem Tode. Nebst einigen Andeutungen über das Kindersterben und über den Spiritismus. pp. 79. Gütersloh, 1883. 8vo. 4257. i. 31.

CREMER, HERMANN. Beyond the Grave. ... Translated from the German by ... S. T. Lowrie ... With an Introduction by ... A. A. Hodge. pp. xxxviii. 153. Harper & Brothers: New York, 1886. 8vo.
4257. g. 30.

PROBATION. Future Probation: A Symposium on the Question, "Is Salvation possible after Death?" By S. Leathes, ... J. Cairns, ... E. White, S. A. Brooke, ... R. Littledale, ... D. Macewan, ... and Others. pp. 324. 1886. *See* NISBET & Co. Nisbet's Theological Library. 1886, etc. 8vo.
4257. m.

LIFE. Eternal Life. pp. 16. Masters & Co.: London [1884]. 8vo. 4255. aa. 1.

BESANT (ANNIE), Mrs. Life, Death, and Immortality.

APPENDIX. 419

pp. 16. Freethought Publishing Co. : London, 1886.
8vo. 4018. aaa. 32 (6.)
SHEDD, WILLIAM GREENOUGH THAYER. The Doctrine of
Endless Punishment. pp. vii. 163. J. Nisbet &
Co. : London, 1886. 8vo. 4257. l. 13.
ARNOLD, ISAAC N. The Layman's Faith: "If a Man
die, shall he live again?" A Paper, etc. pp. 31.
Fergus Printing Co. : Chicago, 1882. 8vo.
4017. d. 3. (1.)
PLUMPTRE, EDWARD HAYES (Dean of Wells). The Spirits
in Prison. New and Revised Edition. pp. xxi.
440. W. Isbister : London, 1886. 8vo. 4257. l. 16.
LIZZI, VINCENTIUS MARIA DE. De diuturnitate poe-
narum quibus in inferno torquentur illi Tartarei
vere infelicissimi habitatores theses theologico-dog-
maticae, etc. pp. 288. Neapoli, 1884. 8vo.
4257. l. 17.
SHEDD, WILLIAM GREENOUGH THAYER. The Doctrine of
Endless Punishment. pp. vii. 163. C. Scribner's
Sons : New York, 1886. 8vo. 4257. l. 18.
PAGET, FRANCIS. Everlasting Punishment. pp. 15. 1886.
See OXFORD HOUSE PAPERS. Oxford House Papers.
No. II. 1886, etc. 8vo. 4017. bbb.
BROOKE, STOPFORD AUGUSTUS. Future Probation. . . .
By . . . S. A. B., etc. 1886. *See* NISBET & Co.
Nisbet's Theological Library. 1886, etc. 8vo.
4257. m.
BERGER, W. T. The Wages of Sin and Everlasting
Punishment. pp. 98. Elliot Stock : London, 1886.
8vo. 4257. g. 28.
JERWITZ, WILHELM. Zum Frieden. Ueber die persön-
liche Unsterblichkeit. pp. 77. Dresden, 1885. 8vo.
4422. b. 33. (2.)
GARRATT, SAMUEL. World without End. pp. xvi. 263.
W. Hunt & Co. : London [1886]. 8vo.
4257. l. 15.

LANDELS, WILLIAM. Future Probation. . . . By . . . W. L., etc. 1886. *See* NISBET & Co. Nisbet's Theological Library. 1886, etc. 8vo. 4257. m.

ALLEN, WILLIAM (Cardinal). Souls Departed: Being a Defence and a Declaration of the Catholic Church's Doctrine touching Purgatory and Prayers for the Dead. First published in 1565, and now edited in modern [s]pelling by the Rev. T. E. Bridgett. pp. xii. Burns & Oates: London, 1886. 8vo.
4257 f. 4.

SWAYNE, ROBERT GEORGE. The Blessed Dead in Paradise. Four All Saints' Day Sermons, etc. pp. 98. Rivingtons: London, 1887. 8vo. 4257. g. 34.

MACKSON, CHARLES. The Blessed Dead with Christ in Heaven, and not in an Intermediate State: their Resurrection and Reunion. pp. 16. Brook & Chrystal: Manchester [1886]. 8vo.
4372. d. 18. (9.)

SHALL. Shall we know them again? [A Treatise on the Future State.] pp. viii. 127. J. Nisbet & Co.: London, 1886. 8vo. 4257. l. 21.

D., E. M. The Fuller Life. Thoughts in Memory of the Departed, and of Comfort to the Sorrowing. Selected from Various Sources by E. M. D. Skeffington & Son: London, 1887. 8vo. 4257. g. 35.

VERNON, S. M. Probation and Punishment. A Rational and Scriptural Exposition of the Doctrine of the Future Punishment of the Wicked, etc. pp. 300. J. B. Lippincott & Co.: Philadelphia, 1886. 8vo.
4257. l. 23.

SPEAR, SAMUEL T. Meditations on the Bible Heaven. pp. 403. Funk & Wagnalls: New York, 1886. 8vo.
4257. l. 24.

SHEDD, WILLIAM GREENOUGH THAYER. The Doctrine of Endless Punishment. pp. vii. 163. J. Nisbet & Co.: London, 1886. 8vo. 4257. l. 22.

APPENDIX. 421

CANTY, MICHAEL. Purgatory, Dogmatic and Scholastic, etc. pp. xii. 271. . . . M. H. Gill & Son: Dublin, 1886. 8vo. 4257.

MÉRIC, ELIE. The Blessed will know each other in Heaven. . . . Translated from the French by Mrs. J. Ringer. pp. xiv. 138. Burns & Oates: London, 1888. 8vo. 4378. a. 3.

ROW, CHARLES ADOLPHUS. Future Retribution, viewed in the Light of Reason and Revelation. pp. x. 429. W. Isbister: London, 1887. 8vo.
4257. m. 16.

KLIEFOTH, THEODOR. Christliche Eschatologie. pp. iv. 351. Leipzig, 1886. 8vo. 4257. m. 7.

WILLINGTON, JAMES WALDYVE. Eternal Scenes from the Poets, and their Views of the After Life. Studies in Criticism and Reflection. pp. 130. Simpkin, Marshall & Co.: London; Dublin, printed 1887. 8vo. 4257. g. 37.

LIVONIA. Ein Deutsches Land in Gefahr! Zustände und Vorgänge in Liv-, Est- und Kurland. pp. 30. Berlin, 1886. 8vo. 8033. g. 27 (4.)

ARNOLD, EDWIN. Death—and Afterwards. Reprinted from the *Fortnightly Review* of August 1885. With a Supplement. pp. 62. Trübner & Co.: London, 1887. 8vo. 4257. g. 38.

SCHWEBEL, OSCAR. Tod und ewiges Leben im Deutschen Volksglauben. pp. vi. 388. Minden i. Westf., 1887. 8vo. 4257. m. 8.

O'REILLY, BERNARD, L.D. Novissima; or, Where do our Departed go? pp. xvi. 332. Baltimore Publishing Co.: Baltimore, 1886. 8vo. 4380. bbb. 33.

STARKEY, NATHANIEL. Man in Solution; or, Thoughts on the Intermediate State, deduced from Certain Scriptures. pp. 24. Elliot Stock: London [1887]. obl. 8vo. 4422. bbb. 50 (3.)

STONEY, H. "Life and Death." A Brief Enquiry into

the Leading Views of the Future State. pp. 38. Hodges, Figgis & Co.: Dublin, 1887. 8vo.
4372. df. 31. (11.)

NEWMAN, FRANCIS WILLIAM. Life after Death? Palinōdia. pp. 51. Trübner & Co.: London; Nottingham [printed], 1886. 8vo. 4372. h. 25. (6.)

ASSIER, ADOLPHE D'. Posthumous Humanity (Essai sur l'Humanité, etc.). A Study of Phantoms....". Translated and Annotated by H. S. Olcott ... To which is added an Appendix showing the Popular Beliefs current in India respecting the Post-mortem Vicissitudes of the Human Entity. pp. xxiv. 360. G. Redway: London, 1887. 8vo. 8632. c. 27.

HENDY, DAVID PONTING. Thirty-six Reasons for believing in Everlasting Punishment. pp. 15. Marshall Brothers: London; Bishop's Stortford [printed], 1887. 8vo. 4372. df. 31 (8.)

REIMENSNYDER, JUNIUS B. Doom Eternal ... With an Introduction by C. P. Krauth. pp. xxiv. 384. Funk & Wagnalls: Chicago, New York, and London, 1887. 8vo. 4257. g. 39.

GREGORY, JOHN ROBINSON. The Coming of the King: Thoughts on the Second Advent. pp. 128. 1887. *See* WATKINSON (W. L.) and GREGORY (A. E.). (Helps Heavenward.) 1887, etc. 16mo.
4400. ee.

NEWMAN, FRANCIS WILLIAM. Life after Death? Palinōdia. ... Second Edition. pp. 55. Trübner & Co.: London; Nottingham [printed], 1887. 8vo.
4257. l. 28.

DODD, ROBERT. An Infallible Sunlight Discourse on Holy Scriptural Rewards and Punishments in a Future State, etc. pp. 130. Carlisle, 1886. 8vo.
4257. f. 10.

HURTER, HEINRICH VON. The Catholic Doctrine about Hell. From the Compendium of Dogmatic Theo-

logy by H. H. Translated by K. D. Best. pp. 15. Burns & Oates: London, 1887. 8vo.
4372. i. 8. (6.)
SCHMICK, J. HEINRICH. Ist der Tod ein Ende oder nicht? Gespräche über das Erdenleben und die Menschennatur . . . Zweite Auflage. pp. 175. Leipzig, 1888. 8vo. 4257. l. 29.
REYNOLDS, JOSEPH WILLIAM. The World to Come. Immortality a Physical Fact. pp. xxv. 310. Kegan Paul & Co.: London, 1888. 8vo. 4257. m. 10.
JEREMIAS, ALFRED. Die Babylonisch-Assyrischen Vorstellungen vom Leben nach dem Tode. Nach den Quellen, mit Berücksichtigung der alttestamentlichen Parallelen, dargestellt von Dr. A. J. pp. 126. Leipzig, 1887. 8vo. 7704. bb. 36.
GIRARD, VICTOR. La transmigration des âmes, et l'évolution indéfinie de la vie au sein de l'univers. pp. 406. Paris, Corbeil [printed, 1888]. 8mo.
8470. bbb. 46.
STOCKWELL, C. T. The Evolution of Immortality; or, Suggestions of an Individual Immortality based upon our Organic and Life History. pp. 69. C. H. Kerr & Co.: Chicago, 1887. 8vo. 4257. m. 11.
ROW, CHARLES ADOLPHUS. Future Retribution .... Enlarged Edition. pp. xlv. 429. Wm. Isbister: London, 1889 [1888]. 8vo. 2210. e.
GURNEY, ALFRED. Our Catholic Inheritance in the Larger Hope. An Essay . . . together with a Historical Appendix by H. H. Jeaffreson. pp. 87. Kegan Paul & Co.: London, 1888. 8vo. 4257. m. 17.
LOVE, WILLIAM DE LOSS. Future Probation examined. pp. x. 322. Funk & Wagnalls: New York, 1888. 8vo. 4257. m. 18.
PETAVEL, afterwards PETAVEL-OLLIFF, EMMANUEL. Quelques difficultés du dogme traditionnel concernant la vie future. Réponse à un article de M. F. Godet.

(Extrait de la Revue de théologie et de philosophie.) pp. 46. Genève, Lausanne [printed], 1887. 8vo.
4372. i. 9. (7.)

CHILD, THOMAS. Is there an Unseen World? Rational Proof of its Existence. (The Unseen World, etc.). ... A Series of Lectures on the Unseen World. 5 pt. J. Speirs: London, 1888. 8vo. 3716. aa. 28. (10.)

PROOF. The Proof of Eternal Hope : A Reasoning-out of Eternal Judgment. ... By a High Church Clergyman. Sin A. pp. 31. J. Heywood: Manchester [printed], 1887. 8vo. 4372. c. 25. (4.)

HEREAFTER. The Hereafter. Twenty-three Answers ... to the question, What are the Strongest Proofs and Arguments in Support of the Belief in a Life Hereafter? [Papers published in the *Boston Herald.*] pp. 123. D. Lothrop Co.: Boston [Mass., 1888]. 8vo. 4257. h. 37.

BAISSAC, JULES. La vie après la mort. Éternité et Immortalité. pp. xii. 245. Paris, Poitiers [printed], 1886. 16mo. 4257. f. 12.

ROMANISM. Romanism Scripturally Analysed. Purgatory. ... By an Oriental Traveller. pp. 32. F. Kirby: London [1889]. 8vo. 3942. aaa. 4. (5.)

REVEL, P. C. Esquisse d'une démonstration scientifique de l'existence de la vie future, etc. pp. 69. Lyon, 1887. 8vo. 4018. c. 7. (2.)

FLEMING, JAMES (Vicar of St. Michael's, Chester Square). Personal Recognition in Eternity: A Sermon [on 1 Cor. xiii. 12] preached ... 1888. pp. 12. Larner & Stokes: London [1888]. 8vo. 4473. g. 29. (9.)

HOBSON, WILLIAM TOPHAM. Conditional Immortality: A Reply to ... C. H. Waller and the *Record*. [Being a Reply to Five Articles by C. H. Waller, printed in the *Record*, and entitled, "Conditional Immortality."] pp. 72. Elliot Stock: London, 1889. 8vo. 4109. aa. 41.

CLARKE, THOMAS (M.D.) The Fate of the Dead: An Address to Laymen. pp. xv. 196. F. Norgate: London, 1889. 8vo. 4257. f. 13.

PORTER, JERMAIN G. Our Celestial Home: An Astronomer's View of Heaven. pp. 116. A. D. F. Randolph & Co.: New York, 1888. 8vo. 4257. b. 12.

FROM POOLE'S
"INDEX TO PERIODICAL LITERATURE."

THIRD EDITION.

[A List of Abbreviations is given in the Index.]

Eschatological Studies. (J. A. Reubelt.) Bib. Sac. 27 : 647.
Eschatology ; Cumming's Great Tribulation. Tait, n. s. 26 : 655.
A New Eschatology. Scrib. 8. 331.
Eschatology of O. T. Apocrypha. (E. C. Bissell.) Bib. Sac. 36 : 320.
Eschatology, Olshausen's. Theo. and Lit. J. 11 : 635.

Eternal Life and Eternal Death. (J. W. Santee.) Mercersb. 23 : 617.
—— in the Gospel of St. John. Lond. Q. 49 : 358.
Eternal Punishment. (L. G. M. Miller.) Luth. Q. 9 : 1.— (G. Porter.) Month, 33 : 358.—(C. H. Robertson.) Kitto, 39 : 56.—(T. J. Sawyer.) Univ. Q. 25 : 205. 27 : 40.—(A. Wolfe.) Kitto, 39 : 299. Kitto, 40 : 152. Chr. Obs. 54 : 433. Nat. R. 16 : 88.—(C. Long.) Bib. Sac. 17 : 111. Meth. M. 25 : 402. Theo. R. 1. 559.

Eternal Punishment and Evil. Kitto, 40 : 152.
—— and Immortality. Kitto, 26 : 433.
—— and Universalism. (H. N. Oxenham.) Contemp, 27 : 222-724. Chr. Rem. 45 : 433.
—— and the Word *Eternal.* Chr. Rem. 27 : 200. *See* Αἰών.
—— Barnes on. Univ. Q. 9 : 377.
—— Belief in, essential to Ordination. (D. Merriman.) Cong. Q. 15 : 225.
—— Christ's Testimony on. (J. Leavitt.) Chr. Mo. Spec. 9 : 617.
—— Doctrine of. (M. Ballou.) Univ. Q. 11 : 72.—(F. H. Hedge.) Chr. Exam. 67 : 98.
—— Farrar's Eternal Hope. Bib. Sac. 35 : 779. (C. G. Thompson.) St. James, 42 : 514. (E. V. Gerhart.) Mercersb. 25 : 600.
—— Papers on, by seventeen Writers. Contemp. 32 : 153, 338, 545.
—— Reply to Critics. (F. W. Farrar.) Contemp. 32 : 569.
—— Sequel to Discussion. (F. Peck.) Contemp. 32 : 694.
—— Grounds of, considered. (T. J. Sawyer.) Univ. Q. 29 : 182. 31 : 306. 32 : 458.
—— in Church of England. Contemp. 19 : 573.
—— in Old and New Testaments. (W. E. Manley.) Univ. Q. 23 : 281.
—— Is it Endless? (F. H. Foster.) Bib. Sac. 35 : 353.
—— Matthew xxv. 46. (A. R. Abbott.) Univ. Q. 20 : 42.
—— Mosheim's Thoughts on. (T. J. Sawyer.) Univ. Q. 12 : 69.
—— Oxenham on. Canad. Mo. 8 : 548.
—— Preaching. Chr. R. 25 : 576.
—— A Result of Character. New Eng. 9 : 186.

Eternal Punishment, Unreasonableness of. (T. C. Druley.) Univ. Q. 30: 215.
—— Untrue. (M. Goodrich.) Univ. Q. 13: 329.
Eternity, Metaphysical Idea of. (C. M. Mead.) New England 34: 222.
—— Realised. (S. R. Andrew.) Chr. Q. Spec. 6: 73.

FUTURE LIFE. (G. Bailey.) Univ. Q. 34: 78.—(A. C. Barry.) Univ. Q. 35: 300.—(J. Bayma.). Cath. World, 25: 494.—(P. Felts.) Luth. Q. 6: 62.—(C. S. Gerhard.) Mercersb. 25: 102.— (J. H. Morison.) Unita. R. 3: 152.—(J. W. Willmarth.) Bapt. Q. 4: 198. So. R. n. s. 20: 459.
—— Ancient and Modern Belief in. (H. Giles.) Nat. Q. 8: 358.
—— and Future Punishment, H. W. Beecher on. (H. R. Nye.) Univ. Q. 35: 83.
—— and the Soul. (F. Harrison.) 19th Cent. 7: 623, 832.—Same art. Sup. Pop. Sci. Mo. 7: 237, 309.
—— Symposium on. 19th Cent. Q. 329, 497. Same art. Sup. Pop. Sci. Mo. 1: 499. 2: 20.
—— Apostolic Doctrine of. So. R., n. s. 24: 404.
—— Bakewell on. (E. Peabody.) Chr. Exam. 49: 37.
—— The Bible and. (J. Boyden.) Univ. Q. 24: 397.
—— Chaldæo-Assyrian Doctrine of. (O. D. Miller.) Univ. Q. 36: 318.
—— confirmed by Nature and Science. (G. W. Quimby.) Univ. Q. 8: 381.
—— Daniel *versus* Zoroaster. (C. H. Hall.) Am. Church R. 16: 355.
—— Degrees of Happiness in. (T. B. Thayer.) Univ. Q. 14: 129.
—— Destiny of Man in. (A. F. Hewit.) Cath. World, 27: 145.
—— Druidical Doctrine of. (W. R. Alger.) Chr. Exam. 62: 88

FUTURE LIFE, Egyptian Doctrine of. (W. R. Alger.) Univ. Q. 13 : 136.
—— Figuier on. O. & N. 6 : 462.—Temple Bar, 35 : 104.
—— Great Future. Hours at Home, 7 : 344.
—— Hebrew Doctrine of. (W. R. Alger.) Chr. Exam. 60 : 1.
—— History of Doctrine of. (W. T. Clarke.) Univ. Q. 21 : 72.
—— Alger's. (O. B. Frothingham.) Chr. Exam. 70 : 1.
—— Hudson on. (J. Strong.) Meth. Q. 18 : 404.
—— in Brahmanism and Buddhism. (W. R. Alger.) No. Am. 86 : 435.
—— Inductive Argument for. (T. B. Thayer.) Univ. Q. 22 : 36.
—— Life after Death. (F. P. Cobbe.) Theo. R. 10 : 438.
—— Life in Death. (W. Walford.) Bib. R. 2 : 19.
—— Natural Evidence for. (W. Walford.) Bib. R. 2 : 108.
—— of the Good. (A. Norton.) Chr. Exam. 1 : 350.
—— of Man and Brute. (C. C. Everett.) Chr. Exam. 67 : 157.
—— Personal Identity in. (G. H. Emerson.) Univ. Q. 11 : 407.
—— Physical Theory of, Taylor's. (Sir J. Stephen.) Ed. R. 71 : 220. Same art. Liv. Age, 87 : 385. —Ecl. R. 64 : 85.—(W. A. Stearns.) Am. Bib. Repos. 8 : 494.—Fraser, 14 : 407.
—— Positive Creed on. (F. B. Lockwood.) Penn. Mo. 9 : 177.
—— Practical Value of Belief in. (C. H. Brigham.) Chr. Exam. 86 : 158.
—— Progressive Knowledge of. Mo. Rel. Mo. 28 : 19.

FUTURE LIFE, Rabbinical Doctrine of. (W. R. Alger.) Chr. Exam. 60 : 189.
—— Spiritual Theory of. (J. Service.) Contemp. 17 : 129.
—— What can we know of? Canad. Mo. 13 : 626.
—— What shall we be in? (W. R. French.) Univ. Q. 17 : 167. 18 : 67.

FUTURE PUNISHMENT. (E. T. Fitch.) Chr. Q. Spec. 1 : 598.—(M. Stuart.) Am. Bib. Repos. 2d s. 3 : 1. —Brit. Q. 7 : 105.—Chr. Exam. 8 : 392.—Am. Church R. 2 : 359.—Chr. Mo. Spec. 3 : 505.— (W. S. Edwards.) Meth. Q. 32 : 546.—(G. P. Fisher, J. M. Whiton, and W. S. Tyler.) New Eng. 37 : 169, 311.—(T. Meritt.) Am. Meth. M. 6 : 201.—(G. S. Mott.) Princ. 43 : 532.— (G. Salmon.) Contemp. 32 : 182. Same art. Ecl. M. 689.—(A. Woodbury.) Unita R. 9 : 673. —(S. Whiting.) Meth. Q. 19 : 414, 614. Am. Meth. M. 3 : 112.—Bentley, 18, 183.—Bost. R. 1 : 113.—Brit. Q. 68 : 107.—Brownson, 19 : 85.
—— and Future Life, H. W. Beecher on. (H. R. Nye.) Univ. Q. 35 : 83.
—— and Rationalism. (E. P. Tenney.) Cong. R. 8 : 161.
—— and Reward, Doctrine of. Ecl. R. 86 : 385.
—— Christ on Duration of. (C. Kent.) Bib. Sac. 35 : 290.
—— Cudworth's MS. on. (C. Kenny.) Theo. R. 15 : 267.
—— Dobney on. Theo. and Lit. J. 3 : 395.—Ecl. R. 82 : 153.
—— Doctrine of. Ecl. R. 85 : 39.
—— Duration of. (E. P. Gould.) Bib. Sac. 37 : 221.
—— Everlasting. Dub. R. 88, 117.
—— Decline of Faith in. (A. S. Chesebrough.) New Eng. 39 : 308.

APPENDIX. 431

FUTURE PUNISHMENT, Pusey on. (J. B. Mayor.) Contemp. 38 : 1025.
—— Foster on. (R. A. Hallam.) Am. Church R. 2 : 359.—(F. Wayland.) Am. Presb. R. 14 : 61.
—— in the Old Testament. (H. Cowles.) Bib. Sac. 35 : 514.
—— of Infants not Calvinism. (L. Beecher.) Spirit Pilg. 1 : 42, 78, 149.
—— Probation after Death. (J. T. Tucker.) Cong. R. 10 : 330.—(J. E Roy.) New Eng. 29 : 400.
—— and the New Testament. (R. D. C. Robbins.) Bib. Sac. 38 : 460.
—— Result of Character. (S. Harris.) New Eng. 9 : 186.
—— Symposium on. Contemp. 32 : 153-182.
—— Verdict of Reason on. (S. Cobb.) Univ. Q. 23 : 151.

See ANNIHILATION—RETRIBUTION—HELL (in *Poole*).

FUTURE STATE.—(G. Grote.) Contemp. 18 : 153.—(W. H. Browne.) So. M. 17 : 250.—(C. Follen.) Chr. Exam. 7 : 390. 8 : 115, 265.—(J. M. Hoppin.) Bib. Sac. 15 : 381.—(C. G. Lyttleton.) Contemp. 21 : 915.—Liv. Age, 110 : 664.—(J. M. C. Breaker.) Chr. R. 22 : 1.—Univ. Q. 9 : 160.— H. Ballou, 2d.) Univ. Q. 10 : 29.—(T. S. Lothrop.) Univ. Q. 30 : 207.
—— Analogy between the Present and. (H. Ballou, 2d.) Univ. Q. 4 : 113.
—— Analogies of, in Nature. (A. Traver.) Evan. R. 18 : 249.
—— Ancient Idea of. (A. Yerrington.) Hogg, 1 : 171. —Am. Bib. Repos. 3rd s. 2 : 686.
—— Future State and Science. (B. Stewart.) Princ. n. s. 2 : 309. 3 : 537.

FUTURE STATE, Antepasts of Chr. Obs. 46 : 513.
—— Apocalyptic Doctrine of. (W. R. Alger.) Chr. Exam. 57 : 1.
—— Buddhistic Idea of. (G. T. Flanders.) Univ. Q. 32 : 428.
—— Clark and Mattison on. (C. T. Moss.) Meth. Q. 27 : 236.
—— Doctrine of, in the Epistle to the Hebrews. (W. R. Alger.) Chr. Exam. 53 : 157.
—— Doctrine of Rewards and Punishments. Bib. R. 5 : 352.
—— Effect of Present Conduct on. (H. Ballou.) Univ. Q. 2 : 39, 251.
—— Egyptian Doctrine of. (J. P. Thompson.) Bib. Sac. 25 : 69.
—— Harpings upon Hades. (C. A. Alexander.) Knick, 42 : 405.
—— Homeric Ideas of. (J. Proudfit.) Bib. Sac. 15 : 753.
—— Hudson's Doctrine of Theo. (Lit. J.) 10 : 592.
—— Life after Death. (F. P. Cobbe.) Theo. R. 10 : 438.
—— Mythology of. Tait, n. s. 21 : 100, 129, 198.
—— Opinions of Contemporaries of the Evangelists on. (T. R. Conder.) Fraser, 91 : 100.
—— Paul's Doctrine of. (W. R. Alger.) Chr. Exam. 54 : 202.
—— Peter's Doctrine of. (W. R. Alger.) Chr. Exam. 55 : 217.
—— Philosophy of. (Dick's.) West. Mo. R. 3 : 596.
—— Physical Speculations on. (W. James.) Nation, 20 : 366. Brit. Q. 64 : 35.—Lond. Q. 45, 49.
—— Place of the Departed. (Mrs. H. A. Bingham.) Univ. Q. 24 : 477. (N. H. Griffin.) Bib. Sac. 13 : 153.
—— Progressive Revelation of. Chr. Obs. 74 : 161.

FUTURE STATE. Proved from the Light of Nature. Theo. Repo. 1 : 236. 2 : 22. 3 : 219.
—— Purgatory, Heaven, and Hell. (J. M. Capes.) Contemp. 22 : 731.
—— Scriptural Doctrine of. (E. P. Barrows.) Bib. Sac. 15 : 625.
—— J. P. Thompson on. (E. C. Towne.) Chr. Exam. 70 : 169.
—— The Unseen Universe. Brit. Q. 64 : 35. Same art. Liv. Age, 131 : 195.
—— Vedic Doctrine of. (W. D. Whitney.) Bib. Sac. 16 : 404.
—— Whateley on. Mercersb. 8 : 384.—Theo. and Lit. J. 8 : 640. 9 : 7.

See HADES—IMMORTALITY—INTERMEDIATE STATE (in *Poole*).

PROBATION AFTER DEATH. (J. E. Roy.) New Eng. 29 : 400.
—— Is there any Limit to Man's? Mo. Rel. M. 37 : 285, 339.
—— Life the only Period of. (A. Hovey.) Chr. R. 16 : 541.

PUNISHMENT OF SIN.—Delay of, Plutarch on. Bib. Sac. 13 : 609.
—— Of Sin. (A. Norton.) Chr. Exam. 2 : 169.
—— Heathen Views of. (E. Fisher.) Univ. Q. 13 : 84.
—— in the Intermediate State. (W. R. Bagnall.) Meth. Q. 12 : 240.

FIRST SUPPLEMENT, 1882-1886.

Eternal Life and Eternal Death. (C. Z. Weiser.) Ref. Q. 33 : 238.
—— of the New England Divines. (F. H. Foster.) Bib. Sac. 43 : 1.
—— of Origen. (A. F. Hewit.) Cath. World, 36 : 563, 721.
—— of Paul. (S. S. Hebberd.) Univ. Q. 39 : 14.
—— of the Psalms. (J. B. Bittinger.) And. R. 2 : 225.
—— Old Testament. (T. Lewis.) Meth. Q. 45 : 231.
—— Relation of Consciousness to. (W. D. Hyde.) New Eng. 43 : 745.
—— Studies in. (P. Schaff.) Presb. R. 4 : 723.
Eternal Life, The New Man and. Church Q. 21 : 271.
Eternal Punishment. Month. 44 : 195, 305.
—— Certainty of. (W. G. T. Shedd.) No. Am. 140 : 153.
—— New Defences of. (T. J. Sawyer.) Univ. Q. 38 : 94.
Eternal Regret. (S. Crane.) Univ. Q. 39 : 460.
Eternity and Eternal, New Testament Meaning of. (G. D. Little.) Presb. Q. 2 : 620.

Future Life, The. (N. Pearson.) 19th Cent. 14 : 262. —(L. W. Ballou.) Univ. Q. 43 : 298.—Spec. 55 : 621. 56 : 958.
—— Annexation of Heaven. Atlan. 53 : 135.
—— Chaldæo-Assyrian Doctrine of. (O. D. Miller.) Univ. Q. 37 : 318.
—— Death—and Afterwards. (E. Arnold.) Fortn. 44 : 218.

APPENDIX. 435

FUTURE LIFE, THE, in the Old Testament. (G. F. Moore.)
And. R. 2 : 433.
—— in the Wrong Paradise. (A. Lang.) Fortn. 40 :
845.
—— Oliphant's Little Pilgrim. Lit W. (Bost.) 13 :
391.
—— Plumptre on. Spec. 58.—Same art. Liv. Age,
165 : 60.—Lit. W. (Bost.) 16 : 132.
—— Possibility of. J. Sci, 12 : 472.
—— Recent Books on. Cong. 14 : 629.
Future Punishment. (E. W. Herndon.) Chris. Q. 2 :
245. — (F. W. Farrar.) No. Am. 140 : 193.
Cong. Q. 15 : 225.—(O. D. Miller.) Univ. Q.
40 : 342.
Future Punishment and Reward. (O. Cone.) Univ. Q.
41 ; 90.
—— Certainty of. (W. G. T. Shedd.) Brit. and For.
Evang. R. 34 : 336.
—— New Defences of. (T. J. Sawyer.) Univ. Q. 37 :
94.
—— Recent Theories on. (J. Cairns.) Cath. Presb.
1 : 81.
Future State, The. Liv. Age, 153 : 634.
—— Darwin on. Spec. 55 : 1249.
—— Hellenic Idea of the After World. (P. Gardner.)
Ecl. M. 105 : 215.
—— Revised Version on. (O. A. Kingsbury.) New
Eng. 42 : 527.
—— Symth's Dorner. Lit. W. (Bost.) 14 : 123.

PROBATION AFTER DEATH. (C. F. Mussey.) Bapt. R. 5 :
440.—(I. E. Dwinell.) Brit. and For. Evang.
R. 35 : 326.—(D. A. Whedon.) Meth. Q. 44 :
121, 316.
—— Dorner on. (W. H. Cobb.) Bib. Sac. 39 : 751.
—— Practical Bearings of. (G. F. Wright.) Bib. Sac.
40 : 694.

PROBATION AFTER DEATH, Conditions and Limitations of. (J. H. Fairchild.) Bib. Sac. 43 : 423.
—— Future. (I. E. Dwinell.) Bib. Sac. 43 : 33.—(S. H. Kellogg.) Presb. R. 6 : 226.
—— Limit of. (W. Rupp.) Ref. Q. 34 : 518.
—— Prentiss, Gerhart, and Edgar on. (E. C. Smyth.) And. R. 1 : 316.

PROBLEM of Human Life, Hall's; Reply to C. Braden. (A. W. Hall.) Chris. Q. 3 : 107.
—— of Man's Destiny. (S. Fitzsimons.) Am. Cath. Q 7 : 137.

www.ingramcontent.com/pod-product-compliance
Lightning Source LLC
Chambersburg PA
CBHW021233300426
44111CB00007B/529